Personal Laws in India

Reconciling Diversity with Gender Justice

Personal Laws in India

Reconciling Diversity with Gender Justice

Tamanna Khosla

Vitasta
LET KNOWLEDGE SPREAD
www.vitastapublishing.com

Published by
Renu Kaul Verma
Vitasta Publishing Pvt Ltd
2/15, Ansari Road, Daryaganj
New Delhi - 110 002
info@vitastapublishing.com

ISBN 978-93-86473-36-3

First Edition 2019
MRP ₹795

Editor: Papri Sri Raman
Cover by Somesh Kumar Mishra
Layout by Ram Kumar
Printed by Vikas Computer and Printers

Dedication

To my Lovely Parents

Contents

Acknowledgements

I am grateful to my parents who nurtured me and loved me to be able to become an able individual who can take her own decisions in life.

I also thank my sisters who have been with me always when I needed them.

I also acknowledge the presence of my brothers-in-law and nieces and nephew.

I thank Professor Gurpreet Mahajan for always guiding me when I needed her advice.

I thank my publisher and editor, Renu Kaul Verma and Papri Sri Raman for always supporting me and being by my side.

More than everything else, I thank the cosmic power of the universe inspiring me and sustaining me and giving me the strength to work through this project.

Introduction

Multiculturalism and Feminism

Culture as a phenomenon is not of contemporary occurrence. Culture has existed since Egyptian and Roman times. In India too, a culturally differentiated environment has existed since time immemorial. The existence of different communities within the same political congregation is also not a new phenomenon.

But mere coexistence of cultural communities does not mean existence of multiculturalism as it currently means. What multiculturalism in its present global context means is not just tolerance of cultural diversity but also simultaneously granting of equal rights to communities in the public sphere. It is this emphasis on equality between cultures that distinguishes the liberal notion of pluralism from multiculturalism.[1]

However, in the Indian context, cultural practices of majority communities are guided by religion. So multi-culture here means multi-religious communities. It also means ethnicity. In India, personal laws of communities are controlled by religion. Especially laws on marriage, divorce, inheritance, adoption and death.

Similarly, if we look at feminism, it is also not a modern political ideology. Plato was a feminist, given his view that women should be trained to rule, even though he was an exception in his historical context. Feminism can to a certain extent be traced to the Renaissance period which regularly challenged conventional wisdom from the medieval period and earlier. Humanism became the new way of looking at politics, science, the arts, education and other fields. Humanism pushed aside the medieval Christian concept of a hierarchical social order that placed regular citizens in a subservient position relative to members of the clergy. While the Renaissance humanists were for the most part 'antifeminist', there were a small number of educated women who had the motivation to challenge assumptions that women should remain submissive to men. Christine de Pizan wrote *The City of Ladies* in 1404, and in it she describes women's gender as having no innate inferiority to men's: Neither the loftiness nor the lowliness of a person lies in the body according to sex, but in the perfection of conduct and virtues.

In the mid-1800s, the term 'feminism' was used to refer to 'the qualities of females', and it was not until after the First International Women's Conference in Paris in 1892 that the term following the French term *féministe*, was used regularly in English for a belief in and advocacy of equal rights for women based on the idea of equality of the sexes. Initially thus, like multiculturalism, feminism emphasised the need for equality between genders. Although the term 'feminism' in English is rooted in the mobilisation for women's suffrage in Europe and the US during the late 19th and early 20th century, the efforts to obtain justice for women did not begin or end with this period of activism. Some have found it useful to think of the women's movement in the US as occurring in 'waves'.

On the wave model, the struggle to achieve basic political rights during the period from the mid-19th century until the passage of the Nineteenth Amendment in 1920 counts as the 'First Wave' of feminism. Feminism waned between the two world wars, to be 'revived' in the late 1960s and early 1970s as the 'Second Wave' of feminism. In this second wave, feminists pushed beyond the early quest for political rights to fight for greater equality across the board, eg. in education, the workplace and at home. More recent transformations of feminism have resulted in a 'Third Wave'. Third Wave feminists often critique Second Wave feminism for its lack of attention to the differences among women due to race, ethnicity, class, nationality, religion and emphasise 'identity' as a site of gender struggle.

As in the case of western feminism, 'universal-sisterhood' acquired significance for Indian feminism too. Until the 1990s, issues of upper-caste/middle-class women were perceived to be the concerns of all women. The 1990s became a crucial decade for feminist politics in India.

There was a radical shift in feminism when Dalit women began to question feminism's exclusive focus over the issues of upper-caste/middle class women. During the 1990s, in India feminism was challenged for being blind to caste. Then the question of caste became crucial and unavoidable for feminist politics. A new need was felt among the feminist groups to critique feminism's lack of engagement with caste. From the '90s onwards, Dalit women established separate organisations to fight for their rights. Dalit feminism can be understood through three major streams: struggle of Dalit women activists who voiced caste and gender intersectionalities and critiqued mainstream feminism for being blind to caste; Dalit women autobiographers and writers who articulated their authentic experiences of caste and multiple patriarchies; and the theoretical formulation of Dalit feminism which has been dominated by a few non-Dalit feminists.

This work refers to the different phases within India's feminist struggle that raised the question of Dalit and minority community women using the ideas of women activists and writers worldwide.[2]

One factor which had to be grappled with was the rise of a new middle-class in the 90s. Indian women too joined the employability bandwagon with men. But patriarchy determined that women had to work not just in the outside but also within the household. Thus, though some kind of independence was perceived for employed women, women in India remained subordinate to their husbands and fathers. Women were overshadowed by patriarchs in the family. Another simultaneous revelation was that the managers of workforces soon realised, women workers were more pliable and less inclined to trade unionism. Workplaces began employing more women at lesser salaries, lesser guarantees and amenities, extracting the same amount of work out of the female employee as one would of the male counterpart. Cutting across class, in India a woman's earning is still mostly under the control of the family. Among the economically disadvantaged communities too, women find it easier to get employed, as a result of which unemployed fathers, husbands, brothers are on the increase, the thinking in the men rapidly changing from traditionally 'responsibility takers', to 'I don't need to earn', family is being taken care of by the daughter/wife.

Rise of this new earning women's middle-class has led to feminists in India attacking obsolete traditions, detrimental social norms, useless customs and restrictions. The latest attack by feminists on restricted entry of women in temples is a case which has been taken into account by the government. Thus, the concurrent rise of Dalit feminism and the subsequent ascendance of the middle-class phenomenon has meant the rise of a new kind of feminism in India.

India has not just seen this new kind of feminism but also a new discourse on minority rights and multiculturalism. The issue of minority rights and multiculturalism, and to a certain extent, gender equality is high on the political agenda of most democratic states today, since most of them comprise a variety of minorities. Here I would like to point out that women are also a 'cultural minority' as their way of life is considered to be a 'minority' way in the public and political space, still male dominated.

Multiculturalism promises a deeper understanding of the demands by marginalised communities, thereby ensuring equality and justice for them. It does so by demanding special consideration for these groups, advocating politics of difference in contrast to the liberal politics of indifference. Feminists too have had close affinity with the politics of difference and therefore, at one level, empathise with multiculturalists and have made claims for another marginalised community—that is women.

However, the multiculturalists' stress on granting cultural rights also opens up possibility for conservative interpretation of ascriptive identities and identitarian politics. This is extremely problematic for feminists, because while multiculturalists pay special consideration to inequalities between groups, they fail to address inequalities within the groups. Thus, the discrimination that exists within the private domain remains unaddressed by multiculturalists. It thus excludes the private sphere within the rubrics of cultural communities from equity. In fact, to the feminist, the granting of cultural rights leads to continued subordination of women within groups. Therefore, multiculturalism is, in fact, bad for women. According to Susan Moller Okin, when minorities gain group rights, women lose out. Women, for example, occupy a subordinate status in most cultures and granting group right ensures the maintenance of their lower status. Thus, they fear that limited gains made by feminist movements over the years may be weakened by increased multicultural sensibilities.

After struggling for so long to increase gender equality and to decrease violence against women, feminists ought to be concerned for their newly-gained ground, which might be lost by way of what starts as 'concessions' to difference. The multicultural readership of culture, community and differences, in their view, leaves many structures of discrimination untouched and it is to draw attention to these dimensions that they interrogate the agenda of multiculturalism. Multiculturalism thus focuses on only one kind of difference—cultural difference—neglecting gender difference.[3]

The focus of this book is to look into the problems created by the interface between multiculturalism and feminism. It intends to study the possibility of reconciliation between multiculturalism and feminism, despite the tension between the two and finds that reconciliation is definitely possible between multiculturalism and feminism. This is possible if both groups understand the exigencies which effect the two. To understand this, we need to look at how multiculturalism and feminism influence each other. It delves into how the two factors influence each other and that multiculturalism is not essentially harmful to women and feminism is not necessarily against multiculturalism. Thus, this book shows how democracy and multiculturalism might not harm women if essential safeguards are taken.[4]

The feminist concern about multiculturalists is primarily that multiculturalist need to 1) Address the issue of intra-group inequalities and 2) Have insight into its central term, culture.

Intra-group Inequality

Feminists sensitise multiculturalists to look not only at internal group inequalities but more carefully at intragroup inequalities and specifically at gender inequalities, when examining the legitimacy of minority group rights. Justice within ethno-cultural groups is as important as justice between ethno-cultural groups. What feminists point out is that multiculturalists like Will Kymlicka need to broaden their concept of internal restrictions (which according to him are those claimed by a group, which involve limiting the civil and political liberties of individual members).[5]

Feminists insist that the ability of women to question and revise their traditional gender roles can be drastically curtailed even when their civil rights are formally protected in public sphere, thus necessitating the need to have a broadened definition of internal restrictions to include operation in the private sphere as well. Multiculturalists tend to prioritise cultural group rights, so feminists stress on the need to strive towards a form of multiculturalism that gives the issues of gender and other intra-group inequality their due—that is to say, adopt a multiculturalism that effectively treats all persons as each others' moral equal.

Definition of Culture

Secondly, feminists and many other groups point out that multiculturalism (as a term) is without much insight into its own central term: culture. How is culture to be defined? Does it refer to ethnic groups, or is it inclusive of religious groups, women etc? This needs to come out sharply in the multiculturalist discourse, otherwise multiculturalism will mean only cultural diversity excluding diversities of sexes, sexual orientations, class, religion etc. This book seeks to understand this aspect and focuses on how the term 'minority' should be defined not just in terms of religions and cultures but also in terms of specific genders.

Multiculturalists points out that feminists need to take care of the following issues:

The Width of Multiculturalism

Firstly, multiculturalism is broader than mere discussion on group rights. Multiculturalists say that feminists need to appreciate the full force of the challenge of multiculturalism and the opportunity it offers to deepen and enrich their self understanding. Liberal feminists like Moller Okin reduce multiculturalism to a discussion about group rights, which is but a small and minor part of it. What is clumsily called multiculturalism is a revolt against liberal hegemony and self-righteousness. For centuries liberal writers have claimed that theirs was a transcultural and universally valid moral and political doctrine, representing the only true or rational way of organising human life. A multiculturalism that rejects this extraordinary claim is not so much a doctrine, as a perspective. Pared down to its barest essentials and purged of the polemical exaggeration of its defenders and detractors, it represents the view that culture provides the necessary and inescapable context to human life.

Understanding of Multiculturalism & Feminism

Secondly, from a multicultural perspective, the liberal view of life is culturally specific and neither self-evident nor the only rational and true way to organise human life. Some of its values, when suitably redefined, may be shown to have universal relevance but others may not. Liberal relations with non-liberal cultures should be based not on dogmatically asserted liberal

> values but on critical and open-minded dialogue. Liberal feminists like Okin offer a liberal theory of multiculturalism in which liberalism is the hegemonic interlocutor and sets the parameters for non-liberal cultures. Feminists, therefore, need to acknowledge that all moral and political doctrines tend to reflect and universalise their cultural origins; that all cultures are partial and benefit from insight of others and that truly universal values can be arrived at only by means of uncoerced and equal inter-cultural dialogue.

This book focuses on examples from India and showcases how each culture is unique and has indigenous tests of cultural diversity and gender equality to clear.

For mainstream feminists the book analyses the need to understand the fact that their perspective may not be the final one.

Minority community women have their own perspective on particular issues affecting their lives, minority women are marked by diversity of perspective within mainstream feminism. The book examines the need to guard against viewing minorities as 'subject' of their cultures of origin, huddled in the gazebo of group rights, preserving the orthodoxy of distinctive cultures in the midst of the great storm of westernised progress.[6]

When this becomes the dominant opinion within the liberal public sphere (strangely similar to views held by patriarchal elders within minority communities whose authority depends upon just such traditions and pieties), then minorities are regarded as virtual citizens never quite here and now, relegated to a distanced sense of belonging elsewhere rather than to a here and then.[7] Uma Narayan points out how western feminist explanations result in third world women emerging as 'victims' of their cultures. It is a matter of perception in the context of the reality of the cultures they are placed in. This is, however, not similarly invoked in cases of forms of violence that affects mainstream western women. Such explanations seem to suggest that that third world women suffer death by culture.[8]

Therefore, theorising on issues of culture is a complicated matter for feminists, lest they be charged of being ethnocentrist and insensitive to others cultures. Liberal feminists need to realise that each culture has its other and discourse in keeping with this requisite sensitivity is needed. In fact, many minority community women critique many practices of western women. Some, in fact, draw attention to practices of silicon implants and anorexia by women in the west. We cannot thus begin to separate the differences from similarities until we understand the history, the culture, the resources, the world view of other women. The first step towards this would be moving beyond the half truth of stereotypes, for example in the difference between sexuality defined by the White women and the Black matriarchs. Feminists need to be cautious—lest they be charged with producing cultural stereotypes. Stereotypes disavow the complex, often contradictory contexts and codes—social or discursive—within which the signs and symbols of a culture develop their meaning and values as part of ongoing transformation progress.[9]

Understanding Patriarchy in a Relevant Context

Thirdly, any understanding of patriarchy needs to be put in a relevant context. Patriarchy in India, for instance, intersects with poverty, caste, illiteracy; Patriarchy in the US is shored up among other things by racism, desultory welfare provision. Okin's historic view of patriarchy and her monolithic deterministic notion of culture itself combine to form a dangerous presumption that many of the world's other cultures—cultures that are not western majority cultures—exist in a time warp.

Thre is a need, therefore, for a multicultural society, to deal with multiplicity of patriarchies and move not towards universal principles that pick up the common elements and flatten them into a core but towards imagining a concretisation of a universal principle, that can take into account both similarities and differences.[10] There is a need to look at the indigenous tradition of reform and resistance, so that minority women are not viewed as passive victims.

> *Western Liberalism as Measure and Mentor of Minority Cultures*
>
> Fourthly, such a campaigning stance obscures indigenous traditions of reform and resistance, ignores local leavenings of liberty, flies in the face of feminist campaigns within nationalist and anticolonial struggles, leaves out well-established debates by minority intellectuals and activists concerned with the difficult translation of gender and sexual politics in the world of migration and resettlement.[11] For example, within the dominant feminist discourse, migrant women have continuously been represented as belonging to an underdeveloped culture in contrast to superior western cultures. The very notion of immigrant women—a discursively created stereotyped category—confirms the popular image of immigrant women as largely subordinated, passive and driven solely by tradition.

Social struggle is conducted through culture. Creative resistance to stigmatising institutional labelling is articulated through women's own culturally derived discourse. In fact, in so far as they deal with current social problems, they are often expressed in broader forms of solidarity that transgress narrow ethnic boundaries; and those emerging forms of consciousness may be defined as modern.

> *Complex Problems of Post-colonial Countries*
>
> Fifthly, while dealing with post-colonial countries, feminists should be able to understand complex problems of modernity. It is the fragile political and economic fate of post-colonial societies caught in the vortex of uneven and unequal forces of globalisation to suffer in a heightened and exaggerated form the contradictions and ambiguities that inhabit the western world. Homi Bhabha to elucidate the point, takes up the case of new divorce laws in China.[12] Formulated to make divorce difficult, to punish male adultery and to protect wives

who are increasingly cast aside for mistresses, the proposed law has met mixed response from the feminist community. Women advocates have been bitterly split, with some calling for the need for protection while younger feminists call this as regressive move in a country where communists have a history of paternalistic meddling.[13] Whether married women should seek progressive state protection or aggressively reject the surveillance of such a pastoral state is an argument that has many resonance with such discussions in the west. A common cause can be made with such controversies on one side or the other but not without taking into consideration the world of cultural translation, which would enable us to specify the concept of paternalistic meddling in relation to the American liberal understanding of patriarchal influence, when discussing policy issues concerned with family laws, role of women and regulatory norms of the state.

This book looks at different minority communities in India and how they have been keeping pace with gender equality. While some have been successful like the Christians, others like the Buddhists and Muslims may not have done so. The book analyses cultures of different communities and sees how equitable they are to women.

Throughout the book we also see how both feminism and multiculturalism influence each other in the Indian context, looking at minority cultures, not just at those who have personal laws but also otherwise. With not much literature available around this particular issue, interviews of prominent minority community people such as priests, intellectuals, women activists and community people have provided the inputs and facilitated this study.

The first chapter focuses on issues which are similar between multiculturalism and feminism. It deals with the notion of difference within multiculturalist and feminist thought, the question which is at the forefront of political theorists today. In contrast to liberal politics of indifference, politics of difference endorses diversity in culture, experiences, lifestyle and gender. It becomes the formative thought of multiculturalist and feminist formulation. The chapter studies similar kind of oppression suffered by both women and minorities, like violence, stereotyping, exploitation, marginalisation, powerlessness, cultural imperialism.

The second chapter looks at the feminist critique of multiculturalism. While the two may converge on certain issues, on certain key area of granting group rights to cultural groups, feminist positions diverge from multiculturalist positions. Feminists look at the issues of veiling, polygamy, Equal Rights Amendment, abortion etc to understand these contexts differently from how multiculturalists do. The solutions vary from granting no group right and granting individual rights, to inter group equality working in tandem with intra group equality. What feminists point out is that culture should not trump all other consideration.

The third chapter looks at models of reconciliation between cultural diversity and gender equality. It looks at four models, namely, exit, liberal multiculturalism, deliberative democracy and multiple jurisdictions. The need to look at these models is to understand which model is best suited to resolve tension between multiculturalism and feminism.

The second part of the book includes chapters which explore Indian experiences in dealing with multiculturalism and feminism. The fourth chapter tries to look at the Indian scenario and see the models presented by Indian thinkers to reconcile gender equality with cultural diversity.

The next three chapters examine the problems of discrimination against women present in Muslim, Christian and the Sikh communities in India. It also looks at how communities are dealing with the problem of discrimination.

The next four chapters examine those communities which do not have their own personal laws but have cultural aspects which discriminate against women. These are the Jains, Buddhists, Parsis and Jews. Some have been using the deliberative democracy model, others are using the internal reforms model in India to resolve the issue of cultural diversity and gender equality.

Multiculturalism is thus seen as a challenge which needs to be dealt with in the present Indian context. If both multiculturalism and women's rights need to coexist, they need to learn from each others positive and negative aspects, thus creating a democracy which is both universal and deliberative in nature.

Common Call for Diversity & Gender Justice

> The idea that I think we need today in order to make decisions in political matters cannot be the idea of a totality, or of the unity of a body. It can only be the idea of a multiplicity or a diversity. To state that one must draw a critique of political judgement today means a politics of opinions that at the same time is a politics of ideas—in which justice is not placed under a rule of convergence but rather a rule of divergence.
>
> I believe that this is the theme that one finds constantly in present day writing under the name 'minority'.
>
> —Jean-Francois Lyotard

DIFFERENCE IS the new doxa of the present century.[1] It is increasingly being used by movements such as feminism and multiculturalism to make claims upon the state. These movements use the concept to show how liberalism, which represents a 'politics of indifference' neglects the concerns of marginalised groups.

This politics of indifference characteristic of liberalism cannot understand group differences.

Thus, modern movements of identity stress on the need for a politics of difference which instead of neglecting, embraces difference. These groups share the pain of being marginalised, stereotyped and misrecognised as a result of liberal politics of sameness. Liberal politics of sameness is unable to address the concerns of groups which are different from the mainstream.

However, the Indian experience shows how politics of *indifference* and *difference* intermix and add flavour to the bowl of diversity. Thus, both of these politics together can help in promoting the rights of minorities and women. The first sections look at similarities in the form of politics of difference between Multiculturalism and Feminism. The last section sees how both politics of difference and indifference can together work for minorities and women's welfare.

Justice, Minorities and Oppression

Before the discussion on the notion of difference and politics of difference advocated by feminists and multiculturalists, it is important to understand why they choose 'politics of difference' over liberal politics of blindness to difference.[2]

'Oppression' is one of the common elements which these segments face and these groups feel a politics of difference can better address oppression. Iris Marion Young,[3] in her work, *Justice and Politics of Difference,* discusses five faces of oppression: Exploitation, Violence, Marginalisation, Powerlessness and Cultural Imperialism. I have included Misrecognition and Stereotyping to understand the category of oppression.

In the most general sense, all oppressed people suffer some inhibition of their ability to develop and exercise their capacities and express their needs, thoughts and feelings. Minorities and women commonly face oppression of certain types such as being exploited, marginalised, they face cultural imperialism, stereotyping and violence, and are rendered powerless and it is that what makes them oppressed.[4]

It would be important to look at certain areas where minorities and women unitedly struggle and give a call for liberation from oppression through a politics of difference. Each of these may entail or cause 'distributive injustices',[5] but all involve issues of justice beyond distribution.[6] Young identifies two problems with contemporary philosophical theories of justice.

a. It tends to focus on thinking about social justice on the allocation of material goods such as things, resources, income and wealth, or on the distribution of social positions, especially jobs.[7] 'This focus tends to ignore the social structure and institutional context that often help determine distributive patterns.'[8]

For example, patriarchy in India and worldwide is not just about material and economic distribution but also about societal structure and institutional context. In this case, family as an institution needs to be considered as a site of oppression. The Indian Parliament at the highest level too represents another site of oppression, which is under-representative of views of women. That is the basis of the whole debate over 33 per cent representation of women in Parliament but most parties governed by needs of patriarchy neglect this necessity. Of importance to the analysis that follows are issues of decision making power and procedure, division of labour, and culture.[9]

b. 'When metaphorically extended to nonmaterial social goods, the concept of distribution represents them as though they were static things, instead of a function of social relations and processes.'[10]

The politics of difference refutes the contemporary theories of justice and envisages a much broader concept of justice. If we follow Young's argument, the concept of domination and oppression rather than the concept of distribution, should be the starting point for a concept of social justice.[11]

Multiculturalists and feminists understand the meaning of oppression in similar manner. Oppression or ideological genocide which effect minorities and women may manifest in following ways:

Exploitation

> Minorities and women feel exploited in the current liberal assimilatory political set up. Exploitation as a concept has been used by several feminist and race theorists. The injustice of class division does not consist only in the fact that some people have great wealth while most people have little. Oppression occurs through a 'steady process of the transfer of the results of the labour of one social group to benefit another'.[12] The energies of have-nots are continuously used to maintain and augment the power, status and wealth of haves.[13]

This is especially true about women all the world over. Feminists have had little difficulty showing that women's oppression consists partly in a 'systematic and unreciprocated transfer of powers from women to men'.[14] Gender exploitation has two aspects, transfer of fruits of material labour to men and transfer of nurturing and sexual energies to men. We need to look at the work of some Marxist feminists to look at certain aspects of patriarchy[15] and how this transfer of labour takes place.

Firstly, Marxist feminists like Christine Delphy point out how in marriage women's labour benefits men without comparable remuneration. She makes it clear that exploitation consists not in the sort of work that women do in the home but the fact that these tasks are performed for those on whom they are dependent.

Secondly, we need to understand the work of another Marxist feminist, Ann Ferguson, who opines that women provide another form of the transference of women's energies to men. Women provide men and children with emotional care and provide men with sexual satisfaction and as a group receive relatively little of either from men.

Thirdly, David Alexander argues that typically, feminine jobs involve gender-based tasks requiring sexual labour, nurturing, caring for others' bodies or smoothing over workplace tensions. In these ways women's energies are expended in jobs that enhance the status of, please, or comfort others, usually men. This is a prevalent work culture and works as a tacit glass ceiling which becomes almost impossible for any woman to crack. Thus, women are suited more as nurses (healers) than as doctors, clerks than as officers.[16]

> *Stereotype*
> Feminists and Multiculturists point out the need to study the stereotyping of women, minorities and other marked groups in popular images, interaction and assumption of which continue to justify exclusion, avoidance, paternalism and authoritarian behavior.[17]

For example, feminists point to cultural practices, such as those of the media, market, cinema, sports, literature and art constructs that are subjective and are mostly gendered. Women are considered in patriarchal imagery to be largely intuitive, emotional, irrational, passive and weak in contrast to men who are assigned positive values of rationality, aggressiveness, independence and strength.[18] Women are generally destined for caring, nurturing roles, men on the other hand are the ones who are to be visible in public and political sphere.

Feminists have, however, had different views on stereotyping. Advocates of the 'equality' perspective believe firmly that the widespread presumption that women are not rational was repeatedly used as a justification for continuation of exclusion of women from full citizenship. Gender differences (such as differing educational aptitude, vocational ambition) are simply the result of generations of sexual inequality. Thus, they advocate transcendence of gender differences.[19]

In contrast, the 'difference' theorists advocate the need to celebrate gender difference. This difference is not to be read as inferiority in any form.[20] They want to place at the centre—which is currently marginalised, against negative stereotyping—the value that is currently devalued in patriarchal culture. The nurturing, peace loving, intuitive and emotional qualities of women are to be celebrated rather than considered as something to be overcome.

The individualistic, competitive, rational qualities of patriarchal society are viewed with suspicion and hostility.

As against the above two, is the 'diversity' perspective which focuses not only on differences between sexes but also on differences between gender groups.[21] They stress against cultural feminists' ethnocentric view of women as an uniform category,[22] as it not only occludes difference between women as category but also results in stereotyping women in the third world as always victimised, out there to be saved—with stereotypical views on issues of veiling, polygamy, sati, arranged marriages, and therefore denying any agency to them.

Post-colonial theorist Homi Bhabha points out that colonial powers stereotyped Blacks as both savage yet obedient and dignified servants; the Black servant was the embodiment of rampant sexuality and yet innocent as a child, he was mystical, primitive and simple-minded, yet most worldly and an accomplished liar and manipulator of social forces. Blacks were depicted as sexually aggressive, libidinous and deceitful. In contrast to the Whites, the cultural politics of racism believed that the Blacks lacked intellect, culture, language and capacity to reason, so biologically they were considered to be people just a rung above the ape on the ladder of evolution.

Similar kind of stereotypes exist for Muslim communities since the 9/11 attack and the Iraq war, as is seen all over the international media. In the media, oriental rulers are shown as being fanatical, cruel, despotic as well as their women at the service of their masters in harems.[23] The American media stereotypes Arab Americans and Muslims as billionaires, belly dancers, bombers and terrorists with little regard for human life, especially in the post-9/11 world.

Native Americans too face extraordinarily powerful stereotypes. Either they are the 'good Indian' who has a handsome physique, unusual stamina, and calm, dignified bearing. He is brave in combat, and devoted to his family. He lives in harmony with nature. Or else he is the 'bad Indian', he is lazy and lecherous, a slippery-fingered thief and he is constantly on the warpath to get revenge on his enemies.[24] There are several stereotypes which are circulated about them. Many believe American Indians are confined to reservations, live in teepees, wear braids and ride horses.

But this is far from the truth. There is nothing that confines Indians to reservations. Few wear braids and ride horses.[25] Fewer still own teepees. Many still believe that Indians were conquered because they were inferior, whereas it was their lack of immunity to European[26] diseases that engineered their conquest. Further, it is a common stereotype that Indians are a vanished race. However, fact is that presently there are 2.1 million United States native Indians today.[27] Many still think Indians had no civilisation until Europeans brought it to them. But the fact is that Indians (also known as Red Indians) were cultured and civilised, with cultures very different from those of Europeans.

Another common stereotype is Indians get a free ride from the government.[28] But the fact is that the benefits native Indians receive from the government derive from treaty agreements, which purport to compensate them for the surrender of some or all of their invaluable lands.[29]

If one were to look at Hispanic Americans, they too are stereotyped in a negative way. They are considered more likely than (non-Hispanic) Whites to prefer welfare to employment and to be lazy, violence-prone, unintelligent and unpatriotic.

In India, Dalits are depicted as naive, without any idea of what is happening around them. Dalits are poor, are employed in lower occupations, do all sort of unclean work such as scavenging, rag picking etc.

Academician KR Durgadas points out that in India, the lower caste experience untouchability even now.[30] Caste has been used by the elite as a tool to exploit and rule, without realising that the nation cannot achieve real progress and grow stronger through disintegration of citizens on the basis of caste and religion.

It is unfortunate that while all the political parties speak aloud on secular values and social justice, none of them have made even an oblique reference to the practice of untouchability. It is believed that because of untouchability and caste-based discrimination that Babu Jagjivan Ram, who belonged to the cobbler community, was denied the office of the Prime Minister of India. If we look at religious minorities, they too have been relegated to backyards. The socio-economic conditions of the Muslim community of India present a dismal picture. They are deprived of due representation in public employment even at the lowest level. Also the representation of the Muslims in Parliament show a downward trend.

Marginalisation

Marginalisation is another concept which engages the concern of feminists, multiculturalists and race theorists. Marginalisation is perhaps the most alarming form of oppression experienced by several kind of minorities worldwide. There is a growing underclass of people permanently confined to lives as social marginals. Marginalisation means that 'a whole category of people is expelled from useful participation in social life and thus potentially subjected to severe material deprivation and even extermination'. Example of such people are racially marked groups such as 'Blacks or Indians in Latin America and Blacks, East Indians, Eastern Europeans or North Africans in Europe'.[31]

'In the United States, a shamefully large proportion of the population is marginal: old people, young people, especially Black and Latinos, who cannot find first or second jobs, many single mothers and their children, pregnant women, American Indians, especially those from reservations.'[32]

Marginalisation means that that these groups are unfairly subjected to severe 'material deprivation'[33] while others in society have plenty.

In India, as far as lower castes are concerned, a complex process of marginalisation is underway. It is the co-option and marginalisation of the Dalits by the dominant castes/classes/parties in the country. The modus operandi is simple. First co-opt the assertive or potentially assertive Dalits and then maginalise them once they want to do something for their community.

Marginalisation of co-opted Dalits is an inevitable process in the Indian society, which retards the rate of their assertion. This process is also very simple. Either the dominant sections do not listen to the co-opted Dalit or exclude him from the process of decision-making or criticise him vehemently and then go on to marginalise him.[34]

It happened to Jagjivan Ram, who was one of the pillars of the Indian National Congress and attracted Dalit votes for it. But once he started asserting himself and she was out of the then current crisis Indira Gandhi created circumstances for his ouster from the party. Ram was also not liked by the leaders of the Janata Party. Being one of the founder members of the party, when the question of his nomination to the Prime Ministerial post came up, he was isolated and marginalised within the party. The marginalising process still continues.

After many years of Congress slumber, President KR Narayanan came out of it and questioned the Judiciary. He only asked for the consideration of appointment of Dalits in the Judiciary, where they have a negligible presence. It shook the whole nation as to how a President can exclusively speak for the Dalits. His words were not taken very kindly by anyone including the print media. And in fact, his message to the nation on the eve of Republic Day 2000, which had a lot of contents about Dalits, was not given much prominence in most of the leading national dailies. His activism at the time of proclamation of President's Rule in Bihar also attracted a lot of criticism.

The decennial censuses or the national sample surveys do not generally address themselves to the living conditions of the Muslims. The socio-economic plight of the Indian Muslims therefore remains clouded in mystery. This despite the veil being lifted in part by the Sachar Committee report of 2006. It is, however, never disputed that the Muslims are not better than the Dalits (Harijans) or the OBC (Other Backward Castes). As VT Rajshekar observes, the Muslims of India 'are in many ways worse than Untouchables and in recent years they are facing dangers of mass annihilation'.

Another case in point is marginalisation of the Sikh quest for justice. The Government of India should seek police reforms and enact a law against communal violence that would hold public officials accountable for complicity and dereliction of duty. Ten government-appointed commissions and committees have investigated the deadly attacks against thousands of Sikhs in 1984, following the assassination of Prime Minister Indira Gandhi by her Sikh bodyguards. Independent civil society inquiries found complicity by both police and leaders of the Congress Party. Yet, three decades later, only 30 people, mostly low-ranking Congress Party supporters, have been convicted for the attacks that resulted in thousands of deaths and injuries. No police officer has been convicted, and there have been no prosecutions for rape, highlighting a comprehensive failure of the justice system.

Apart from material deprivation, however, we need to understand the other concomitant concepts of injustice to understand the concept of marginality.

The provisions of welfare seem to produce new injustices and thus seem to produce new victims. These victims are generally the ones who are dependent on the welfare system. And because they happen to 'depend on bureaucratic institutions for support or services, the old, the poor (who happen to be racially marked groups or women) are subject to patronising, punitive, demeaning and arbitrary treatment by the policies and people associated with welfare bureaucracies'.[35] Dependency of these section of classes 'gives sufficient warrant to suspend basic right to privacy, respect and individual choice'.[36]

As leading economists in India have pointed out, any tampering with the existing scheme will hurt its beneficiaries—most of them Dalits, tribals and women.[37]

A letter jointly sent by several leading economists to Prime Minister Narendra Modi in 2015, urging him not to dilute the Mahatma Gandhi National Rural Employment Guarantee Act (MNREGA) renewed attention on the importance of welfare schemes in the development trajectory of India. The economists voiced their concern over the Modi government's move to dilute or restrict some critical provisions of the Act. 'Wages have been frozen in real terms, and long delays in wage payments have further reduced their real value', they wrote. The goal of poverty alleviation programme should not aim at merely increasing the income level of individual, householder groups but at mainstreaming the marginalised in the development process of the country. The country cannot claim economic growth when a section of the people is marginalised and pushed to the periphery of the society. The rapid economic growth process should accelerate the access to services like education and healthcare for all, especially the marginalised citizen', the letter said.[38]

Further, marginalisation does not just have a distributive angle. Many old people, for example, may have sufficient means to live comfortably but remain marginal in the form of uselessness, boredom and lack of self-respect.

Thus, marginalisation involves not just material loss but also deprival of cultural, practical and institutionalised conditions for 'exercising capacities in context of recognition and interaction'.[39]

Powerlessness

Powerlessness certainly means three things: that such groups lack decision-making power, they are inhibited in development of one's capacities and remain exposed to disrespectful treatment because of status one occupies. These injustices have 'distributional consequences but are more fundamentally matters of division of labour',[40] ie. those who plan and those who execute. In the

American context, women especially of colour, Blacks, Latinos, American Indians and Chicanos who happen to be in the latter position. They are mostly employed in non-professional jobs.[41] The situation of the powerless is perhaps best described negatively: the powerless lack the authority, status and a sense of self that professionals tends to have.

In India, to a large extent, the most exploited classes in our society constitute the most socially oppressed castes. These castes and classes are generally employed in low paid jobs.

> The life of such powerless groups have been described by Young as: (i)the life of a non-professional in contrast to a professional is powerless in the sense that it lacks orientation towards the progressive development of capacities and avenues for recognition.[42] (ii) Nonprofessionals, unlike professionals, lack autonomy and in both their working and their consumer client lives often stand under the authority of professionals.[43] (iii) The norm of respectability in the society are associated specifically with professional culture. Professional dress, speech, tastes, demeanour, all connotes respectability.[44] 'In daily interchange women and men of colour must prove their respectability'.[45] At first they are often not treated by strangers with respectful distance or deference. 'Once status as say, a Puerto Rican college teacher or a business executive is revealed, they are then treated more respectfully', says Young.[46]

Similarly, in India, Dalits and religious minorities like Christians and Muslims have to prove themselves constantly. Power, thus, has not just a distributional dimension but also is associated with issues of division of labour.

Cultural Imperialism

Several feminist, Black liberation and minority right theorists have brought to focus that the nature of oppression is not just confined to exploitation, marginalisation, powerlessness and violence. A more expansive approach to viewing oppression would require considering what Young would call 'cultural imperialism'.

> Cultural imperialism involves 'the universalisation of a dominant group's experience and culture, and its establishment as the norm. These dominant groups have exclusive access to means of interpretation and communication in a society. As a consequence, the dominant cultural products of the society, that is those most widely disseminated, express the experience, values, goals and achievement of these groups. Often without noticing they do so, the dominant groups project their own experience as representative of the whole of humanity as such. For example, patriarchy is represented as universal. It accepts the inferior position of women politically, socially and economically.

But here it is pertinent to point out that it is not an extremely good idea to describe patriarchy as universally acceptable because some cultures do not accept patriarchy.

Polyandry in India refers to the historical practice of polyandry, whereby a woman has two or more husbands at the same time. The popular Hindu epic *Mahabharata* provides the first striking example: Draupadi, daughter of the king of Panchal, was married to five brothers.

While polyandrous unions have disappeared from the traditions of many of the groups and tribes, it is still practiced by some. Apart from Kinnaur in Himachal Pradesh, polyandry was practised in south India among the Toda tribes of the Nilgiris, Nairs of Travancore and Ezhavas of Malabar.

Polyandry and polygamy were prevalent in Kerala till the late 19th century and isolated incidents were reported till mid-20th century. The castes practicing polyandry were the Nairs, Thiyyas, Kammalans and a few of the artisan castes. In the case of the Nairs and other related castes, a man's property is inherited by his sister's children and not his own. Several unrelated men had a common wife in the Nair polyandry. Under the Nair polyandry, the only conceivable blood-relationship could be ascertained through females. However, polyandry among Nairs is a contested issue with opinion divided between the ones who support its existence and the ones who do not support it, based on the fact that no stable conjugal relationship is formed in Nair polyandry.

A distinct group of people called Paharis live in the lower ranges of Himalayas in Northern India from southeastern Kashmir all the way through to Nepal. Polyandry has been reported among these people in many districts but is still practised and studied in great detail in Jaunsar-Bawar in Dehradun district in Uttarakhand. The practice is believed to have descended from their ancestors who had earlier settled down in the plains from the Himalayas. Polyandrous union occurs in this region when a woman marries the eldest son in a family. The woman automatically becomes the wife of all his brothers upon her marriage. The brothers can be married to more than one woman if the first woman is sterile or if the age differential of the brothers is high. The wife is shared equally by all brothers and no one in the group has exclusive privilege to the wife. The woman considers all the men in the group as her husbands and the children recognise them all as their father.

Fraternal polyandry exists among the Khasa of Dehradun and among the Gallong of Arunachal Pradesh, the Mala Madessar, the Mavilan etc. of Kerala. Non-fraternal polyandry exists among the Kota and among the Karvazhi, Pulaya, Muthuvan and Mannan in Kerala.

In the *1911 Census of India*, EA Gait mentions polyandry of the Tibetans, Bhotias, Kanets of Kulu valley, people of the State of Bashahr, Thakkars and Megs of Kashmir, Gonds of Central Provinces, Todas and Kurumbas of the Nilgiris, Kallars of Madurai, Tolkolans of Malabar, Ishavans, Kaniyans and Kammalans of Cochin, Muduvas of Travancore and the Nairs.[47]

Race, Caste, Religion

Young points out how race is a structure of oppression at least as basic as class or gender. According to her, there is no doubt that racial groups in the US, especially Blacks and Latinos, are oppressed. For example, wherever there is racism, according to her, there is the assumption that members of the oppressed racial groups are or ought to be servants to the privileged groups. High paying, skilled and unionised jobs are reserved for Whites. Thus, there is transfer of energy whereby the server enhances the status of the served.

In most White racist societies, this means that many White people have dark or yellow skinned domestic servants and, in the US today, there remains significant racial structuring of private household service: anyone who goes to a good hotel or a good restaurant can have servants. Servants often attend to the daily and domestic activities of business executives, government officials and other high-status professionals. In the US there remains a strong cultural pressure on the Black people.

Similarly, Dalits and religious minorities like Christians and Muslims in India have to prove themselves constantly. Power has not just a distributional dimension but also is associated with issues of division of labour.

MN Srinivas speaks of 'Sanskritisation as the process by which a "low" Hindu caste, or tribal or other group, changes its customs, ritual, ideology and way of life in the direction of a high, and frequently, "twice-born" caste'. This means cultural imperialism of the lower castes by the upper castes.[48] Consequently, the difference between women and men, American Indians or Africans and Europeans, Jews and Christians, homosexuals and heterosexuals, workers and professionals, upper caste and lower caste becomes reconstructed as deviance and inferiority. These groups get marked as *the other*. These dominant cultural expressions often have little place for experience of other groups, at most only mentioning or referring to them in stereotyped or marginalised ways.

While it does not mean that the dominant sections are not stereotyped but the male WASP section (White Anglo-Saxon Protestant) hold major means of communication. Feminists and multiculturalists point out how stereotyping can harm a whole life cycle of the concerned group.

Misrecognition

Not only multiculturalism but also contemporary feminist and race relation discussions are ungirded by the premise that withholding of recognition can be a form of oppression.[49]

> According to Taylor, 'hegemon or dominant cultures possess the power to bestow or fail to bestow recognition'. The term indicates that people need the approval and respect of others in order to develop self-esteem, self-confidence and self-respect. According to Axel Honneth, 'the failure to recognise or misrecognition can inflict a grievous wound on another culture, saddling its victims with crippling self hatred'.[50] 'An internalised picture of their own inferiority develop amongst these groups', according to him, 'so that even when some of the objective obstacles to their development and growth falls apart, they may be incapable of taking advantage of new opportunities.[51]'

This kind of misrecognition is also true of Dalits in India. Taylor points out that 'the depreciatory image which women in patriarchal societies or Blacks in White societies have been induced to adopt, become the most potent instrument of their own oppression'.[52] 'The victim misrecognised and marginalised is the other, the voice that is submerged.'[53]

According to Nancy Fraser, 'misrecognition is perpetrated through institutionalised pattern'.[54] For example, the link between the androcentric norms that devalue activities coded as *feminine* on the one hand and low wages of females on the other. Likewise, heterosexist norms delegitimise homosexuality and deny resources and benefits to gays and lesbians.

The aim, therefore, is to deinstitutionalise patterns of cultural values that impede parity of participation and to replace them with patterns that foster it. What multiculturalists, feminists and

Marxists advocate is 'a politics of recognition, a politics which aims to repair internal self-dislocation by contesting the dominant cultures demeaning picture of the group'.[55]

This politics proposes that 'members of misrecognised groups reject such images in favour of new self representation of their own making, jettisoning internalised negative identities and joining collectively to produce a self-affirming culture of their own, which when publicly asserted will gain the respect and esteem of society at large'.[56] According to these theorists the result, when successful, is recognition.

Violence

Finally, feminists and multiculturalists point out that several groups suffer oppression and systematic violence. Violence is a social practice. 'It is a social practice given that everyone knows—that it happens and will happen again.'[57]

> 'The oppression and violence consists not only in direct victimisation, but in the daily knowledge shared by all members of oppressed groups that they are liable to violation, solely on account of their group identity.' Members of some groups 'live with the knowledge that they must fear random, unprovoked attacks on their persons or property, which have no motive but to damage, humiliate, or destroy the person'.[58]

Iris Young points out that 'in American society women, Blacks, Asians Arabs, gay men and lesbians live under such threats of violence, and in at least some regions Jews, Puerto Ricans, Chicanos and other Spanish speaking Americans must fear such violence as well'.[59] 'Any woman, for example, has a reason to fear rape. Regardless of what a Black man has done to escape the oppressions of marginality or powerlessness, he lives knowing he is subject to attack or harassment.'[60]

Thus, advocates of politics of difference say that violence is a form of injustice which distributive justice alone is unable to cover. According to a report by Human Rights Watch,

'Dalits and indigenous peoples, known as Scheduled Tribes or Adivasis, continue to face discrimination, exclusion and acts of communal violence'.

> Laws and policies adopted by the Indian government provide a strong basis for protection but are not being faithfully implemented. The Christians have taken a strong exception to the programme of hate and religious nationalism of the Hindu radicals, which they say are a blatant attempt to sabotage the Constitution of India that guarantees freedom of faith. The Christian community in India has been feeling a sense of apprehension and fear at the incidents of violence against churches and their personnel in various parts of the country. Enumerating several cases of social boycott, physical assaults and cases of desecration of and restrictions on chapels or building churches, the statement expresses a hope and prays that such discrimination and targeted violence will be ended by strong political will and administrative action. The Christians, who are a small religious community, have also demanded an assurance from the government that they are protected, with security and safety in their motherland. Some of the other incidents briefly outlined below are representative of the hostility and discrimination being faced by Christians across India.[61]

Social Boycott

The entry of and propaganda by non-Hindu missionaries, especially Christians, is banned in more than fifty villages of Chhattisgarh's Bastar region by the local gram panchayats.

In February 2004, in the Deogarh district of Odisha several tribal Christian families were expelled from their village. Three Christian families were deprived from enjoying common facilities of the village road, water and forest land because of their faith in Christ. The well commonly used by the Christians was polluted by adding filth to it. And the Christians have been forbidden to mix or talk to anybody, to take part in any social functions or walk on the main road. The fundamentalists also threatened to snatch away the government land allotted to the Christians, to cancel their BPL Cards and demolish their houses if they did not renounce Christ.

Physical Assaults

In the 1990s, a mob of religious extremists brutally beat up ten Christians including two women who were later rushed to the hospital in Sirisguda, Bastar town in Jagdalpur district of Chhattisgarh. About a 100 Christians who were denied rations for two months for their faith in Christ and were beaten up by this mob. Christians from fifty-two families had gathered before the district Food Inspector's office when the mob rushed in and started to beat the Christians indiscriminately. The mob beat up the Christians with sticks, kicked and punched them and hurled stones at those who were trying to escape from the scene. Two women were pulled to the ground while the perpetrators stood on them and hit their genital organs. No FIR was registered against members of the mob.

Religious-political extremists locked up a church after they beat up a Christian family in Balwanazir, Kaliyanganj, Bihar in 2014. The mob comprising Hindu extremists beat up Sadanandan Singh and his family for their faith in Christ and finally locked up the church of the Indian Evangelical Team. Singh and his family were dragged on to the road and the entire family, including two minor girls, were beaten up mercilessly. The extremists told Singh that he would not be allowed to pray in the future in the village.

Desecration of and Restrictions on Churches

Local religious political groups threatened to harm Pastor Bhikanlal Dhurvey several times for conducting prayer meetings in Bhopal, Madhya Pradesh the 1990s. However, the pastor continued to conduct worship services and later started to build a prayer hall on his land. Subsequently, the extremists filed a police complaint against the pastor, accusing him of illegal construction. The construction has since been stopped and prayers are now being conducted in the homes of local Christians.

In Karnataka the properties of two churches were allegedly damaged by unidentified miscreants. In 2014, an ornamental pot at the entrance of the Holy Rosary church was broken and a signpost leading to St Antony church in Koteshwar also was uprooted.

India is a land where different religious faiths have for long flourished and our founding fathers have made special efforts to ensure that the rights of all are safeguarded irrespective of our religious beliefs, gender or caste. India is committed to secularism and any attempt to weaken the socio-religious fabric of the nation must be dealt with swiftly and effectively.

Notion of Equality which focuses on Sameness

Apart from the seven faces of oppression, both feminists and multiculturalists critique the liberal notion of equality which focuses on *sameness* rather than on *difference*.

Equality as Sameness

According to multiculturalists and feminists, treating different groups equally and in similar manner may result in discrimination. They, therefore, emphasise on the mantra of different but equal rather than equal and the same. 'Treating non-similar similarly results in discrimination' is the message emphasised by both multiculturalists and feminists. Multiculturalists and feminists critique liberalism's blindness to difference. This blindness to difference has two consequences:

a. Blindness to 'difference' disadvantage minority groups. This is because the liberal policy of blindness to difference implies assimilation of these minority groups to the mainstream. And this liberal strategy of assimilation implies 'coming into the game after it has already begun', that is after the rules and standards have already been set, and 'having to prove oneself according to those rules and standards'.

b. The liberal ideal of neutral universal humanity without social group differences allows privileged groups to ignore their own group specificity. Against such a neutral universalistic ideal, only the oppressed minority groups are marked and objectified, not the privileged groups.

The controversy around the Sikh turban case and uniform dress code case reflect how minorities stand discriminated in multicultural polities. This was illustrated in Britain, where all motorists were required to wear helmets.[62] Sikhs raised objection, saying that the turban was a religious requirement for them and they could not replace it with a crash helmet. The presiding judge, however, was not convinced and argued that if for some reason they were unable to wear helmets, they could not ride motorcycles as turbans were not safe. Sikhs, however, campaigned against the law, arguing that the turban was as safe as a crash helmet and that if they could fight for the British in two world wars without anybody considering their turbans to be unsafe, then they surely could ride motorcycles. The law was subsequently amended to exempt Sikhs from wearing crash helmets.

Similarly, in Canada, the Royal Canadian Mounted Police did not allow its personnel to wear turban.[63] However, the trial division of the federal court of Canada ruled objection to turban as quite speculative and vague and that turbans did not compromise the non-religious character of the RCMP.

Thus, in both Britain and Canada, discrimination against Sikhs was resolved to accommodate minorities.

However, we also need to see that different multicultural societies react differently to multicultural questions raised. In France, for example, the courts upheld the expulsion of three Sikh children from school for wearing a turban. In March 2004, a law was passed in France that banned so-called conspicuous religious symbols in classrooms. Under the law, school children are banned from wearing the Christian cross, the Jewish skull cap, the Islamic head scarf and the Sikh turban. Thus three Sikh boys were expelled from school for not removing their turban.[64]

Not just the turban but also dresses have been sites of controversies in multicultural polity. In USA, for example, an orthodox Rabbi serving as clinical psychologist in the US Air Force was discriminated against and asked to resign when he refused to stop wearing his yarmulke which was against its standard dress requirement. The Secretary of State argued that the uniforms of the armed forces were cherished symbols of service, pride, history and traditions and allowing any variation in them would go against the order of the US Air Force. The Congress, however, asked the armed forces to introduce greater flexibility in dress codes.

There was another case of discrimination and disadvantage against many Asian women. Many Asian women have disregarded the rule to wear uniform in hospitals, stores and school. In Britain, a Sikh woman who refused to wear the required uniform of nurse was denied a training place on a nursing course by her health authority. While the industrial tribunal upheld her complaint on cultural ground, the employment appeal tribunal took the opposite view. However, the General Nursing Council made the rules culturally more flexible and allowed the women who were qualified as nurses to wear grey trousers and white shirt.[65]

Multiculturalists, by citing above examples, point out that if the yalmulke, turban and other religious head dresses were to be disallowed, Jews, Sikhs and others would be denied both an avenue of employment and an opportunity to serve their country. Furthermore, most liberal democracies are multicultural and thus there is no obvious reason why its national symbols, including military uniform, should not reflect the fact. Besides, according to Bhiku Parekh, if uniforms are likely to detract from unity then it would be even more so in terms of difference of race, colour, accent etc.[66] Thus, Jews, Blacks and Asians would be banned from joining these services. What the multiculturalists point out is that while the uniform should not be discarded, appropriate cultural differences need to be accommodated.[67]

Feminist too, like multiculturalists, emphasise on the jargon of 'different but equal'. According to feminists, women-specific experiences such as pregnancy, child bearing and rearing need to be considered by policy makers. Abstract general principles cannot take care of women-specific experiences.

What both feminists and multiculturalists are trying to point out by these examples are the following:

a. Different cultures, sexes, races need to be treated differently. They cannot be treated similarly, which would otherwise result in discrimination against these minorities. This 'different' principle does not however divorce it from treating these populations in equal and fair manner.

b. A liberal society has to strike the right balance between the value of equality and right to culture. According to Parekh, 'The nature of balance depends on number of factors such as the importance of minority practices to its way of life, the kind, extent and cost of the changes without seriously damaging its coherence and stability'. The balance will naturally be struck differently in different societies and by the same society. This was seen in the case of different reactions in France and Britain over the Sikh turban row.

Thus, unlike equality as sameness, both multiculturalists and feminists emphasise on equality as recognition of relevant differences. Difference has been defined by both as recognition of diversity.

Difference as Diversity

Multiculturalists and feminists both emphasise on diversity as a value.

Multiculturalists advocating against the liberal stress on politics of indifference, advocate politics of difference, endorsing diversity not only as a fact but as a value. Difference is not merely to be understood as discrimination or as otherness in an absolute sense, with no dialogue possible, but more so as representing diverse opinions and voices of marginalised groups which are now not only of race, religion and gender but also difference of culture.

Contemporary discourses on multiculturalism make a plea for a heterogeneous public sphere where all sorts of relevant differences are fostered. Will Kymlicka in his work *Multicultural Citizenship* explicitly rejects the political principle which assumes that a single polity must coincide with a single common culture. According to him, political societies today consist of at least two cultural groups and often more than two.

Multiculturalists, in fact, cherish the principle of difference as diversity. The notion of diversity receives positive value within multiculturalism. It does not simply indicate the absence of cultural homogeneity. Rather it points to the presence of several distinct and homogeneous cultures. It asserts that individuality of each culture needs to be respected, cherished and protected. Multiculturalism further asks us to recognise and even foster particularity. The belief that different cultures cannot be compared or collapsed into each other gives a distinct flavour to the multicultural notion of difference and diversity.[68] Parekh argues that different cultures represent different systems of meaning and visions of good life. One's life is likely to be richer if it enjoys contact with other cultures. This new interdependent world leads to 'fusion of horizons' as we learn to move in broader horizons.[69] Multiculturalists are of the opinion that 'culture deserves some respect because of what it means to its members and the creative energy it displays'.[70]

Now if we were to look at feminism and its relationship with diversity, postmodern feminist and third world feminist work emphasises on this aspect, unlike the works of first and second wave feminism. While there is much variation in postmodern feminism, there is also some common ground. Postmodern feminists accept the male/female binary as a main categorising force in our society. Following Simone de Beauvoir, they see *female* as having being cast into the role of the *other*. They criticise the structure of society and the dominant order, especially in its patriarchal aspects.

Many postmodern feminists, however, reject the feminist label, because anything that ends with an 'ism' reflects an essentialist conception. Postmodern feminism is the ultimate acceptor of diversity. Multiple truths, multiple roles, multiple realities are part of its focus. There is a rejection of an 'essential nature of women', of one way to be a woman. Poststructural feminism offers a useful philosophy for diversity in feminism because of its acceptance of multiple truths and rejection of essentialism. They do not talk about fixed female entity but address the problem of diversity, which to them is embedded in complex historical and cultural contexts.[71]

Apart from postmodern feminists, post-colonial feminists too critique first world feminists' essentialist leanings and emphasise the need to address diverse needs of women worldwide. Post-colonial feminists affirm the irreducible particularity and complex diversity characterising the lives of non-western people. Chandra Talapade Mohanty shows how the category of third world women is appropriated by western feminists as ultimate proof of patriarchy and female bondage. She is depicted both as part of putative global sisterhood and yet as the mysterious other. Against such an ethnocentric perspective, Mohanty argues for context-specific differentiated analysis of ways in which women are produced as a socio-political group within particular historical and cultural locations. Such analysis of the complicated intersection of gender with ethnicity, religion, class, region and numerous other determinants inevitably undermines an established western feminist narrative of male power and female powerlessness.[72]

Sylvia Walby would point to the fact that there are different sites of oppression and potentially different sites of struggle. Thus, she notes that sites of struggle for women of colour may be different from those of White women.[73]

Politics of Difference

Multiculturalism and feminism based on the notion of difference as discussed above works on a very different rationale than that of liberalism. Liberalism, which can also be referred to as 'politics of indifference', functions on three primary principles. First is that, the liberal theory is individualistic in asserting or assuming the moral primacy of the person against the claims of any social collectivism. Second, that it is egalitarian or based on equality, because it confers on all such individuals the same moral status and denies the relevance to legal or political order of difference in moral worth among human beings. Third, it is universalistic because it affirms the moral unity of human species and accords a secondary importance to specific historical association and cultural forms.[74]

Politics of difference, however, works from a different logic than that of politics of indifference. Liberalism or 'politics of indifference' celebrates diversity but only at the level of the individual. Liberalism values differences of tastes, opinions and lifestyles but values less the differences of culture.[75] Advocates of politics of difference, however, assert that attachment to specific traditions, practices, languages and other culturally specific forms is crucial.

Notion of Difference

Politics of difference stands for *a specific notion of difference.* It is against the oppressive meaning of group difference which defines it as the *absolute otherness.* This is because of the fear that any admission by oppressed groups that they are different from the dominant groups, risks marking and exclusion of these groups. Since the calls for return of women to kitchen in the west and India, Blacks to servant roles and separate schools, and disabled people to nursing homes and Dalits in India to scavenging roles are not absent from contemporary politics, 'the danger is real'.[76]

The notion of difference which these groups stand for is indeed 'ambiguous, relational, shifting, without clear borders that keep people straight—as entailing neither amorphous unity nor pure individuality'. Difference now comes to mean 'not otherness, exclusive opposition, but specificity, variation, heterogeneity'.[77]

So, Dalit scholars like Kancha Illiah advocate the need for *dalitisation*, meaning in a sense reverse discrimination, and sociologists like MN Srinivas stress on Sanskritisation, but the reality lies somewhere in between. Sanskratisation and dalitisation intermingle to hybridise and create a new culture. One needs to look at colleges in India to see the impact reservation has on culture amongst students in India.

Several multiculturalists and feminists point out that group differences should be conceived as relational. A relational understanding of difference 'relativises the previously universal position of privileged groups, which only allow the oppressed to be marked as different'.[78] For example, when group difference appears as a function of comparison between groups, Whites are just as specific as Blacks or Latinos, men just as specific as women, able-bodied people just as specific as disabled people, and Dalits are just as specific as General category people in India.[79]

Different groups are always similar in some respect and potentially share some attributes, experiences and goals.[80] Gay men, for example, may be Black, rich, homeless or old. Dalit women, for example. may share same problems as general category women in India—for example, rape, sexual harassment at workplace and even problems which several male politicians create as far as reservation for both category of women are concerned in the Parliament.

Group Representation

Multiculturalists in the west and India (especially those advocating reservation for the Muslim community through the Sachar Committee report) and feminists have called for special representation of minorities which have been depressed and oppressed for centuries. The group representation principle calls for representation only of the backward and the oppressed and not the privileged as these groups have been already dominantly represented.[81] Representation ensures an opportunity for some to express their needs or concerns which would not likely be heard without that representation. Group representation best institutionalises fairness under circumstances of oppression and domination of some groups. Until and unless group oppression or disadvantages are eliminated, public places ought to include special representation of those oppressed groups through which these groups express their specific understanding of issues before the public and register a group-based vote.[82]

Women, Dalits and Muslims should be given these rights according to several theorists in India. The Justice Ranganath Misra Commission called for reservations to be 'delinked' from religion and make them 'religion neutral'. It said:

> We recommend that para 3 of the Constitution (Scheduled Caste) Order 1950, which originally restricted the Scheduled Caste net to the Hindus and later opened it to Sikhs and Buddhists, thus still excluding from its purview Muslims, Christians, Jains and Parsis etc. should be wholly deleted by appropriate action so as to totally delink Scheduled Caste status from religion and make the Scheduled Castes net fully religion-neutral like that of the Scheduled Tribes...We further recommend that all those groups and classes among the Muslims and Christians, etc. whose counterparts among the Hindus, Sikhs or Buddhists, are included in the Central or State Scheduled Castes lists should also be covered by the Scheduled Caste net.

According to Young, group representation should have the following provisions:

Self Organisation of Group Members

There is need for and the development of institutional mechanisms and public resources so as to support self organisation of group members. Several women's organisations and workers organisations have come forward with this strategy in India and abroad. But this has not percolated to the very 'below poverty line' people in India. They need to group together to get their voices heard.

Analysis that takes Group Concerns into Consideration

The existence of group analysis and group generation of policy proposals in institutionalised contexts where decision-makers are obliged to show that their deliberations have taken group perspectives into considerations. Parliament committees in India, the corporate sector worldwide, all need to show that they have taken care of the concerns of women, Blacks, Dalits, HIV patients etc.

Veto Power

Granting of group veto power regarding specific policies that affect a group directly, such as reproductive rights policy for women, or land use policy for American Indian reservations.[83] In India, tribes are yet to have this right over land and women in Parliament also do not have such power, for example, over policy of caste-based reservation in India.

This kind of representation is required wherever the interest of group members is specifically affected and when the groups' perceptions and interests are not likely to receive expression without that representation.

Unlike Young who uses the term 'group representation', Will Kymlicka uses the term 'polyethnic rights' or cultural rights. These give political autonomy to a particular community in a defined geographical area. Minority of a particular area is converted into majority and are given right to deliberate upon its own affairs. The hope is that this would allow a community to govern and protect its own interests.

These are most frequently used in liberal democracies. Unlike polyethnic rights, self government rights are rights given to communities such as indigenous populations and national minorities like the Quebecois. Kymlicka justifies group rights for aboriginal communities. By aboriginal community, Kymlicka means a stable and geographically distinct historical community with separate language and culture. It is a community which has been rendered a minority by conquest or immigration or redrawing of political boundaries.[84] The special measures demanded by aboriginals serve to correct an advantage that non-aboriginal people have before anyone makes their choices.[85] For aboriginal people (unlike the White population), the security of the cultural community is in question and therefore it is necessary to outbid the non-aboriginal people just to ensure that their cultural community remains intact and that non-aboriginal people do not dominate and erase the cultural structure of the original people.[86] Thus temporary affirmative action programmes are not sufficient even if material deprivation is no longer the issue.[87]

Bhikhu Parekh, unlike the above two, uses the term *collective rights*. According to him collective rights are required by groups under some specific conditions.[88]

Preservation of indigenous populations in Canada and India are essential for fundamental interest of the nations. Communities like the Amish enjoy moral status in the eyes of its members. These community members then wish to preserve their indigenous culture. Many Muslim communities in India find it difficult to integrate into the mainstream without certain special rights. Muslims across India may have different experience, but the fact remains that they are universally discriminated against. While Bengali Muslims and UP Muslims might have different experience with regards to discrimination, but there are certain features which unify the experience of oppression of Muslims across India. Untouchables in India, a group which has long been subjected to oppression, need opportunity to compete with mainstream communities.

Thus, collective rights, according to Parekh, may vary according to each community's specific need. For example, 'some collectives might merit only the right to interference, some might merit exemption from certain general requirements, yet others might rightly claim positive support of the state and other public institution'.[89]

Assertion of Positive Sense of Group Difference

New social movements do not disagree with the benefits that elimination of difference, and the principle of treating everyone similarly, has brought about for minorities and women. The problem they have, however, is with the conclusion of liberalism, which is the belief that with time these differences will die out. According to these movements, achievement of formal equality does not eliminate social differences. Thus, both feminists and multiculturalists assert (as against sameness) the need to understand how important is understanding difference. For example, on the issue of citizenship[90] and national identity[91] both feminists and multiculturalists assert against the 'sameness' argument, voicing their concern for the differences of immigrant and aboriginal to be incorporated.

The politics of difference challenges the second important principle of liberalism, that is egalitarianism.

As against liberal individualism, politics of difference asserts the need for a positive sense of group difference. In this vision, the good society does not eliminate or transcend group difference. Rather there is 'equality among socially and culturally differentiated groups, who mutually respect one another and affirm each other in their differences'.[92] 'The politics asserts that oppressed groups have distinct cultures, experiences and perspectives on social life with humanly positive meaning, some of which may even be superior to the culture and perspectives of mainstream society.'[93]

Those promoting a politics of difference doubt that a society without group difference is either possible or desirable. Attachment to specific traditions, practices, languages and other culturally specific forms is a crucial aspect of social existence. This negates the first and third principle, that is *individualism* and *universalism*, which define the notion of good society by liberalism. The politics of difference also promotes a notion of group solidarity against the individualism of liberal humanism. 'Where the dominant culture refuses to see anything but the achievement of autonomous individuals, the oppressed assert that we shall not separate from people with whom we identify in order to make it a White Anglo male world.' In the Indian case it would be the Brahmanical male culture. 'The politics of difference insists on liberation of the whole group of Blacks, women, American Indians and this can be accomplished only through basic institutional changes.'[95]

Dual System of Rights

According to advocates of politics of difference, the need is for dual system of rights. A general system of rights, which is the same for all, and also a more specific system of group-conscious policies and rights. In India, we already have group-specific rights and universal rights for citizens. Right to equality, for example, is guaranteed to the general citizenry, while right to culture is guaranteed to minority communities (Article 25-30).

Just provision of group-conscious policies, however, cannot be used to symbolise inclusion. This is because in the past, group-conscious policies were used to separate those defined as different and exclude them from access to the rights and privileges enjoyed by dominant groups. Thus arises the need to treat citizens belonging to certain caste, class, gender both differently and similarly in a particular context. For example, the debate on women's rights focuses on granting women on the one hand equal general rights, while granting them group specific rights such as reservation in panchayats and parliament. The emphasis here is on oppression which women have faced for centuries. Similarly, in India SC and ST communities have been granted similar general rights as well as specific rights, taking care of backwardness of these communities for centuries.

Rainbow Coalition

Young advocates that the politics of difference would require a rainbow coalition of social groups and not traditional coalition of groups.

> In traditional coalitions, diverse groups work together for specific ends which they agree interest or affect them all in a similar way. In contrast, in a Rainbow Coalition 'each of the constituent groups affirms the presence of the others as well

as the specificity of their experience and perspective on social issues'.[96] A Rainbow Coalition of social groups arrives at a 'political programme not by voicing some principles of unity that hide difference, but rather by allowing each constituency to analyse economic and social issues from the perspective of its experience'. 'This implies that each group maintains significant autonomy and requires provisions for group representation.' For example, in a Rainbow gathering, Blacks do not simply tolerate the participation of Gays, labour activists do not grudgingly work alongside peace movement veterans, and none of these paternalistically concede to feminist participation. In India, women activists work with their male counterparts for the welfare of HIV + patients. So, not just the health (both mental and physical) of women is of concern to these organisation but also that of men. Activists like Medha Patkar work not just for displacement of families as a result of building of dams, but also against corruption with Anna Hazare. We can, thus, concede, India is a diverse country and already has this principle of rainbow coalition in functioning.

Specificity of the Indian Experiences

The Indian experience has been one of intermixing of *universal* and *group-differentiated* citizenship. In India, there has been a juxtapositioning of universal concepts of citizenship and group-specific notions of citizenship. In the pre-independence period too, there were these two models which were competing side by side.

Universal citizenship was also a concept which was envisaged by the Congress party, the Hindu organisations and the women's movement.[97] For example, the Motilal Nehru committee report rejected separate electorates but did propose their replacement by reservation for Muslims in provinces in which they were in a minority. The Congress election manifesto emphasised universalism, qualified only by the need to enable cultural diversity to thrive and social justice and inequality to be remedied, as an instrument of making the larger universalist goal more robust. The Congress stood for equal rights and opportunities for every citizen of India, man or woman. It stood for unity of all communities and religious groups and for tolerance and goodwill between them.[98]

The conception of citizenship advanced by Hindu nationalist politics may also be interpreted as proto-universalism. Sarvarkar coined the word 'Hindutva' and defined it in terms of the geographical unity of the Indian nation and its association with territory, race and culture, with religion being ostensibly only one component of culture. Sarvarkar asserted commonality with Muslims in terms of their inheritance of Hindu blood, almost unaffected by an alien adulteration.

A third assertion of universal citizenship was contained in the claims advanced by women's organisations in the early years for the franchise and equal political status with a simultaneous rejection of special provisions such as separate electorates or quotas.

The colonial regime in India invoked the need for group differentiated subjecthood. The chief justification in the colonial period was not so much about disadvantage or oppression as it was about special interests. *The assumption* underlying separate representation *was the conviction that the intensity of group differences in India precluded any possibility of commonality* and the task of colonial governance was therefore to manage these differences by allowing each group to have its point of view and its interests. Seperate representation of Muslims was sought by this argument.[99]

Both these experiences are also visible in independent India. The universalism was the right to equality and freedom while group differentiated rights were the need for affirmative action for SC, ST and OBCs. In the last 70 years, there has been a proliferation of claims to group differentiated citizenship—largely in the form of quotas. Today, there are claims to quotas not only in public institutions, but also in private and non-governmental sectors. The Indian experience of universal and group-differentiated citizenship should be viewed less as a dichotomy and more as an antinomy. Multiculturalists and feminists advocating politics of difference need to keep in mind the unique nature of the Indian context where universal concept of citizenship and group-differentiated citizenship sees an intermixture.[100] Thus, it would be a kind of critique of a pure politics of difference approach. India is a unique case where difference and sameness are juxtaposed against each other. In fact, this diversity of thought is respected, as shown even in the Constitution.

The Health of Democracy

While issues of social justice envisaged through such group representation entails democracy it, on other hand, raises certain other vital questions about the health of democracy.

· Does a differentiated citizenship entail group hostility and irreconcilable difference, with no dialogue across groups?

Some might, for example, object that implementing a principle of group representation in governing bodies would exacerbate conflict and divisiveness in public life, rendering decisions even more difficult to reach. According to Young, especially if groups have veto power over policies that fundamentally and uniquely affect members of their group, it seems likely, it might be claimed that decision-making would be stalled. This objection presupposes that group differences imply essential conflict of interest. Groups may have differing perspectives on issues, but these are often not incompatible and may in fact enrich everyone's understanding when they are expressed. While there might be differences between Jains and Buddhists on the one hand and Muslims and Christians on the other (for example, former lower classes being granted reservation right as SCs and latter not being granted rights of SCs), they may similarly think on the lines of the need for rights to minorities. Therefore, a discussion between minorities on the issues of reservation or a Uniform Civil Code may enrich the already heterogeneous public life in India.

A just society should bring such differences into the open for discussion. Insofar as structural relations of the privileged and oppression are the source of the conflict, group representation can change those relations by equalising the ability of groups to speak and be heard.

Young's concept of 'heterogeneous public'[101] acknowledges difference as 'irreducible', however, communication across those differences is possible. Therefore, she advocates communicative ethics, which recognises the need for a significant interdependence, a commitment to equal respect and agreement on procedural rules of fair discussion and decision-making.[102]

To Parekh, a dialogically constituted multicultural society is fundamentally committed to culture and morality of dialogue.[103] It believes that common good and collective will, that are vital to any political society, are generated not by transcending culture and by the thrust of a dialogue. 'It has a strong notion of common good consisting in respect for basic rights, maintenance of justice, institutional and moral precondition of deliberative democracy and it cherishes not static and ghettoised but interactive and dynamic multiculturalism.'[104] Thus the need would be, for example, in India to have a dialogue of inter-and intra-minorities and the need is for dialogue between these minorities and the majority community.

Conclusion

As far as contentious issues are concerned, Amy Gutmann advocates deliberative universalism, which recognises that some conflicts over social justice cannot be resolved here and now. These conflicts are best addressed and provisionally resolved by actual deliberation, the give-and-take of arguments that is respectful of reasonable differences.[105] For instance, on the issue of abortion, deliberation provisionally resolves fundamental moral conflicts here and now, but not necessarily once and for all. The debate over Uniform Civil Code in India is such a contentious issue, which requires continuous dialogue as while some communities like the Parsis agree on a UCC, Muslims, represented by the All India Muslim Personal Law Board, are strictly against a UCC. They fear, the UCC would reduce the male-domination and control over the community's women.

Here, the fact is that we can potentially learn more about political morality from listening and responding to reasonable arguments with which we disagree rather than thinking on our own.[106] Deliberation thus 'calls upon people both, to affirm the moral status of their own position and also to acknowledge the moral status of those reasonable positions with which they may disagree'.[107] Multiculturalism, thus, can aid deliberation. Our moral understanding of many-sided issues like legalising abortion, Uniform Civil Code etc is furthered by discussion with people with whom we respectfully disagree, especially when these people have cultural identities different from our own.

Therefore dialogue, be it on different experiences, perspectives, cultures, is a necessity for developing a common sense of belonging among citizens.[108]

So far, I have argued that feminists and multiculturalists take a united stand against the liberal politics of indifference. This politics is unable to tackle oppression of minorities and women. Against liberal politics, they advocate the need for politics of difference. They believe, the ideal of a just society is accommodating difference as eliminating group differences is both unrealistic and undesirable. '... justice in a group-differentiated society demands social equality of groups and mutual recognition and affirmation of group differences.'[109]

'Attending to group-specific needs and providing for group representation, both promote that social equality'[110] and provides the recognition that undermines cultural hegemony. Justice and undoing of oppression requires much more than distributive issues. It involves studying deeply the causes of injustice. Only then do the multiculturalist and feminist feel that a holistic concept of justice can be understood. Thus, as the Indian experience will show, it is not just politics of difference but also politics of universalism which need to be understood by multiculturalist and feminist.

While multiculturalists and feminists agree on several issues, in this book we will also consider how they disagree on many aspects.

Conflicting Practices of Diversity & Feminism

Sexual difference is one of the major philosophical issues, if not the issue of our age. According to Heidegger, each age has one issue to think through and one only. Sexual difference is probably the issue in our time which would be our salvation, if we thought it through.

—Luce Irigaray

Writing on the field of multiculturalism and feminism was more like stepping on to a 'political minefield', some might even say like throwing a verbal 'grenade' into a simmering discussion.

—Susan Moller Okin

IN THE previous chapter, I have pointed out how 'multiculturalism and feminism are allies engaged in related struggles for a more inclusive conception of justice'.[1]

However, we need to understand that the 'muddle of multiculturalism'[2] leads us towards a situation where there are 'no simple questions or simple answers'.[3] The point where the two meet leads to considerable tension. As Susan Moller Okin points out:

I think we—especially those of us who consider ourselves politically progressive and opposed to all forms of oppression—

> have been too quick to assume that feminism and multiculturalism are both good things which are easily reconciled. I shall argue instead that there is considerable likelihood of tension between them—more precisely, between feminism and a multiculturalism commitment to group rights for minority cultures.[4]

According to Katha Pollitt, 'feminism and multiculturalism might find themselves as allies in academic politics'. However, in this chapter I look at 'how, as political visions in the larger world, they are very far apart'.

While 'multiculturalism demands respect for all cultural traditions',[5] feminism on the other hand 'interrogates and challenges all cultural traditions'.[6] Feminism, in its demand for equality, places itself virtually against all cultural traditions present. According to Pollitt, 'fundamentally the ethical claims of feminism run counter to the cultural relativism of group rights multiculturalism'.[7]

Tension areas between the two need to be highlighted and discussed.

Is Multiculturalism bad for women?

Feminists fear that 'the fragile gains of feminism may be attenuated by heightened multicultural sensitivity'. According to Bonnie Honig, 'after struggling for so long to increase gender equality in hiring, wages and promotions, and to decrease violence against women, feminists really ought to be concerned that their newly gained grounds, such as it is, might be lost by way of what starts out as concessions to so called difference'.[8]

Before looking at the cases specifically pointed out by feminists, we need to understand the reason for the feminist critique of multiculturalism.

Multiculturalists' call for group rights for minority cultures is found extremely problematic from the feminist point of view. Cultural communities, for them, suppress women and, therefore, granting of group right would only mean sanctioning their oppression. All cultural communities restrict women's choices. They prescribe sexual division of labour.[9]

According to Bonnie Honig, 'It is not at all counter intuitive to think that in a few years, group rights that are tensely related to women's human rights, may get extended not only to national minorities (as Kymlicka would like it) and immigrant groups and ethnic groups, but also to cultural and religious groups until virtually all of the population is covered in one way or another by some cultural exemption'.[10]

Groups are considered problematic because they are generally governed by elders of the tribe, who determine the groups' norms and interests. These groups lack formal democratic decision-making processes and endorse orthodox points of view. Women and minorities thus find themselves oppressed within these groups.

Feminists focus also on a different side of the cultural debate. In the debate on cultural purity, it is not just women who are silenced but equally within the group, the reformers, non-conformists and dissenters are also marginalised. Granting non-democratic communities group rights thus amounts to siding with the traditionalist (often even the reactionary) against the non-conformist, the reformer and dissenter. This can be especially said about the Muslim and the Parsi communities in India.

Problem with contemporary theories of multiculturalism arise because:

a) One of the liberal feminist argument is that advocates of group rights pay little or no attention to the private sphere. Some of the most persuasive liberal defences of group rights urge that individuals need a culture of their own and that only within such a culture can people develop a sense of self-esteem or self-respect. But such arguments typically neglect both the different roles that cultural groups impose on their members and the context in which the persons' sense of themselves and their capacities are first formed—the realm of domestic or family life.[11]

b) Advocates of group rights for minorities tend to treat cultural groups as monoliths to pay more attention to differences within them. Specifically, they accord little or no recognition to the fact that minority cultural groups like the societies in which they exist, are themselves gendered with substantial differences in power and advantages between men and women.[12]

c) Also, one of the major reasons for multiculturalists for ignoring gendered nature of the problem is due to association of cultural diversity with non-discrimination, which provides a powerful rationale for not interfering with or restricting in any ways the existing community practices. 'Thus, the conflation of two quite distinct concerns relating to non-discrimination and preservation of culture provides powerful rationale for non-interference in community rituals and practices.'[13] This results in multiculturalists taking no cognisance of intra group inequality, stressing on equality between groups. Thus, multicultural theorists overlook the link between culture and patriarchy.

Most cultures, feminists point out, have as their principal aim, the control of women by men.[14]

Feminism might be of varied kinds. The issues covered by Chinese feminism may be different from their western counterparts. For example, while female foeticide, the one child policy, might be a matter of concern in China, the same is not true in the west where there is no ban on sex determination, nor any problem related to female foeticide.

Russian feminism may be located differently from Black feminism. Recent Russian political narratives have increasingly depicted the role of women as belonging to the domestic sphere, especially in the context of the very low birth rates of the last two decades. Awareness about gender inequalities in the USSR, including job discrimination, the exclusion of women from decision-making levels, the double hat of paid and domestic work, as well as patriarchal societal and family structures have increased.

The hope of a shift towards 'liberal' democracy in Russia further encouraged the formation of new political and civil society groups, such as the political party, Women of Russia, gender research groups and non-governmental organisations. However, in modern Russia, liberal hopes of democracy and westernised feminism were soon to wane.

Mikhail Gorbachev has been a strong advocate of 'ridding women of their double burden' by letting them return to domestic work, their 'natural domain'. This is very different from the situation of women in Africa, India or China. In fact, within a country there could be different kinds of feminism. For example, in India, mainstream feminism may be different from Dalit feminism.

Concerns of Community Practices

Tension areas between the two need to be highlighted and discussed.

Feminists stress that all cultures have shades of patriarchy, which attempt to control women's sexual behaviour, establishing control over their bodies. This can be demonstrated in different countries by looking at issues in both majority and minority cultures, varying from female circumcision, forced marriage, polygamy, personal laws, rape in minority cultures, abortion and the Equal Rights Amendment.

Historically, discussing the thousand-year-old custom of foot binding in China, Bonnie Honig seems to have drawn her conclusion from a pre-conceptualised theory that men created submissive women and used foot binding as 'the ultimate tool to deny women the physical expression of freedom' and that foot binding was 'the pre-eminent symbol of sexual oppression' in China.

The practice of female circumcision in African countries is explicitly defended on grounds of necessity for controlling women's sexual behaviour, making her more marriageable.[15] Such circumcision is built upon a complex mythology that has been elaborated with the primary purpose of controlling women's sexuality for benefits of men. Feminists point out that cultural arguments in favour of circumcision by traditionalist females uncomfortably parallel the invocation of culture or ethnicity as a defence or excuse for violence, injustice and a host of other ills. Most advocates of female circumcision appear to equate culture with history and tradition, but they fail to recognise the many ways in which their present actions and life style reinforce a notion of culture that comprises not only the traditional but the contemporary as well. Feminists point out that circumcision has fatal medical, psychological and sexual consequences.[16]

Matters become more complicated when it concerns immigrant communities as in France. On the level of fundamentals, there is thus little or no disagreement among [17] feminists. It is, however, at the 'level of strategy, cultural sensitivity and dilemma of taking legal action against women in the name of, paradoxically, women's rights that serious divergences appear'. While the pro-trial feminists take the stance that excision is under no circumstances defensible or excusable, for it is a physical, sexual and psychological mutilation of the female child, anti-trial feminists split with the former over the issue of criminalisation. 'The position they take is that bringing cases of excision to trial does more harm than good, particularly as it is other women who are being judged and sentenced, while men who hold the real power of this decision are less and less likely to be brought to trial.' 'The responsibility of their husbands in contributing to their isolation (from welfare networks) has been stressed by both pro-and anti-trial feminists and in particular by African feminists who work closely with the immigrant communities.'

This brings to fore the case of how women can be doubly disadvantaged. Not only do women have subordinate roles within their communities, but they are also being victimised by state laws. France has signed bilateral conventions with all three Maghrebian countries, Algeria, Morocco and Tunisia, allowing marital laws of those countries to prevail in case of immigrant families, even though laws in question run contrary to French laws. 'This could be seen as a legal precedent for the respect of their patriarchy in case of excision.' This points to the fact that even the nation state as a category is not always very helpful to the women's cause.

Honour killings and coerced marriage first and foremost consider girls and women as sexual servants of men, that their virginity before marriage and fidelity within it are their preeminent virtues. Honour killings have been frequently documented in countries such as Bangladesh, Brazil, Ecuador, Egypt, India, Israel, Italy, Jordan, Morocco, Pakistan, Sweden, Turkey, Uganda and the UK. Honour killings have been defined as 'the killing of women for suspected deviation from sexual norms imposed by society'.[18]

Honour killing are extreme acts of violence perpetrated upon women when an honour code is believed to have been broken and perceived shame is brought upon the family. Women can also carry the burden for the shame of male violation of their sexual honours and have been killed because they have become pregnant, as victims of incest and rape. Being suspected of sexual deviancy such as pregnancy outside marriage or adulterous behavior is also seen as enough to justify punishing a woman.[19] What marks so called honour killing is that it is not just the husband or partner that may carry out the act but also the community and other family members such as mothers, brothers, uncles and cousins. It is often younger women in their late teens and early twenties who are victims of these crimes. At this age, the young woman's sexuality comes under increasing regulation and control by the family and the wider community. It is the young woman's sexual purity and honour that is seen to define the status and regard with which ther family is held in the community.[20]

Multiculturalism, which is underpinned by notions of respecting diversity and valuing cultural differences, unwittingly supports non-intervention when dealing with domestic violence routed in cultural and religious practices in the private sphere of the home. The affected women slip through the cracks of both domestic violence and the multiculturalism discourse.

As Beckett and Macey argue, 'Multiculturalism does not cause domestic violence, but it does facilitate its continuation through its creed of respect for cultural differences, its emphasis on non-interference in minority life-styles and its insistence on community consultation (with male self-defined community leaders). This has resulted in women being made invisible, their needs ignored, and their voices silenced'.

As for child marriage or otherwise coerced marriages, this practice is clearly a way not only for controlling who the girls or young women marry but also of ensuring that they are virgins at the time of marriage and often of enhancing the husband's power by creating a significant age difference between husbands and wives.

Polyandry in India refers to the historical practice of polyandry, whereby a woman has two or more husbands at the same time. While polyandrous unions have disappeared from the traditions of many of the groups and tribes, it is still practiced by some Paharis, especially in Jaunsar Bawar region in northern India. This leads to sexual competition among husbands and problems with deciding paternity. This might lead to conflict amongst spouses. Jealousy may be bred amongst them. A general theory presented for polyandry is the insurance of marriage for all eligible individuals in societies where there is a surplus of men (Heath 1955, cited in Berreman 1962).

In Jaunsar Bawar, there is a great shortage of women. However, in nearby and monogamous Garhwal, there is a high surplus of women (Berreman 1962), a trend which suggests that polyandry may be the cause and not the solution to a shortage of available wives. Starkweather and Hames noted that they 'found that an imbalanced operational sex ratio in favour of males is the only variable robustly associated with polyandry (2012, p. 166)'.

Kinnauri women have been quoted as saying that, 'the role of a polyandrous wife is the most crucial and the most difficult, yet it is the co-husbands that fight and leave'. This kind of polyandry is in practice in many villages of Kinnaur district of Himachal

Pradesh. Fraternal polyandry (where husbands are related to each other) is mainly in practice in villages where the societies are male dominated and which still follow old rituals and customs. There are many forms of polyandry which can be found here. Most often, all the brothers are married to a woman and sometimes the marriage to brothers happens at a later date. The wife alone can ascertain the blood-relationship of the children, though recently there have been a few instances of paternity tests using DNA samples to solve inheritance disputes.

Fraternal polyandry exists among the Khasa of Dehra Dun and among the Gallong of Arunachal Pradesh, the Mala Madessar, the Mavilan etc. of Kerala. Non-fraternal polyandry exists among the Kota and among the Karvazhi, Pulaya, Muthuvan and Mannan in Kerala.

Female infanticide, for example, in Punjab has resulted in polyandry.

There is practice common in much of Latin America, South East Asia and parts of West Asia, of pressuring a rape victim to marry the rapist. It is believed, by marrying his victims, the rapist can help restore the family's honour and relieve it of a daughter who as 'damaged goods' has become unmarriageable. In fact, in many cultures, 'rapists are legally exonerated if they marry or simply offer to marry their victims'.[21]

However, worst fates do exist in some cultures, notably in Pakistan and parts of Arab Middle East 'where women who bring rape charges quite frequently are charged themselves with the Muslim offence of Zina or sex outside of marriage'. Law allows for the whipping or imprisonment of such women and culture pressurises them to commit suicide. The law in Pakistan requires evidence of four Muslim males without the witness of whom rape cannot be proven.[22]

The Hudood ordinance defines rape in a very discriminatory manner for women and children, since they generally have no access to legal counsel and also have low economic status. Women can now be accused of rape as can children. 'Laws of mutual consent may easily convert a case of child abuse into prosecution of child for Zina.' 'Furthermore,[23] unmarried men and women can be convicted of having committed rape against each other, since a subsection of Zina offense defines rape as one where a man or woman has illicit sex knowing that they are not validly married to each other.'

In polygamous cultures too,[24] men readily acknowledge that practice accords with their self interest and is a means of controlling women. French African immigrant women deny that they like polygamy and say that not only are they given no choice in the matter but their female forbearers in Africa did not like it either. Feminists point out that polygamous marriages breed insecurity and jealousy. Since each wife knows she is replaceable and dispensable, they lack a sense of bonding. Economically, pressures increase on women and family. Neither does it provide ideal condition for growth of children, which requires a secure and stable environment.

However, feminists are aware that not only minorities, but also majority cultures have shades of patriarchy, which cannot be overlooked. I would like to highlight the controversies which the issue of abortion has generated across communities. The issue continues to generate divisions within both minority and majority community in the US.

Anti-choice communities—Catholics, Orthodox Jews, Mormons and Fundamentalists consider it to be a moral sin to kill a foetus. In USA, the issue of abortion revolves around, whether abortion is crime, that is, murder of human being/foetus as a fundamentalist would put it or is it about reproductive rights and control of women over their bodies as feminists view the matter. The current battle for feminists raises the most potent danger to women's autonomy, because now the 'womb has been pitted against women'. 'With creation of this preborn and invisible citizenry, a woman's quite legitimate expectation of privacy and control in pregnancy is being obliterated.'

The question that goes abegging is, 'what is a woman? Private citizen or a pregnant subject?'[25] 'Furthering the sanctity of foetal life, government and its policies ignore the need of its existing citizens and already-born children and constitute a national betrayal of feminists.' National betrayal of feminists constitute amendments like the Hyde Amendment which allowed the state to refuse funding for women on grounds such as parental consent, spousal notification etc. leading to access of women already having limited access further reduced.

While in the USA, the *Roe vs Wade* case legalised abortions, tensions continue to exist with the *Muller and Monson* case, where the judiciary pronounced the principle of foetal endangerment and feotal neglect, saying all women are potentially accountable for the outcome of their pregnancy and condition of their offspring at birth. Feminists demanded empowerment not only at the level of public/political sphere, but also at the intimate sphere, that is, at the level of womb.

The Equal Rights Amendment (ERA, the United States Constitution amendment designed to guarantee equal legal rights for all American citizens regardless of sex) has held importance across the feminist spectrum, which basically meant prohibiting legal sex discrimination. The issue was, however, not only over ERA as it also covered issues such as equal pay, affirmative action, lower value given to women's work, in fact showing the sensitive nature of the issue. Its non-passage would have been seen by feminist and women's movements as representative of women's secondary status.

Powerful reaction against ERA came from communities such as Catholics, orthodox Jews and Mormons in both the USA and Europe. The 1977 international women's year was condemned by moral majoritarian forces as immoral women's year. The Mormon community excommunicated one feminist of their community from their church for mobilising Mormons in favour of ERA. Anti-feminist groups such as the now-defunct Moral Majority or

Eagle Forum, promulgate an ideology in opposition to child care, welfare, reproductive rights, sexual autonomy, affirmative action and racial integration.

Pro-family groups point out that the whole talk about equal rights was devaluing women's role and taking away protection for women such as alimony and child support. In fact, ERA is a stark reminder of the communities' power and pressure over the state so as to withhold any rights being provided to their women (because it would entail altering the existing hierarchical and oppressive patterns within the communities). However, what is worth pointing out in case of ERA is that not only minority communities, but also majority communities (Protestants) allied in the cause, which saw the non-passage of the amendment.

Feminists thus raise the larger issue of citizenship and public/private dichotomy within feminist theory. To feminists, multicultural political theory is plagued with the same problem of public/ private dichotomy as liberal theory; as they now place private sphere within the community's jurisdiction. A non-interventionist accommodation policy permits identity groups to surround themselves with barriers so inviolable that whatever happens within those groups, happens outside the jurisdiction of state law. Hence if a violation of citizenship rights occurs within an identity group, then violation is categorised as a private affair. The state as an outside entity has no right to intervene.

So, the important question in context of all multicultural societies would be—are women granted citizenship rights as citizens or are they considered to be citizens subsumed within communities? What kind of citizenship right would exist for women if cultural rights are granted? To feminists this would be 'male centred' citizenship with both achieving citizenship rights differently as per their roles, as Carole Pateman would bring out, men as soldiers and women as reproducers, which would lead to women being again relegated to the private realm.

Feminist Critique of Multiculturalist Thinkers

Despite all this evidence of cultural practices that control and subordinate women, most of the prominent multiculturalists do not address the troubling connection between feminism and multiculturalism.[26]

To multiculturalists, giving cultural rights to groups triumphs all other considerations. Model provided by theorists like Kymlicka elevate cultural membership to the status of primary good.[27] The stress is on need to reduce minority groups' vulnerability to the economic or political power of the larger society (which, however, overlook internal restrictions that they posit on their group members). Multiculturalists like Parekh take recourse to 'operative public values' that are enshrined in the constitution, which can be the basis of determining what kind of cultural diversity may or may not be protected.

However, feminist are deeply sceptical of multiculturalist claims to inter group equality; while Kymlicka acknowledges the need for internal liberalism, feminists like Susan Okin point out that far fewer minority cultures than he seems to think will be able to claim group rights under such a justification. While Kymlicka regards culture that discriminate overtly and formally against women by denying them education or right to vote or hold office—as not deserving special rights—but the fact is, sex discrimination is often far less overt, subordination of women is often informal and private and that virtually no culture in the world today—minority or majority—can pass its 'no sex discrimination test', if it were applied in the private sphere.

Multiculturalist emphasis on *operative public values* and *shared public norms* may themselves buttress structures of discrimination. Who makes and determines what values are enshrined in a nation's constitution and laws? Certainly not women (be it from minority or majority cultures). This is very much evident when we count the number of women represented in parliaments and political parties. Parekh, for example, contends that public values can be challenged in case of sexist regimes. However, how do women simply challenge entrenched patriarchal values, which are reflected not only in constitution and laws but also societal values, as in marital rape laws? How can a dialogue be open ended and free floating, when prevailing values are patriarchal in nature? Operative values are definitely not working in favour of women—least of all minority community women.

Another prominent critique of the multiculturalist position has been provided by Iris Marion Young.[28] Young says, the multiculturalist focus on cultural inequality ignores issues of structural inequality. Young discusses at least three unfortunate consequences of the multiculturalist position.

i) Where structural injustices do build on perceived cultural differences, a politics of cultural differences and its emphasis on liberty does not make visible enough issues of structural inequality.

ii) Because the politics and political theory of cultural difference tends to focus on what state policy properly should allow, forbid or remain silent about, it tends to ignore civil society as a crucial site for working on injustice.[29]

iii) According to Young, most of the issues that arise both in theoretical writing and public discussion about the politics of cultural difference concern state policy, regulations or the organisation of state institutions. However, movements of African-Americans, people with disabilities, feminists, gay men and lesbians, indigenous people as well as many ethnic movements realise that societal discrimination, processes of segregation and marginalisation enacted through social networks and private institutions must be confronted in their non-state institutional sites.

While law can provide a framework for equality and some remedy for egregious violation of rights and respect, the state and law cannot and should not reach into every capillary of everyday life. A *politics of positional difference*, thus, recommends that churches, universities, production and marketing enterprises, clubs and associations all examine their policies, practices and priorities to discover ways they contribute to unjust structures and recommends changing them when they do so.

Seyla Benhabib distinguishes such a 'dual track' approach to politics, which she associates with critical theory, and argues that liberal political theory typically ignores non-state dimension of politics.[30]

In *deliberative democracy* as distinguished from *political liberalism*, the official public sphere of representative institutions, which includes the legislature, executive and public bureaucracies, the judiciary and political parties, is not the only site of political contestation and of opinion and will formation. Deliberative democracy focuses on social movements and on the civil, cultural, religious, artistic and political associations of the unofficial public sphere as well.

Recent discussions on the politics of cultural difference finally admit, especially regarding the status of women within cultural minorities, that too often multiculturalists themselves tend to elevate particular group-based standards as normative for a whole polity without specifically noticing this normalising move. 'Framing issues of difference in terms of toleration, however, often introduces a normalising logic in the debates on multiculturalism.'

'The political question debated often has this form: shall we tolerate this expression or practice that we find of questionable value or morality, for the sake of mutual accommodation and civic peace? Should we allow methods of processing animals for food which requires that the animals be conscious at the time of slaughter?' 'The point of view of the dominant culture, which assumes itself to have the power to influence the authorities who allow or forbid certain practices prevails… While those holding the point of view debate among themselves whether toleration is the appropriate stance in this case, they all presume themselves to occupy a position as normal, which means not only in statistical majority, but also holding values that lie within the range of acceptable and even good.'

Young makes a different point as far as the politics of cultural difference is concerned. According to her, 'a funny inversion often happens to gender issues in this politics of cultural difference, utilising the normalising logic implicit in many debates about toleration'. 'The politics of cultural difference obscures many issues concerning gender and justice that are matters of structural inequality.' An example of such inversion in India would be the Shah Bano case.

'In many theoretical writings on multiculturalism, gender issues serve as the test to the limits of toleration. The questions of concern in this regard are many. To cite a few, they are on the lines of: "Can we tolerate rules of a national minority that refuse to recognise the women who marry outside as group members?" "Can we allow Muslim women to accede to the pressure or expectation that they wear the hijab?" "Surely we cannot permit arranged marriages of teenage girls or female genital circumscision under any circumstances."'

Young's purpose in calling attention to the ubiquity of gender issues in contemporary political and theoretical debates on cultural difference is 'to bring them up as instances of the normalising of the discourse of toleration typical of logic of the politics of cultural difference'. The *we* in these questions occupies the position of the majority western liberals. *We* can raise these questions about the extent to which the gender practice of the minority culture can be tolerated because among *us* women have the same freedom and autonomy as men. *Our* gender individualism is the norm against which the practices of many cultures come up deviant. 'Debates about gender in the politics of cultural difference thus serve the double function of positioning some cultural groups beyond the pale and encouraging a self-congratulatory arrogance on the part of the *we* who debate these issues.'

In the process, according to Young, 'the real issue of gendered structured inequality may be ignored'. Thus, according to her, the fact that politics of cultural difference has occupied political theorists more in recent years than a politics of positional difference is lamentable. 'It tends to narrow the groups of concern to ethnic, national and religious groups, and to limit the issues of justice at stake to those concerned with freedom and autonomy more than equal opportunity of people to develop capacity and live a life of well-being.' Its reliance on a liberal paradigm, moreover, tends to limit politics to shaping state policy and to reintroduce normalising movements.

'Young's objective in making these distinctions and arguments has not been to reject the politics of cultural difference, but to encourage political theorists to refocus their attention to group difference generated from structural power, the division of labour and constructions of the normal and the deviant, as they continue also to reflect on conflicts over national, ethnic, or religious difference.'

Liberal Feminist Response to Multiculturalism

Securing Individual Rights and Autonomy

Liberal feminist prioritise individual rights over group rights. Some of them are opposed to granting of group rights. Feminist like Susan Moller Okin, for example, regards it not to be clear from feminist point of view that group rights are part of the solution. 'They' according to her, 'may in fact increase the problem'.[31]

According to Okin, 'no argument can be made on the basis of self respect or freedom that the female members of the culture have a clear interest in its preservation'. 'In fact, they might be much better off if the culture into which they were born were either to become extinct (so that its members would become integrated into the less sexist surrounding culture), or preferably be encouraged to alter itself so as to reinforce the equality of women—at least to the degree to which this value is upheld, in majority culture.'

Many instances of private sphere discrimination against women on cultural grounds are never likely to emerge in public. It is thus especially important to consider inequalities between the sexes, since they are likely to be less public and thus less easily discernible.[32]

Establishing group rights to enable some minority cultures to preserve themselves may not be in the best interest of the girls and women of those cultures, even if it benefits the men. Thus, to Okin, those who make liberal arguments for rights of groups must take special care to look at inequalities within those groups.

According to her, 'unless women, and more specifically younger women (since older women often are coupled into reinforcing gender inequalities), are fully represented in negotiations about group rights, their interest may be harmed rather than promoted by granting such rights'. 'What we need to strive towards is a multiculturalism that effectively treats all persons as each other's moral equals.'

Just like Okin there are several feminists in American politics who believe in *secularism* as a value special for protection of women's rights.[33] To cite two prominent works, Alison Jagger's *Feminist Politics and Human Nature* and Catherine Mackinnon's *Towards a Feminist Theory of State* are the two best anthologies of feminist social-political thought that devote no space to religion, although they discuss many topics only contingently linked to feminism such as environmentalism and vegetarianism.

In law for example, feminists more frequently take on religion. According to some of the legal feminists, 'religion perpetuates and reinforces women's subordination and religious freedom impedes reform'. 'Religion contributes to women's subordinate status, not only within the religious community's hierarchies, but also in broader culture.' 'Religion encourages women to live with the status quo rather than destabilising it by insisting on equality.'

The secular feminist tends to view religion itself as irredeemably patriarchal, and powerful ally of women's oppression throughout the ages. 'The secular feminist is not unhappy to muzzle it and does not see it as doing a whole lot of good in anyone's life.' 'Many secular feminists are Marxists; and following Marx they are bound to take a negative view of religion and are unlikely even to give the free exercise of religion a high degree of respect.'[34]

Yael Tamir feels the need to empower individuals by granting them individual rights. In so doing, 'we may protect the rights of the less powerful and less conservative members of each group to live their lives[35] and preserve their identity the way they see fit. In so doing, we may provide help and support for the agents of cultural and societal change in general and in particular for defenders of women's rights'.

Many multiculturalists state the need to disassociate special rights granted for systemic discrimination of minorities within the nation state from the rights that may be necessary for preserving minority cultures. 'Preservation of cultural practices' can be and often is an excuse to continue with customs that perpetuate discrimination of some groups. Within the community, special rights cannot be justified for this end. Thus, respect for other cultures is always premised on first respecting individual citizens.[36]

Here I would also like to point to some Muslim feminists who proclaim the need for separation of religion and state.

Valentine M Moghadam somewhat answers this when she discusses her personal reasoning for secular feminism.[37] Her assertion is that as long as feminist movements are 'focused on theological rather than socioeconomic and political questions, and so long as their point of reference is the Qur'an rather than universal standards, their impact will be limited at best'. According to her, unlike the American feminists, 'Islamic feminists are seeking revolutionary change to political and social institutions by questioning the exclusive right of clerics to interpret the Islamic texts and on Islamic jurisprudence'. She even points out that it is particularly Islam which puts in danger feminist movements because 'it defines citizenship rights on the basis of religion'.

Haideh Mohissi, as a Marxist feminist, is open about her dim view of religion, specially 'as a driving force for meaningful social change'. As far as Islamic in *Islamic feminism* is concerned, Mohissi view is that 'not only is a religion based in gender hierarchies incompatible with "gender equity and... women's rights", but it has no libratory potential either'.[38]

Hameed Shahidian is critical of attempts by Arab scholars such as Fatima Mernissi and Aziza Al-Hibri, and the Pakistan-born Rifat Hassan at the reinterpretation of Islamic texts. According to him, these attempts are futile given the strength of conservative, orthodox, traditional and fundamentalist interpretations, laws, and institutions. He is especially critical of a growing trend in Middle East Women's [39] Studies wherein authors justify Muslim women's veiling, domesticity, moral behaviour and adherence to Islamic precepts as signs of 'individual choice' and identity.[40]

Nadje Al Ali, in her work, points out that 'all women interviewed were united in their opposition to the establishment of an Islamic state, the implementation of the Shariah, the existing personal status law and an imposed dress code that is compulsory veiling. They also shared a sense that religion should not be conflated with politics'. The majority of the activists concurred with the view that 'the personal status law is a source of inequality and discrimination'. 'For many activists, the aim to change the laws regulating marriage, divorce and child custody is the only aspect of their conceived goals that touches on women's private lives.'[41]

However, some feminists believe that religion is important and the only need is to interpret religion in a progressive manner. Martha Nussbaum, another liberal feminist, focuses on the need for religion. She agrees with Okin that 'current liberal interest in multiculturalism holds grave dangers for equality of women'. The danger has, according to Nussbaum, increased by the fact that issues of sex equality have rarely been seen as urgent and central by major political thinkers of our times. However, Nussbaum takes a totally different view on religion despite agreeing with Okin for the need for exit for women members. She makes three points with regards to religion.

Firstly, 'several movements such as abolitionism and US civil rights movement, the movement against racism, even the Indian struggle for Independence have had a religious base'.[42]

Many feminists worldwide have been deeply religious. Nussbaum says, because 'Okin and other secular feminists do not acknowledge these instances, they cannot well describe the complexity of the issues raised by the relationship between religion and feminism'.

Secondly, Nussbaum insists that *political liberalism* unlike *comprehensive liberalism* is far more capable of accommodating the very great value of citizens' religious freedom. Political liberalism insists that every citizen has a wide range of liberties and opportunities; so it agrees with comprehensive liberalism that a non-autonomous life should not be thrust upon someone by the luck of birth. Nonetheless, it respects such lives—given a background of liberty and opportunity—as lives that reasonable fellow citizens may pursue. 'Political liberals will be likely to judge that religion merits special deference from the liberal state, given its central importance to citizens in their search for meaning and given the content of religious convictions, which frequently specifies their central importance and the non-optional character of demands they make.' Nussbaum favours the 'traditional stance of giving religion special deference, on the grounds that minority religions have been especially vulnerable in all societies and are consequently in need of this special protection'.

Thirdly, according to Nussbaum, 'no religious tradition consists simply of authority and sheep-like subservience'. All contain plurality of voices—including the voices of women which have not always been clearly heard. Nussbaum acknowledges that secular humanist feminists like Okin do mention existence of more progressive, reformed versions of major religions. But this characterisation is simple and simplistic.[43]

As a reformed Jew, to Nussbaum, 'the core of Judaism is a set of timeless moral ideas that are imperfectly revealed in both text and rabbinic history'.Thus reform means, a reform of 'defective historical practices in the direction of a more authentic realisation of Judaism'. By treating the original core of religion as equivalent to certain patriarchal stories these feminists simply bypass centuries of debate within each of the religions, debate highly pertinent to religion's role in search of women's equality.[44]

While Nussbaum does not like the idea of a all-male priesthood any more than Okin does, she feels a strong sense of solidarity with Roman Catholics who are trying to open the church more fully to women through internal reform.'Yet she feel that we need to respect different lives our fellow citizens choose to lead and a sense of complexity of our task.'

Fourthly, many feminists argue against orthodoxy of religion which does not change for centuries. Jewish and Islamic feminist scholars have taken a further step by entering the 'temple' of religion by undertaking the most revered of its internal mechanisms of cultural reproductions: theological study. Their strategy has been to highlight the potential within the constitutive religious texts for alternate readings that are better able to mesh with women's freedom and equality.

As Susan Heschel, a Jewish feminist, writes, 'We examine what the text reveals but also explore what the same text conceals'.[45] Thus, 'by infusing religious study with feminist perspectives, women are asserting not only their membership in the community, but also their contribution to it as full participants'. For instance, female and progressive scholars have offered revisionist readings of the Qur'an, readings which are inclusive of women and which treat women and men as equals before Allah.

Thus, a quiet revolution has involved not only scriptural learning but also prayer leading and marriage officiating by Muslim women.[46] According to them, 'Most important for our discussion is the recognition that entering the charged field of theological study and knowledge production has allowed women to demonstrate the importance of their agency and their voice in their creation of more egalitarian cultural religious norms and practices'.

One of the most prominent Islamic Feminists, Irshad Manji, in her work establishes the need for reform in Islam. Irshad has founded *Project Ijtihad,*[47] an initiative to renew Islam's own tradition of critical thinking, debate and dissent. Project Ijtihad is helping to build the world's most inclusive network of reform-minded Muslims and non-Muslim allies.

Her basic argument is that the Qur'an is a complex, contradictory, human book. Its proscriptions are many and conflicting. 'Abandoning the role of a thinking person is not something that should be required of any religious individual.' Reason and faith, Manji wants to believe, are not in conflict. 'And yet, as Islam is frequently practiced, reason is deplored as something that should defer in every instance not simply to the Qur'an but to the political authoritarians who reserve to themselves the sole right to interpret it.'

What Manji discovered in the madrasas was a symptom of what she sees as a broader and deeper problem, 'that Muslims have stopped thinking, that their faith has been hijacked by tyrants and bullies, and that it has become infested with all kinds of hatred—of Jews, of women, of gays, of the West'.And instead of confronting these issues directly and openly, most western Muslims—perhaps the only group of Muslims with the actual freedom to question, criticise and debate—have decided to retreat into playing victim and appeasement. Aided and abetted by the moral nihilism of academic postmodernism, these people have surrendered to the new fascists of the Arab world.[48]

However, despite her critique of present-day Islam, she continues to work within the folds of Islam. 'She wants to embrace her faith by understanding it fully, by realizing its vision of human equality, by resuscitating the ancient Islamic tradition of ijtihad: questioning, asking, thinking.' Even the Egyptian feminist

Nawal el Saadawi writes that, 'We have to compare the Qur'an to other holy books before we judge Islam'.'A fair comparison will help us to discover that the Qura'n or fundamental teachings of Islam are relatively progressive in relation to women and democracy.'[49]

'A striking feature of contemporary political philosophy is the emergence of the nature of the political itself as central theme of discussion.'[50] Both feminist and multicultural political theory have contributed towards this trend by maintaining that the story of western life to date has beenone of arbitrary exclusion, in the course of which various victim groups have been created—in case of women by patriarchy and minorities by majorities. This trend has been compounded at the practical level by development and acceptance of multiculturalism as a value and fact of life.

Feminists point to the need to consider not only inter-cultural but also intra-cultural equality. Anne Phillips says, 'The need is for us to consider equitable treatment of minority and majority cultures alongside other considerations of equity, that is between men and women'.[51] She cautions against elevating cultural membership to the status of primary good as it potentially triumphs all other considerations. Feminists say that respect for other cultures is always premised on first respecting the individual citizen—which is not abstract but a gendered, differentiated citizenship within which multiple differences and diverse perspective of the previously excluded *other* might be recognised, affirmed and represented.[52]

The fate of a culture, a language, or a religion ought to be determined by its members. For that purpose, one must grant cultural, religious, national rights to individuals rather than to the community as a whole. The difference between granting cultural or religious rights to individuals and granting them to groups is evident if one compares the status of the Jewish reform movement in Israel and in the United States.[53] In the US, for instance, religious rights are individual rights—under these conditions the reform movement flourishes, as a large percentage of American Jews choose to affiliate with it. In Israel, on the other hand, religious rights are granted to each religious community. The search for a unified voice that represents the Jewish community provokes a struggle among the different Jewish movements. The Orthodox, who succeeded early in presenting themselves as the sole authoritative representatives of Judaism, attempt to disqualify all other versions, especially the reformed ones. The reform movement is thus presented as a threat to the continued existence of the Jewish people and its members are deprived of their religious rights. Unlike Orthodox institutions, reformed ones receive almost no financial support from the state; the teachings of the 'reform movement' are not part of Jewish studies in schools; and reformed rabbis cannot perform marriages. Consequently the 'reform movement' finds it very hard to form an Israeli branch. As a result, in Israel (unlike in the US) individual Jews are unable to make a free choice concerning the way they would like to practice their religion.

This analysis can teach three lessons: first, we should have a realistic, a less sentimental view of traditional communities and less static view of culture. We ought to recognise that cultures are permanently changing and developing, and that there is no reason to freeze a culture in order to preserve it. Cultures hostile to change are less likely to trust the ability of individuals to withstand change and reform their traditions and lifestyle without surrendering completely their particular identity.

Second, we must entrust the faith of community to its individual members. According to Yael Tamir, we ought then to empower individuals by granting them individual rights. In so doing, we may protect the rights of the less powerful and less conservative members of each group to live their lives and preserve their identity the way they see fit. According to her, in so doing, we may also provide help and support for agents of cultural and social change in general, and in particular, for defenders of women's rights.

In fact, if culture and tradition are seen in less static light, then reformers could be seen as contributing to the preservation of the communal identity no less than conservatives.

Therefore, from a feminist perspective, 'Multiculturalism is a problem today and foreseeable future—a problem for politics and ethics of politics'. This is because feminists and many such other issues still need to be addressed in their true complexity, within the domain of present multicultural societies.[54]

Diversity & Feminism: Theories of Reconciliation

> Contemporary social struggles are bringing to the fore this contradictory movement that the emancipatory discourse of both religious and modern secularized eschatologies had concealed and repressed. We are today coming to terms with our own finitude and with the political possibilities that it opens. This is the point from which the potentially liberatory discourses of our postmodern age have to start. We can perhaps say that today we are at the end of emancipation and at the beginning of freedom.
>
> —Ernesto Laclau

WE HAVE looked at the areas of tension between multiculturalism and feminism in the previous chapter. In this chapter I will examine the models which look at reconciliation between the two. Several theorists have attempted to answer this. The answer to this conflict, they say, can have several possibilities such as the exit option, the liberal multicultural method, deliberative democracy and the multiple jurisdiction method.

The Exit Option

An exit system means that women and men have a fundamental right to move out or disassociate from the system they are linked with. According to theorists like Chandran Kukathas, exit option proceeds with the fundamental assumption that women and other marginalised groups have the right to disassociation in this 'liberal archipelago'.[1] It means that if the practices of any group are unacceptable to its members, they have the option to move out or leave the group.

Thus, the right of the individual should not be taken away from group members, for example, a woman's right to move out of a community should be an inalienable right of the community. In multicultural theory, thus, *exit* is called upon to protect vulnerable group members against oppression which they may suffer at the hands of their group members.[2] While minorities have the right to practice their traditional ways, any liberal or illiberal culture should provide choice to individual members to cease to be part of the community. An example would be the Amish community or the Dalits of India who often declare they are Buddhists, exercising an exit option from the dominant community.

If members of a cultural community wish to continue to live by their beliefs, the outside community has no right to intervene to prevent those members from acting within their right. For example, the state need not interfere in internal functioning of the community. It is the prerogative of the individual alone. No authority has a right to coerce people into becoming members of any community or association. Or remain within its fold either. Right to exit is thus a necessary condition against any sort of cultural oppression. It is neither the group nor the state which has absolute rights, it is the individual rights which are protected by this approach.

However, critics point out that the exit option expects the already disadvantaged section of a community to move out, thereby increasing their vulnerability.[3]

Even when community members use the exit option, especially through religious conversions, there have been cases of constant harassment and threats to such individuals by the original community's orthodox members. In India, for example, Hindu extremists have reacted in similar manner aganist members of their community converting to other religions. Similarly, there have been cases when Muslims who converted to Christianity were threatened by Islamic radicals even when they migrated to western countries. Here too, liberal arguments for tolerance of other cultures have been used to suppress dissent within communities. Thus apostates even in western countries have been forced to maintain low profiles.

Another aspect is that exit might not be a real option because of the overall attitude of stereotyping of minorities within a larger society. While certain individuals of a community may not be associating with traditions of their community[4] in public sphere, they are negatively stereotyped. Thus, even though individuals may not wear turban or offer namaz five times, they may still get 'ostracised as Sikhs or Muslims'[5]. In such a situation, exit is not much a matter of individual choice but is 'thrust upon individuals from the outside'.[6] If individuals are categorized because of 'their names and identity with which they are born rather than with their beliefs and actions', then exit can never be choice with individuals.

In fact, this right of exit solution offers no comprehensive policy approach at all and instead offers a case by case approach, imposing the burden of resolving the conflict upon the individual and relieving the state of any responsibility for the situation, even though as the accommodating entity it, still has fiduciary duty towards all citizens. Specifically, the right of exit argument suggests that an injured insider should be the one to abandon the very centre of her life, family and community. This solution never considers that obstacles such as economic hardship, lack of education, skill deficiencies may make exit all but impossible for some.[7]

Exit option, as a legal strategy which has been provided in India, has not been a popular strategy. This is because it expects the individual to choose between community or state. This is Hobson's choice as it penalises the vulnerable sections who have to opt out of their cultures to be governed by secular laws of state.[8]

Establishing Boundaries for Just Treatment

Liberal multiculturalists argue that multiculturalism need not accept all kinds of cultural diversity. It is only the specific kind of cultural diversity which needs to be accepted in liberal democracies. According to theorists like Bhikhu Parekh, Will Kymlicka and Joseph Carens, all cultural practices cannot be accepted within liberal democracy as they tend to harm minority sections within minorities, like women.

Will Kymlicka draws a distinction between special rights and group rights. Special rights, according to him, are those rights which are given to protect communities against external pressures. Group rights, however, are those rights which are given to strengthen communities against pressures of disintegration that come from within.[9] Kymlicka, however, sanctions only special rights for marginalised communities. Further, these rights are to be granted *to national* and *not ethnic* minorities. Ethnic minorities to Kymlicka are those who choose to stay in some other country, leaving behind their homeland. Hence no special rights need to be granted to them.[10] Issues of ethenic identity, however, dog India's tribal populations in matters of their rights to land and cultureand their concerns are not addressed by Kymlicka's classification.

Similarly second generation immigrants too cannot claim the right to preserve their culture. This particular right can only be claimed by national minorities whose homeland has been incorporated through conquest or colonisation of some sort.The Rights of second generation Algerian Muslims in France is today a contentious issue and this is a matter of liberation of nations and consequent migration.

Kymlicka acknowledges that special rights may only be claimed by groups that respect the rights of internal minorities. Thus, the requirement of internal liberalism rules out the justification of group rights for many fundamentalists of all political and religious stripes.[11]

However, special rights may be granted initially to shelter the community from pressures that come from the outside, but once they are granted, the community may use them in a way that it deems best.[12] The Pueblo Indians can, with the right to self-governance, decide that protecting their religious identity is crucial to their identity. Hence they may ban conversions, or penalise members who convert to another religion. Likewise, indigenous communities may receive special rights to land for the sake of protecting their culture against external pressures, but since the land-population ratio is important for sustaining their way of life, these communities may well stipulate restrictions upon their members. The fact that many groups have denied women who marry outside of the community rights to reservation land only reaffirms the possibility of special rights being used for limiting the options of some members. Kymlicka realises that rights obtained for the sake of minimising external pressures to assimilate may be used to curb individual choices. He argues that just as liberal states are extremely careful about intervening in the affairs of other independent states that do not endorse liberal cultures, likewise they should be extremely cautious about interfering in the lives of illiberal national minorities. Thus, the possibility of special rights being used for perpetuating oppressive communitarian practice remains.[13]

Any internal restrictions on individuals (particularly women) to revise, question or abandon traditional cultural rules cannot be acceptable to liberal theory of minority group rights. Joseph Carens espouses certain principles of human moral equality which all cultural communities seeking cultural rights must abide by. Thus, any practice (such as genital mutilation of young girls) which goes against the equal moral worth of persons cannot be supported[14]. Instead of specifying the rights that should be granted to particular minorities, Carens recommends an approach which is 'contextual' in nature. This means that specific claims of each minority have to be considered separately. These would include specifics such as history of the community, nature of nation-state etc. Thus, it cannot be said that religious, ethnic or national minorities would be given special rights. Each case has to be considered individually and in a certain moral context. However critics point out that 'in a situation of considerable inequality, a contextual approach that advises each case to be considered separately, allows a lot of room for the politics of patronage'.[15]

What theorists like Parekh argue for is that multiculturalism need not simply endorse all sorts of cultural diversity. He says, the 'operative public values' enshrined in the constitution should provide the basis for what is acceptable in a society. In a democracy, the need is to draw the boundaries for permissible diversity. Therefore minority practices which do not violate operative public values are permissible within a liberal democracy.

It includes respect for human dignity, equal respect for person etc. Though in each society, emphasis on these values may vary, it is operative public values which become important in giving concrete meaning to these. The practices of the minority which do not violate public values can be permitted within a liberal democracy. There are a set of principles which minorities need to respect and abide by. Alongside, the majority community also needs to check its biases. It needs to, for example, see whether clitoridectomy and polygamy goes against the operative public values.[16]

However, Parekh misses the point that constitutions reflect the consensus in society when they were initially formed.[17] 'The constitution is to be viewed as a historical text.'[18] What is equally important is that the constitution does not always speak in a single voice. For instance, right to equality and right to religion were agreed upon as tied in the same vein in the constitution.[19] In India, thus, community personal laws were granted despite the fact that there were voices that, these laws are discriminatory against women's rights to being equal citizens of the country. Consequently, operative values do not always provide safeguard against discriminatory practices.[20]

Critics have pointed out that responses by these thinkers have largely been focused on extreme cases. Practices such as female genital mutilation, *sati*, polygamy, which involve grave physical and psycological injuries to women in these groups are the primary triggers. Kymlicka too advocates against slavery, and mass tortures. Defenders of cultural rights have taken examples of these practices, which have caused bodily harm to women.[21] These are softer issues, as most of these practices represent clear cases of human rights violation, to a large extent, voices within these communities already exist against these discriminatory practices and initiative are already being taken to bring about change. The tougher issues are of laws of marriage, divorce, inheritance, and adoption that are discriminatory against women. This is a problem, which has not been addressed by these theorists.

Deleberative Democracy

The deliberative democracy model assumes a heterogeneous public and the democratic process involving primarily a discussion of problems, conflicts and claims of needs or interests.[22]

Thus, any conflict between women's rights and claims of culture can be resolved using this model. According to Monique Deveaux, 'the best way to resolve tensions between traditional cultural practices and liberal principles in socially, plural, democratic states is to defend and strengthen deliberation and the decision-making practices that reflect a radical principle of democratic legitimacy'.[23] She states that an approach to mediating disputes about the value and status of cultural practices will require that women members of cultural groups have a direct say in these matters, through the expansion of sites of democratic contestation and the inclusion of women in formal decision-making.

The *deliberative democracy* theory offers for women and disadvantaged section a robust, egalitarian model of power-sharing in public deliberation and decision-making. It also provides a political framework for democratic and respectful resolution of both inter-and intra-cultural conflicts in socially plural, liberal democratic states. According to Seyla Benhabib, strength of deliberative democracy consists in its dual track approach to politics. This dual track approach on the one hand focuses on established institutions, like the legislature and the judiciary in liberal-democratic societies; and on the other hand, the political activities and struggles of social movements, associations and groups in civil society are brought sharply into focus through the theory of democratic public sphere. In contrast to other models of democracy, a deliberative democracy model emphasisesthe 'need for inclusive decision making' which can contribute towards 'more just and political judgement'.[24]

Amy Gutmann's *deliberative universalism* advocates that conflicts are best addressed and provisionally resolved by actual deliberation; the give and take of arguments, that is respectful of reasonable differences.[25] It advocates the need for openness of politics to all reasonable people and perspectives, providing especially to marginalised groups like women and minorities access to deliberation on forums and admitting all reasonable arguments to the political agenda for decision-making purposes.

Our moral understanding of many-sided issues like legalising abortion, female genital mutilation, polygamy is further enhanced by discussion with people whom we respectfully disagree with, especially when these people have cultural identities different from our own. In policy matters, a deliberative process produces preferences which are more emphatic and better informed as they are more considered and more far reaching in approach.[26] In contrast to other models of democracy, a deliberative democracy model emphasises on the 'need for inclusive decision-making' which can contribute towards 'more just and political judgment'.[27]

Young cites four normative ideals for the deliberating parties.[28]

a) *Inclusion*: A deliberative model presupposes the need for those effected to be included in the process of decision-making. However, inclusion also raises the question of how this inclusion needs to come about in large democracies.[29]

b) *Equality*:People should not only be included in decision-making, they should be included on equal terms. All ought to have equal effective opportunity to question one another and to question and criticise each other's proposals. The ideal model of deliberative democracy is that it promotes free and equal opportunity to speak.[30]

c) *Reasonableness*:The principle of reasonableness requires the willingness to listen to others who want to explain why their ideas are incorrect or inappropriate. Reasonable people enter into discussion to solve collective problems with the aim of reaching agreements. Reasonable people understand that dissent often produces insights and that decisions and agreements should in principle be open to new challenges.[31]

d) *Publicity and Accountability*: A public consists of a plurality of different individuals and collective experiences, histories, commitments, ideals, interests and goals discussing a set of problems under a set of procedures. When members of such a public speak to each other, they know that they are accountable to plurality of others. Therefore, they must explain their particular background experiences ,interests or proposals in ways that others can understand.[32]

Any conflict between cultural diversity and gender equality can be resolved by this model.

Deliberative Democracy: Some Concerns

While one cannot do without deliberative democratic procedures given the nature of current conflicts, there are certain other issues which I would like to draw attention to.

Firstly, deliberation seems to work for softer issues but as far as the so-called 'irreconcilable' issues are concerned, deliberation has seemed to yield lesser results. This is largely the case in issues where opinions between camps have got polarised such as abortion, pornography. On these and several such issues reconciliation becomes difficult.

Secondly, deliberation may work in certain societies at certain times over certain isssues. This might, however, not work for all societies. Deaveux suggests an example in England of how deliberation worked in England with a committee comprising of various racial, ethnic and religious communities being formed.[33] The fact, however, remains that a lot depends on the relation between state and minorities but also between minorities and within minorities. These three would determine the outcome of a deliberative procedure. The nature of a problem too determines its outcome. So, success of a certain deliberation process in a certain context cannot lead to generalisation about overall success of procedure as suggested by some theorists, like the case of the UCC implementation in India.

There have to be certain conditions which are essential to make deliberative procedures in a democracy successful:

> No deliberation procedure can succeed till certain level of trust and mutual respect is established between groups, within groups and between state and groups. A society needs to fulfill conditions of 'minimal decency'. No group should be in a more advantageous position. A balance of power should exist between deliberating parties. Deliberation for groups is not possible from position of inequality.
>
> Deliberation also works, depending on the group in question. While with some groups, mediation might be a relatively easier task, with others due to hostilities shared with society at large, reaching the stage of negotiation might be a tough option. So deliberation is a complex process. Right confidence-building measures need to be initiated by parties in power which decreases hostilities between deliberating parties. Otherwise any policy which is not conceived properly might increase

hostilities between groups. This is because mediation is being brought on terms of the majority, rather than minority. So the right political will to resolve the issue with involvement of civil society is a must in cases where there are past incidences of hostility. An ill-conceived policy might increase suspicion and hostilities between groups, which might only increase polarisation.

Multiple Jurisdiction Model

The most interesting case for reconciling women's and children's rights and multiculturalist concerns have been made by Ayelet Shachar. She is acutely aware of what she terms as the 'paradox of multicultural vulnerability'—namely the unintended consequence of well meaning state policies that aim at cultural accommodation but result in the women and children of this group bearing a disproportionate burden.[34] The multiple jurisdiction model, in contrast to the other three models, is essentially a model for governance and addresses policy issues. Shachar, in her work, *Multicultural Jurisdictions*, specifically addresses the issue of conflict between community groups and women's rights in a multicultural polity.

She suggests a resolution model based on joint governance. Unlike the deliberative democracy model, multiple jurisdiction seeks to resolve a somewhat irreconcilable issue—that of personal law. While there are other multiple jurisdiction models which address the issue of accommodating cultural diversity and gender equality,[35] the best model for Shachar is the one based on joint governance principle. The *joint governance model* establishes multiple jurisdiction authority through allocation of jurisdiction along submatter lines. An example would be the marriage customs of the Nomoi people from Micronesia. Among them, marriage may be sanctified by the Nomoi groups, by law, by custom and traditional norms of the society, where the state alone can retain the authority to determine children's allowances and to allocate family assets and other benefits. 'The joint governance system for dividing and sharing authority promises to establish more than one set of standards that would jointly govern or co-prevail in contested social arena. It hopes to replace all division of authority with a more fluid and dynamic conception of power and jurisdiction.'[36]

The most attractive variant of joint governance to Shachar is transformative accommodation.[37] This is a variant which takes the two loci of authority—the population under study, that is the Nomoi group, and the state—and instead of viewing their conflict of interest as a problem, considers it as an occasion for encouraging each entity to become more responsive to all its constituents.

This is based on three core principles. They are:

a) *The sub-matter allocation of authority.*[38]

Like other separation of power models, transformative accommodation intentionally eschews the idea of exclusive or absolute authority. Instead, transformative accommodation envisions a new way of allocating jurisdiction. It observes that contested social arenas (such as education, family law, criminal justice, immigration, resource development and environmental protection) are internally divisibleinto sub-matters, which are: multiple, seperable, yet complementary legal components.

Transformative accommodation capitalises on the divisibility of each social arena by allocating jurisdictional authority along sub-matter lines. The principle of sub-matter can be clearly seen in the arena of family law. The complexities of family life create several legal sub-matters within this single social arena. For example, in the context of marriage, there are at least two sub-matteres which come into play. There is a *demarcating function* which regulates, among other things, the changes of one's marital status or one's entitlement to membership in a given community. And then there is a *distributing function* which covers, among other things, the definition of the rights and obligations that married spouses are bound to honour, together with determination of the economic and custodial consequences of this change in marital status (in the event of divorce for example).These demarcating and distributive functions parallels the two legally distinct sub-matters. Meaningful consideration of marriage and divorce rules thus requires an examination of both jurisdictions: the authority which governs each distinct legal sub-matter, as well as complementary authority which jointly governs in a contested social arena.

b) *The no monopoly rule.*[39]

According to this rule, neither the group nor the state can ever acquire exclusive control over legal sub-matters, and have to consider the intersection of multiple affiliation among individuals.

c) *The establishment of clearly delineated choice options.*[40]

In order for constituents to register their response to the competition between state and group, they must have clear options which allow them to choose between the jurisdiction of the state and the Nomoi group. Choice here means that they can remain within the submatter jurisdiction of the original power holder (approval), or that they can resist that jurisdictional authority at pre-defined reversal points (disapproval). As a last resort, they can discipline the relevant power-holder by opting out of a jurisdiction if the jurisdiction power-holder fails to effectively respond to constituent needs. It is precisely the fact that members are no longer locked in that ensures the capacity for change from within.

However, there are certain drawbacks of such a model. In a country like India according to Shachar herself, the religious groups must be convinced to voluntarily surrender their power over family law or other issues.The deeper the cleavages run between the communities comprising a body politic, the more difficult it becomes to alter the current balance of power between state and the group.[41] In Shachar's argument there is a certain privileging of the legal at the expense of the political and cultural aspect of this power.[42]

Conclusion

Benhabib has this to say:

> Multicultural accommodation may result in a kind of multicultural cold war: there may be peace but no reconciliation; there may be bargaining but no mutual understanding and there may be stalemates and standoffs, dictated less by respect for the positions of others than by fear of others.

According to her, precisely because multiculturalism, in so many of its manifestations, challenges key assumption of liberal democracies, it needs to release its conflictual and explosive potential in the public civic sphere through dialogue, confrontation and give and take of ordinary citizens.

All models have their own drawbacks. Looking into specifically the Indian context and seeing what models have emanated from India to solve the dilemma of cultural diversity and gender equality, we will see what model appears best to solve the conundrum between cultural diversity and gender equality. Attempt will be to resolve issues and answer questions regarding cultural diversity and gender equality as I move forward in my work.

Personal Laws in India: Laws for Hindus

> I believe the main question we are faced today in the present age of diversity is not whether the accommodation of different cultures can conflict with the protection of certain member's citizenship right's. Undeniably it often does. The mere recognition of this fact represents, however, only the initial stage in any serious rethinking of the tangled dynamics inherent between the group, the state, and the individual. It tells us very little about how we can best redress the troubling fact that well-meaning accommodations aimed at mitigating power inequalities between groups may end up reinforcing power hierarchies within them. Some scholars have suggested that this tension should lead us to abandon any attempt to enhance the autonomy of minority cultures or to respect their distinct way of life. But I take the paradox of multicultural vulnerability to raise a different, and more complicated, challenge. We need to develop a concept of differentiated citizenship which is guided by ambitiously innovative principle: one that strives for the reduction of injustice *between* groups, together with the enhancement of justice within them.
>
> —Ayelet Shachar

I LOOK at the tension between multiculturalism and feminism in this chapter by focusing on Indian personal laws. This, unlike other cases we have discussed earlier, is one of the most complicated of issues. This tension was first reflected during debates over making of the Indian Constitution. In seventy years of existence as a free country and a democratic republic, India has been unable to resolve the inherent conflict in the provisions of its constitution, open to amendments and upgrades.

Independent India adopted for a model of separate personal laws for each of its religious communities, a process in which ethnicity was ignored and their faiths, traditions and practices unguarded. Like in so many other matters, in later decades, when conflict arose, these issues were conveniently clubbed under the all-prevailing concept of the law for the dominant community.

As per this model, religious communities in India govern a broad range of family law issues including marriage, divorce, maintenance, guardianship, adoption and succession. Under such a model, each religious community is given autonomous powers to demarcate its membership boundaries and preserve its cultural distinctiveness. The personal laws and cultural rights of tribes from the north-east, south-west and central Indian regions were left unsecured.

After independence, some scholars and many indigenous political leaders believed that a system of separate personal laws for religious minorities could be an important source of cultural autonomy in divided societies, contributing to ethnic stability and facilitating the preservation of minority cultures. On the whole this was the model to accommodate multiculturalism and cultural diversity in India.

However, this model of cultural diversity or extreme religious particularistic model[1] perpetuated other kinds of inequalities. While the cultural diversity model maintains the autonomy and sovereignty of different minority cultures (upholding the demarcating function of family law), it is problematic in terms of women's rights, particularly when the jurisdiction it extends to religo-cultural groups reaches beyond pure status issues and includes matters of property relations between spouses.[2]. These relations can be structured so as to be of disadvantage to women, or even exploit women. In so doing, they put at risk women's rights to fair and equal treatment and may interfere with their capacities to make and pursue significant life-choices.

While in India women are guaranteed on paper full and equal citizenship rights by state law, in practice their basic rights may be circumscribed with impunity by their group's family law traditions. Hence, the preservation of a group's cultural distinctiveness through multicultural accommodation often imposes severe internal costs, which are disproportionately allocated in a way that tends to compromise the citizenship status of certain sub-sections of the groups by upholding the structural impediments imposed upon them by a rigid reading of all such groups' traditions.[3]

Supremacy of Personal Law over Uniform Code

The Constitution Assembly Debate (CAD) in the late 1940s saw heated discussions on whether personal law should exist for communities or whether a common uniform code should be applied for the entire country, once it is free.

In the Constituent Assembly (1946-1949), members had to resolve the issue of religion and minority rights in the immediate context of partition and its accompanying communal slaughter. Protecting communal rights, restoring communal harmony even while unifying the new nation of India after the subcontinent's vivisection over religious differences became the pre-eminent goal.

However, the minority community members of the Constituent Assembly were especially against a common code. The debate in the Constituent Assembly on draft article 38 (now Article 44 of the Directive Principles of the Indian Constitution) show that some Muslim and Sikh members were against such a provision. Five Muslim members,[4] led by B Pocker Sahib Bahadur, unhesitatingly branded this article as a tyrannous measure which ought not find a place in the Indian Constitution[5]. These members also contended that the personal laws of a community were part of their *religion and way of life* and in any case, so far as Muslims were concerned, their law of succession, inheritance, marriage and divorce were completely dependent upon their religion. Accordingly, imposition of a Uniform Civil Code for the entire country would not only conflict with the *freedom of religious practice* guaranteed in the fundamental rights of the constitution, but also amount to tyranny over those who want to follow their own personal law.[6]

There were several other members in the Constituent Assembly who raised objection to inclusion of Uniform Civil Code in the Directive Principles of State Policy. They pressed for need to transfer the clause regarding UCC from Chapter Two to Chapter One after making suitable modification in it. BR Ambedkar observed that:

> We have in this country a uniform code of laws covering almost every aspect of human relationship. We have a uniform and complete criminal code operating throughout the country, which is contained in the penal code and the criminal procedure code. We have the law of transfer of property, which deals with the property relations and which is operative throughout the country. Then there are the Negotiable Instrument Acts and I cite innumberable enactments which would prove that this country has practically a civil code, uniform in its content and applicable to the whole country. The only province the civil law has not been able to invade so far is the marriage and succession.[7]

KM Munshi pointed out that freedom of religious practice was subject to power of the state to make any law (a) regulating and restricting any secular activity which may be associated with religious practices, (b) for social welfare and social reform. *If personal law of inheritance, succession etcetera was considered a part of the religion, then equality to women which has been guaranteed in the Fundamental Rights could never be given.*

Rajkumari Amrit Kaur pointed out that the *right to religion may invalidate legislation against anti-social customs which have the sanction of religion.*[8] She noted that nowhere in the then advanced Muslim countries, the personal law of each minority was recognised as so sacrosanct as to prevent the enactment of a civil code.[9] She pointed out the disadvantages that would perpetuate if there was no civil code.[10] Alladi Krishnaswamy Aiyyar also supported the view of KM Munshi and pointed out that there was 'no question of religion being in danger' because of Uniform Civil Code.[11]

Minoo Masani, Hansa Mehta and Amrit Kaur expressed complete dissatisfaction with the inclusion of the Uniform Civil Code in the Directive Principle of State Policy. According to them, one of the factors that kept India back from advancing to nationhood was the existence of personal laws based on religion that keeps the nation divided into 'watertight compartments'[12] in many aspects of life. Seventy years later the status quo regarding UCC continues.

Nehru insisted, in deference to the Sikhs and Muslims, that the framing of a UCC be a goal set out in the Directive Principle, the implementation of whose provision was neither mandatory nor justiciable.[13] The nationalist Muslims in the Assembly, having chosen to remain in India instead of joining Pakistan, opposed even this.[14] Nonetheless Article 44 of Directive Principle became part of the Constitution. It promises, the state shall endeavor to secure for the citizens a Uniform Civil Code throughout the territory of India.[15]

Indian Model of Accommodating Diversity

What I call the 'Indian model of accommodating cultural diversity' was largely about letting each religious community retain their personal laws. So far, it has been against a uniform civil code ever being implemented in the country. However, Article 44 of the Constitution makes it obligatory for the 'state to secure for citizen a uniform civil code', when the situation is ripe for the same.

The Indian model encompassed two basic ideas:

a) To begin with, the Constitution established difference in the public sphere.
b) This was supposed to graduate towards greater uniformity in public sphere.

This Indian model was in fact in sharp contrast to the western model, which was based on a reverse trajectory. Western democracies were based on:

a) First a difference-free, neutral, uniform, secular public sphere was sought to be established, where ascriptive identity of individual citizen did not matter. This was when Enlightenment Principles got shaped.
b) Slowly, the realisation came that the uniformity created out of 'indifference to difference model' led to several exclusions within the society. Then the need was felt to accommodate these sections. So, while some were as a result assimilated, others were granted special rights. Only when such enlightenment projects were completed, principles of pluralism, diversity and multiculturalism got accommodated in western societies.[16]

So what in effect happened in the west was that, first the parameters of a modern society based on principles of Enlightenment were fought for and laid. Once the goal of establishing such a society was achieved, issues of difference and diversity were addressed.

The purpose of drawing out this comparison is to bring out how a model which attempts to accommodate differences in the original position itself (like the Indian model) compromises on principles of a modern society, based on principles of Enlightenment. In fact, it would not be an exaggeration, if one were to add that the compromises led to a direct assault on any national plan based on modernisation and Enlightenment principles, which needed to be vigorously launched in a post-colonial society like India's. Such Enlightenment projects need to be truly realised in countries like India where revolution has come from above and not below (unlike the French, English and American revolutions).

One of the prominent principles on which enlightenment stood was the need for a scientific approach, belief in human reasoning and above all, separation of church and state. The power of religion and the aristocracy diminished gradually in England, and in France they were violently uprooted. Prominent philosophers Derrida and Habermas write that the project of enlightenment that promoted separation between *the religious* and *the political* has yet to be completed. The philosophical experience of Europe in the 17th and 18th centuries has left in the European political space original marks with regard to the religious: they both identify Europe as the *only secular actor* on the world stage today.[17]

Both thinkers place their hopes in the 'new figure of Europe' and the inherent possibility of discourse and politics, different from the current American rhetoric or Islamic fundamentalism. Europe being 'a way out of this double theological-political programme'.[18] According to Derrida, our responsibility is to prevent a 'return of the religious' and promote the Enlightenment spirit. Habermas and Derrida call on Europe to finish the uncompleted project of Enlightenment.[19]

Multiculturalism, on the other hand, has stood for the opposite. Centrality to religion in public sphere, somewhere also gets linked to abandoning the human ability to reason. It has stood for rigid support to custom, privileges and fundamentalism. However, not only in India, the task is incomplete according to Derrida and Habermas in the older democracy, that is America. American polity clearly contradicts Enlightenment principles of separation of religion and state.[20]

My contention is that *in India, the introduction of the system of separate personal laws struck at the roots of Enlightenment principles (which has been the aim of both liberal and socialist societies).* By this arrangement, India temporarily made space for cultural diversity, but sacrificed values of a scientific society based on Enlightenment. In free India, the constitutional scheme helped establish a legal system based on certain underlying assumptions.

Personal Laws and Underlying Assumptions

Unlike polities based on uniform laws for all citizens, in India, a polity based on separate personal laws stands on certain primary beliefs.[21] These are:

Primacy to Religion over Secular Principles

Unlike western societies, where a secular public sphere, based on the principle of separation of the church and the state, was established and religion was relegated to the private sphere, in India (due to historical reasons) something very different happened. The system of personal laws gave sanctity to establishing primacy of religion in the public sphere of the country.

Community Rights before Individual Rights

Governance based on personal laws recognises the rights of a cultural or religious community to be governed by their own laws. The premise here is that this will lead the community to have autonomy in deciding on its internal matters. Neither the state, nor the majority community will have any right to interfere in minority community matters.

However, we must admit that a system, which is based on primacy to religion and community rights, is exploitative to a large section of the country's people.

This is because by establishing religion in the public sphere, one is giving primacy to laws made during earlier times which do not have much relevance in today's times.

A law needs to address the problems of the times we live in and therefore needs to be for 'here and now'. Also religion gives automatic sanctity to community rights, which in turn gives orthodox elements within these communities an opportunity to rule community matters; who in face of dissent from within or outside the community, use the slogan of 'community in peril'. This goes against all individual rights as members are often made to toe the community's line.

Models for Reconciling Diversity with Feminism

Feminists have provided not only a critique of blind multicultural accommodation policies[22] and their effects on women but have also simultaneously emphasised on the need for a multiculturalist model which is accommodative of concerns of women and other minority population within any community.[23]

The Uniform Civil Code Model

The compulsorily uniform civil code model has been suggested by several women's groups in India who have been advocating for a common gender-just code differentiating the'When metaphorically extended to nonmaterial social goods, the concept of distribution represents them as though they were static things, instead of a function of social relations and processes.'10mselves. However, they clearly differentiate their stand from the rightist agenda for a uniform civil code. Women's groups like Saheli and Peoples Union for Democratic Rights argue that plurality of laws work against the interest of women. And so the need is for a compulsory civil code which would override personal laws.

They say, cultural and other aspects of personal laws which do not offend the provision of equality in the Constitution can be retained. Such a code can be brought into effect through separate acts of legislation, issue by issue, not necessarily in one sweep. This entire exercise is to be carried out in the context of understanding that the right of minorities is to live in safety and dignity and this must be ensured by the state.[24]

Special Marriage Act – the Exit Model

The Special Marriage Act is the Indian Constitution's answer to hardships caused by the presence of separate personal laws. This is, in fact, the exit option provided by the Constitution.

The enactment of the Special Marriage Act in 1954 had been one of the significant moves in post-independent India not only to secularise but also to bring some kind of uniformity in family laws. 'This Act has been described as the first step towards the attainment of the objective of a Uniform Civil Code contemplated in Article 44 of the Constitution.'[25] 'The Act provids for a civil marriage of two Indians, without the necessity of renouncing their respective religion.'[26]

The Act contained several redeeming features. It introduced the *concept of breakdown theory or a divorce by mutual consent.*

The Act also provided for the 're-registeration of marriages solemnised in accordance with the customs or rituals of the spouses'.[27] This provision of *subsequent registration* enabled parties 'to avail of secular and uniform remedies despite the solemnisation of the marriage through the performance of religious ceremonies'.[28]

'Since a marriage under this Act is a secular and civil contract, conversion or apostasy of the spouse is not a ground for divorce.[29] The marriage is contracted at the civil registry in the presence of a marriage officer appointed by the state and a certificate is issued to the parties which constitutes a clear proof of a valid marriage having been performed for all future litigation purposes.[30] This serves as a restraint against husbands contracting subsequent bigamous marriages.'

Once the parties opt for such a secular form of marriage, in matters of succession they are governed by the Indian Succession Act, 1925 which is more egalitarian and gender-just and not by provisions of their respective personal laws. 'This was a concrete step towards gradual unification of family.'[31]

However, this option has not been very popular with Indians. Amendments to the SMA and the Hindu Succession Act, 1956 are partly responsible for this.

'If one were to look at the provisions of this act, any Hindu couple married under the Act were taken out of the purview of the Indian Succession Act of 1925 and were permitted to be governed by the Hindu Succession Act.[32] This move was to ensure that coparcenaries, and male privileges within it, are not dissolved by the contracting of a civil marriage by means of the act.' The interests of a Hindu male who contracted a civil marriage were protected so long as he married a woman within the broad Hindu fold (which would include inter-caste and inter-regional marriages, as well as marriages with women from the Buddhist, Jain and Sikh religions and also Brahmos, Prathana Samajis and Arya Samajis or even atheists).[33]

'At one level, it gave a further lease to coparcenaries, which in any case, are anti-women.'

'The move was deemed progressive because it protected the interests of a Hindu male contracting a civil marriage.'[34] Even if one concedes to this reasoning, why a similar benefit was not conferred upon a Hindu male contracting an inter-religious civil marriage remains unexplained.[35]

'In effect, the amendment was a deterrent to a Hindu male wishing to marry a woman from any minority religious communities, ie. a Parsi, a Muslim or a Christian. Such an event would result in the dissolution of coparcenary.'[36] Progressive Hindus who married under the secular Act were not given a choice to be governed by a uniform and secular law of succession.

The benefits conferred on a Hindu male contracting a civil marriage were deemed a progressive step for the Hindu community. Hence the deterrence the SMA amendment poses to marriages of Hindu males with women from minority communities and to secular principle of the nation, did not ever figure in the public debate.

The Act actually had 'the potential of being developed further into a comprehensive code of marriage and divorce which could incorporate adequate safeguards for women, without invoking the controversy of freedom of religion'.[37]

'The premise that the Act is merely a facilitating measure which would apply only to consenting couples had already been accepted both politically as well as legally.'[38] Hence equitable principles of gender justice could easily have been incorporated into this Act. Unfortunately, the Act has not been well publicised and there seems to be a manipulation to subvert its provisions. Also, despite its secular credentials, the Act leans towards the dominant Hindu upper caste practices, which prohibit marriages between first cousins and close family relatives. Such prohibitions are not found in the customary practices of several lower castes, as well as among the practices of Muslims, Christians, Parsis and Jews. Among several south Indian communities, including among the Brahmins, marriages between uncles and nieces and first cousins are a norm.[39]

Reverse Optionality Option

The argument this model employs is similar to arguments presented by theorists on right to exit.[40] This option too, like the right to exit, provides options to exit from cultural communities' personal laws and choose what is acceptable to the self.

> The proposal for *reverse optionality* has been put forward by the Working Group on Women's Rights (WGMR) of Delhi which hopes, through this device, to break through the impasse created by the polarisations of the state/community and the community/women. WGMR critiques the demand hitherto put forward for a UCC on the grounds that such demand have either been explicitly foregrounded or have been appropriated for the idea of national integrity rather than being about gender justice. On the other hand, reform from within personal laws has proved to be blocked by patriarchal pressures from within the communities. Therefore, while supporting all feminist initiatives for reform from within, the WGMR feels this to be a limited strategy. Communities in the public domain demand democratic rights between communities whilst denying the same to the women of their communities.

Personal laws depend on the accident of birth and do not give the dissenting individual the choice to opt out. The concrete aspects of the present proposal are three central planks to contribute to the democratic space of individuals:

1. Development and implementation of certain comprehensive packages regarding rights of women to marriage, adoption, property against domestic violence, to work, equal remuneration etc.[41]
2. These laws would be the birthright of every citizen and also apply to all naturalised citizens.
3. All citizens would have the right to opt for the personal laws of their community at any point of their lives. This option would be revocable at any time, including the time of dispute. In case of difference in the options between the parties to a dispute, the secular law would prevail.

The right to choose provides for the democratic space. In order to attract women to choose the personal laws, the communities will have to take gender considerations into account while framing/interpreting personal laws. This will trigger the process of change within the communities to keep persons within the bounds of religious communities. This will also help stem the rise in fundamentalisation and can be seen as a way out of the present impasse. This proposal is not opposed or in violation of minority rights.

Reform from Within

This model is similar to the model for accommodation of multiculturalism and gender equality provided by liberal theorists, who have advocated the need for change to come from within the cultural community.[42] It requires deliberative democracy to operate so as to achieve this model. It requires deliberation to exist within inter-and intra-groups to resolve conflict. It is a popular model with deliberative democrats, in fact, one of the most popular models with the multiculturalists.

> In similar vein, the proponents of reform from within argument in India advocate the need for change from within the communities.

This is because in today's communalised politics, any change suggested either by the state or the majority community is perceived as imposition from above. Several theorists in India have variously upheld this position. It has also been the most popular model with the community leaders. Most communities have agreed to the need for reform only when it comes from within the community itself.

Many scholars in India have advocated the need for internal reforms. Partha Chatterjee, upholding the groups' right to their culture, says that minority communities have no reason to justify their actions to the state or other groups, presumably on issues related to their culture, so long as they have internal democracy within the group.[43] He suggests that the Muslims should set up a Muslim parliament. The state must recognise whatever this parliament decides on Muslim personal law.

According to Rajeev Bhargava, any position for a UCC or personal laws are implausible positions.[44] Thus the need for 'a full and free deliberation' over the entire issue becomes a precondition to reform.[45] Muslims as a group have the right to their personal laws. It does not follow, however, that Muslims have a right to the protection of existing interpretations of laws grossly unjust to women. This position, however, rules out in an unabashedly individualistic vein the violation of basic individual human rights in the name of group rights.

Freedom from domestic violence, a right to share in inheritance and right to maintenance for divorced and destitute women must be legally enforceable, irrespective of the group to which the women belong. The state must enforce the exercise of such rights, no matter how incompatible this is with the personal laws or customary practice of any group. Any custom or law of say Muslim orthodoxy that violates these basic rights must be set aside.

Alongside, there ought to be the precondition for Muslim women to be given the right to exit the system of personal law.

Another suggestion by Imtiaz Ahmed is that communities themselves should undertake to rationalise those aspects of their personal laws that are in conflict with constitutional provisions for equity or which fail to pass the test of equity, justice and good conscience. This will provide both external protection to minorities vis-à-vis the larger society, as well as ensure internal restrictions on these communities to ensure the rights of sections of their own population.[46]

Groups like Nikahnama and Women's Research and Action Group(WRAG) feel that women in the community are not willing to accept changes that come from outside the community, or which seem to threaten community identity. In their opinion. the only practicable alternative at the present moment is to focus on smaller changes which will provide greater rights for women even if they do not measure up to absolute gender justice. Nikahnama, for instance, suggested the following:

a) Modification of permission for polygamy to include the option of divorce for earlier wives.
b) Comprehensive and adequate maintenance and inheritance rights.
c) Outlawing the triple *talaq*.

Similarly, groups like Majlis suggest that along with support to initiatives for reform within the community, Feminists should work towards smaller, specific and focused statutes that will address some of the immediate problems faced by women, particularly in areas of domestic violence and economic rights. Since these areas do not fall within personal laws, there will be no room to communalise the issue and at the same time, this will protect the right of women.[47]

An all-encompassing code is likely to do more harm than good in a multicultural and diverse society like India, since it will be imposition from above.

The leftist group, AIDWA, also advocates a step-by-step approach which is similar to the strategy suggested by Majlis. That is, it reiterates the need for common laws based on equality for all women, in every sphere: economic, social, political and legal. However, rather than advocating any state legislation across the board, it suggests the strengthening of the common legal ground for women by bringing in legislation in specific areas with immediate effect. These areas are rights to property acquired after marriage, registration of marriages regardless of the religious rituals followed and domestic violence. Clearly, AIDWA sees immediate reform possible only in areas which do not directly conflict with existing personal laws. Its analysis of the present political conjuncture, therefore, appears to be similar to that of the positions advocating reform from within, although this is never explicitly stated.

Thus the debate regarding personal laws have continued from the Constituent Assembly debate to till today. While several women's groups and people from the legal fraternity have expressed the need for a Uniform Civil Code, minority communities, especially the Muslim community, harp on the need for separate personal laws. However, several Indian thinkers and communities have felt the need of certain models to accommodate cultural diversity with gender equality. In this book, I have looked at models which have either suggested legal mechanisms like reverse optionality, already existing constitutional provisions like the SMA or communities' internal mechanisms (internal reforms model) to deal with conflict between the two. In the following chapters we look at how India's minority communities have taken to the reform process in their personal laws since independence. Each community has aired its views on its own ways of bringing about reform but in many areas, such reforms still remain matter of debate, rather than practice.

Laws for the Indian Muslim Community

CULTURAL ACCOMMODATION policies adopted by the independent Indian state, which justified separate personal laws for each religious community, had severe adverse effects upon the members of the Muslim community, in comparison to other minority communities in India.

This is because, in post-independent India, hardly any changes were visible in the Muslim personal laws. It continued to exist as it was compiled and practiced during the British era. Apart from the two laws which were codified in the 1930s (unlike the Hindu law which got codified in 1954), no other law got codified in post-independent India. This laid open the scope for regressive interpretation of Muslim Personal Law.

Since there was no uniformity in laws, it could be interpreted anyway and anyhow.[1] This affected the lives of millions of Muslim women in India, especially their legal status, in whose case several discriminatory provisions such as triple talaq, polygamy, unequal inheritance rights and petty maintenance amount were justified in the name of culture.

The Muslim leadership too doggedly resisted any reform in certain aspects of the law, particularly pertaining to marriage and divorce.[2] Unlike other religious communities in India, if one were to analyse the history of personal laws of Muslims, it becomes evident that it became a highly politicised issue only in the recent decades.

What happened, in fact, was that Muslim Personal Law became a representative of Muslim culture in independent India. A false campaign was spread by the orthodox section within the community that preservation of 'Muslim culture' was equivalent of preservation of 'Muslim Personal law'.[3] This Muslim Personal Law was thus in need of protection from intrusion from the majority culture—that is, the 'Hindu' culture. The personal laws became a Hindu vs Muslim issue, without considering the different cultural practices of Muslims of different regions. In India, the Muslim personal laws are today interpreted according to their convenience by local religious leaders—marriage, divorce and inheritance laws are interpreted differently by the Shias and Sunnis, by north Indian clergy and south Indian clergy, interpreted differently by even the local courts and regional high courts.

It is because of this politics of cultural preservation that Muslim laws in India have remained essentially unchanged since independence. There were hardly any efforts made to reform these laws, even though reforms have come about in other Muslim countries.[4] As a result, in modern democratic India, it is the voices of the orthodox section that has come to the forefront to represent the interest of the community while the voices of internal minorities and progressive sections are rendered invisible.

On the plus side, what has also lately been visible is the clamor for reform of the current situation from within. Muslim feminists, women's organisations and liberal Muslims are bringing about reform initiatives within the community.[5] As a result of their efforts, the orthodox sections have of late become more open to bringing about changes for the benefit of the community as a whole. There have also been several court initiatives too in the positive direction.

Sharia and Muslim Women

Muslim Personal Law as a British Enactment

It is important to note that the *Muslim Personal Law is a British enactment* and is being followed by Indian courts by virtue of this enactment, and *not because it is divine law.*

The British rulers had their own agenda and made personal laws totally static by this enactment. The Sharia Law had been quite dynamic even during the Mughal period.[6] According to Asghar Ali Engineer, the *Fatwa Alamgiri* sets out the fatwa (rule/law) as compiled during Aurangzeb's period on various questions pertaining to Sharia. These are far more dynamic and liberal to women than the Muslim personal law enacted by the British. Even the provision for maintenance to women is much more progressive in the Fatwa Alamgiri and if followed, could have avoided the notorious Shah Bano incidence.

The British themselves significantly called the enactment—not the Sharia Law—the Anglo-Mohammedan Law, which itself is indicative of the fact that it was believed to be a secular enactment by a colonial government, a pre-1937 practice.

Ashghar Ali Engineer is of the view that the Muslim leaders need to understand this today and work sincerely for the much-needed reforms in the Muslim personal laws being practiced in India, particularly in matters of marriage, divorce and maintenance. They should not treat the enactment by a colonial government as divine and static. They should also note that cases are decided not by the Qazis but by secular judges of free India. The secular judges, as is obvious, cannot follow the spirit of Islamic law but the law as laid down by the colonial enactment. They should also take into account that India is an evolving, changing democracy and all its citizens are equal and Muslims in India need to take advantage of this modernisation. Unfortunately, it is commonly believed by the Muslims that the personal laws, as enacted in India, are divine. There is urgent need to remove this misconception and pave the way for necessary reforms within the Islamic framework.

Orthodox Nature of AIMPLB

The All India Muslim Personal Law Board was a body which was basically formed to protect the Sharia law in India. The Board members remain orthodox and conformist in their views. They have robbed the Sharia laws of their dynamism and are perpetrating old formulations, which were arrived at centuries ago. *We must first assert that the Muslim Personal Law Board does not represent opinion of all Muslims in India.* Let alone any voting, it was not even constituted by any broad consensus among Muslims. A few ulama, Muslim educators and others got together and decided to constitute the board and later gave representation to other Muslims, sectwise. No opinion of other schools of thought or liberal Muslims was ever sought about its representative character.[7] The AIMPLB should, therefore, not claim in the first place that it is representative of all Muslims sectwise. And the way it has functioned, it has represented at best only ultra-conservative sections of Muslims. The Board has seriously failed in protecting the real Sharia laws. It missed great opportunities repeatedly. It always showed its conservative face. The Shah Bano judgement is the best example.[8]

It is true that among Muslims in India, there is no unanimity about application of the Sharia. Not only are there sectarian differences but also polarisation among them on the lines of progressive and conservative. It is not easy to push through any decision unanimously among 172 million Indian Muslims and differences are bound to arise.

The Shah Bano case of 1985 was a great opportunity for the Board members to give healthy lead to Indian Muslims and set a healthy precedent in terms of legal reforms, reverse the hitherto followed unjust practices versus women and regularise just maintenance for properly interpreting the Qur'anic verse 2: 241, which says: make provisions for the divorcees in godly manner.[9]

As Ashghar Ali Engineer notes, it should be remembered that Qur'anic laws are very progressive and equitable and give equal status to women with that of men. It was the first religion in the world which kept interests of divorcees also in view and required men to make provisions for their divorced wife/wives.[10] The Qur'an did not mention any period for such provision and left it to the requirements of time. It was the opinion of early jurists that provisions be made at least for three months of *iddat* (waiting before she can remarry after divorce).

The Muslim Personal Law Board in India gave in to ambitious Muslim politicians who exploited the Supreme Court judgement for their own political ambitions, without regard to the interest of Muslims in general and Muslim women in particular. Engineer points out, the ulama in the MPLB simply protected the opinion of early Muslim jurists rather than the true spirit of the Qur'anic injunctions, ie. to protect the rights of divorcees and do justice to them. As a result, all non-Muslims in general and many Muslim women think that Islam is unjust to women's rights. The reality is quite the contrary. The Qur'anic pronouncements in respect of women are far ahead of time.[11]

The Need for Unification of Different Schools

Muslim personal laws in India are generally in uncodified form, with at least four kinds of Islamic laws prevalent. All these schools have conflicting doctrines. To illustrate, the Ithna Ashari laws (generally called in India the Shia Law) recognises the validity of bequests in favour of heirs but the two locally prevalent Sunni schools regard it as invalid. The scheme of inter-state succession is entirely different from its counterpart under the Shia law. There are also serious differences in the realm of procedure. So, while the Sunni laws require the presence of witnesses at the time of marriage but not at the time of divorce, the rule under the Shia law is exactly the opposite of this.

The Sunnis in India are not prepared to recognise the authority of the Shia Ithna Ashari and Ismaili schools. Similarly, the Shia Indians do not accept the validity of the Hanafi, Shafi and other Sunni schools. This is a pitiable situation which unfortunately keeps the Sunni Muslims of India deprived of some of the liberal laws of the Itna Ashari jurists and on the other hand, does not allow the Shia to benefit by some of those Sunni legal principles which are more conducive to modern social conditions than the corresponding principles under their own law.[12]

According to Tahir Mahmood, the Shia and Sunni schools should not be regarded as mutually exclusive.

The principle of equality of the schools of Islamic law, Sunni as well as Shia, has now been implicitly accepted in many Muslim countries. In these countries, no discrimination has been made in practice against the Shia legal doctrines during the course of the codification of personal laws on the basis of an eclectic choice of provisions made from conflicting legal principles of the various schools. Instances of these are found in the enforcement, under the Egyptian, Sudanese and Iraqi laws, of the Shia principle, like upholding the validity of a bequest in favour of an heir (which is denied by the Sunni schools).[13]

It will be difficult for the Muslims of India to agree to the unification of their personal laws unless they too accept the sound principle that the various schools of Islamic law, whether Sunni or Shia, are interchangeable and not mutually exclusive.[14]

The advantages of codified laws are: its certainty, simplicity and uniformity, whereas its sole disadvantage is its artificial rigidity. It cannot, however, be denied that re-codification of a Muslim Personal Law is necessary in India in order to remove uncertainties, prevent it from being tampered with by the introduction of alien rules and avoid the evils of judicial legislation.[15]

Problems faced by Muslim Women

In post-independent India, Muslim women face a lot of problems due to uncodified Muslim personal laws and an orthodox leadership. The issues are iniquitous inheritance laws, maintenance laws, triple talaq and polygamy.

Maintenance

One of the issues which has affected Indian Muslim women severely is the issue of providing maintenance to divorced women. Maintenance is the amount paid to the wife and children by the husband for their sustenance after divorce. However, in case of Muslim women this amount has been low and paid till just the mandatory iddat period, even if the woman does not remarry. These maintenance rules and customary practices cause havoc in the lives of Muslim women. In India today, the provisions of the Sharia are being abused by Muslim men to deny women their basic human rights.[16]

The plight of Muslim women came to fore during the 1980s when Shah Bano, an elderly Muslim woman from Indore in Madhya Pradesh, was divorced at the age of seventy by her husband. Shah Bano appealed to the court for her right to maintenance under section 125 of IPC.[17] Her husband refused to pay her maintenance beyond the iddat period ie. three months of the waiting period after divorce before which she cannot remarry according to Muslim law.

The Supreme Court maintained that Sec 125 is common for all citizens of India. It said, Muslim women can claim right to maintenance under this law and this would also not be contrary to Muslim Personal Law. The SC said that the provision of CrPC Section 125 is supported even by the holy scriptures of Islam.

This, however, created an uproar within the community. Muslim leaders, particularly the ulema, took great offence and opposed the SC judgement tooth and nail and maintained that it is 'blatant interference' in the Muslim Personal Law. The ulema declared that the apex court has no right to interpret the holy Qur'an and claimed, the Qur'an is against maintenance beyond ninety days.

This was despite more progressive maintenance laws having been in place for other community women in the 1080s. The Muslim Personal Law Board stll maintains that the SC has no right to rule for maintenance of Muslim women. Therefore, even when the Maintenance legislation was passed in 2001 by Parliament, it excluded Indian Muslim women from its benefits.[18]

Iniquitous Inheritance Rights

Muslim women in India are given unequal share in inheritance rights, especially in matters of agricultural land. For many, these prospects have been enhanced by the Hindu Succession

(Amendment) Act 2005 (HSAA) which deleted the gender discriminatory clause on agricultural land. But the benefits of this Act has been limited only to Hindu women, leaving intact the disabilities facing non-Hindu women, especially Muslim and Tribal women.

In contrast, under the Sharia, a daughter and widow cannot be excluded by any other heir and are protected by the overall testamentary restrictions, even though their shares are always lower than men's and the Sharia is not equitable in this matter.[19]

History records that it was the 1937 British enactment that excluded a critical form of property, agricultural land from being inherited by Indian women. Section (2) provides that:

> Not with standing any custom or usage to the contrary, in all questions (save questions relating to agricultural land) regarding inter-state succession, special property of families, including personal property inherited or obtained under contract or gift or any other provision of personal law, marriage, dissolution of marriage including Talaq, Ila, Zihar, Lian and Mubaraat, maintenance, dower, guardianship and waqfs (other than charities and charitable institutions and charitable and religious endowments) the rule of decision in cases where the parties are Muslims shall be the MPL (Shariat).[20]

While in many States in India, reforms were brought about in this law after independence,[21]other States such as Delhi, Jammu & Kashmir, Haryana, Himachal Pradesh and Punjab continue to practice highly discriminatory tenurial laws and customs at considerable variance with the Sharia.[22] In Uttar Pradesh, for instance, non-Hindu women are still governed by the UP Zamindari Abolition and Land Reforms Act, 1950. Section 171 of this Act gives primacy to male line of descent. Only in their absence, a widow can qualify. Daughters come lower. Tenurial law in Delhi, Punjab, Haryana, Himachal Pradesh and J&K give similar primacy to the male heir. This is contrary to laws granted under the Sharia. This virtually excludes Muslim and other non-Hindu women from rights on agricultural land.

Countries like Turkey and Somalia have full gender equality in inheritance laws. Even situation in neighboring countries of Pakistan and Bangladesh is much better as far as inheritance laws for women are concerned. In Pakistan, the 1937 Act was superceded by later laws. The West Pakistan Muslim Personal Law Act of 1962 includes agricultural land and extends the Sharia to all of west Pakistan, except 'Tribal Areas' in the NWFP.[23] The Act entitles Muslim women to inherit all property including agricultural, with shares as prescribed by the Sharia. Pakistani women's groups played a key role in this reform.

Muslim women of East Pakistan (now Bangladesh), however, continue to come under the 1937 colonial enactment. But here, women were not disadvantaged, since even before this Act, customs contrary to Islamic law were not enforced in (undivided) Bengal. Here the Sharia also applies to agricultural land, as outlined in Mulla's *Principles of Mohammedan Law* 1990.[24]

However, in India, not only in case of agricultural land but whatever rights Muslim women have according to the Sharia,[25] are not implemented. This has caused immense distress to Muslim women as loss of property, especially agricultural land, is of particular concern to poor Muslim women in the large Indian States.[26]

Equitable inheritance laws would require the need to delete the phrase, 'save questions relating to agricultural land' in section 2 of the Anglo-Muslim Law and bring all property, including agricultural, in line with the Sharia. State laws, just like personal laws, have been equally inequitable to Indian Muslim women.

Triple Talaq, Instant Oral Divorce

Triple divorce is a system where, by uttering the statement of divorce thrice, marriage ends instantly. It is a system wherein a man can divorce his wife in a matter of minutes. This issue has been highlighted after many Indian Muslims have taken to divorcing their wives by mail, over the phone and even through mobile phone text messages.

For generations, countless Muslim men have invoked the triple divorce that have left equally countless women (and children) destitute. The All India Muslim Law Board has responded to recent cases by pronouncing this form of divorce as *sin* and the need to discourage it. However, they also claim that this form of divorce is *legal* and once pronounced, is binding and therefore the ulema cannot go against what is written in Sharia.[27]

The practice of instant divorce is banned in several Islamic countries including Pakistan, Bangladesh, Malaysia and Indonesia. In Pakistan (where the majority, as in India, follows the Hanafi tradition), a husband has to notify an arbitration council/Sharia court about the talaq immediately after its pronouncement. The effect of the notice is to freeze the talaq for 90 days, during which the council tries to bring about reconciliation.

Only after the expiry of 90 days, the talaq takes effect unless there is a patch-up. Moreover, the man has to apply to the council to marry a second time, giving exact reasons why he wants to do so. Similar to the Pakistani system, other Muslim nations like Syria, Lebanon and several others do not term talaq pronouncement legal unless the matter is brought to the notice of the court or the arbitration council.

It is only in India that the single utterance of triple divorce has been valid until recently. India's lower House of Parliament has passed a bill that seeks to criminalise 'triple talaq', a style of instant divorce used by some in the Muslim community despite the country's top court suspending the practice in August 2017. The Muslim Women's (Protection of Rights of Marriage) Bill 2017, introduced by the Narendra Modi government in the Lok Sabha, provides three years' jail term for men found guilty of divorcing their wives through triple talaq. The Bill is, in part, the result of decades of campaigning by Indian Muslim women's groups and victims against a vicious practice.[28]

The Mumbai-based women's rights group BMMA or the Bharatiya Muslim Mahila Andolan (Indian Muslim Women's Movement) was party to the legal battle and has chronicled more than a hundred cases of triple talaq in India.

Polygamy

Polygamy is the form of marriage in which a person has more than one spouse. According to Islamic law, a husband can have up to four wives. In India, the Muslims are allowed to have multiple wives. There have been several cases of desertion of a first wife and marrying another without giving justice to the first wife or providing for her and the children.[29] There have been increasing number of women who are approaching the judiciary against this practice.[30]

While this practice has been banned in several Muslim countries, in others there are checks in place to prevent degeneration of the practice. In South Asia, countries like Pakistan and Bangladesh require that all matters of extra judicial and arbitrary divorce, and second and subsequent marriages be submitted before an arbitration council. They also require written permission of the first wife before a second marriage can be contracted.[31] These kind of arbitration councils are missing from the Indian scene.

Egypt, Indonesia, Pakistan, Bangladesh, Tunisia and Turkey have enacted laws requiring permission from a court of law to remarry. Increasing incidence of polygamy has impelled the Islamic court of Dar-ul-Qaza to lay down the condition that polygamy will be allowed only if a person shows sufficient cause, and satisfies the authorities that he will be able to bear the additional economic burden and not divorce the first wife.[32]

Scholars of Islamic law also point out that as far as polygamy is concerned, the Qur'an has given permission for it *in particular circumstances* and *most reluctantly* and if the two verses on polygamy ie. 4:3 and 4:129 are read together, it becomes impossible to practice polygamy. *It is wrong to think that the Qur'an has permitted polygamy without any conditions.* Its conditions are most rigorous and very difficult to fulfill and hence even in earlier Islamic periods, it was believed that it is as good as banned.[33]

In a recent update, the Supreme Court of India stated that the Muslims, like every other community in India, have the right to follow their religion but in terms of equality and as per the Constitution of India, those rights do not allow them to have multiple wives.[34] The judges ruled that for public order, equality and justice in India, it was essential to regulate marriage issues within the country, especially those dealing with polygamy practices although in India, people have the freedom to practice their own religions.

While some see the ruling and new laws as injustice to Muslims, banning triple talaq and polygamy in India is the best justice for Muslim women in India and their children. It is nowhere relevant to any particular religion but it's a question of morality. As a man cannot bear his wife being with another man, similarly it is not easy for a woman to share her husband with another woman either. The empowering judgment came from Justices TS Thakur and AK Goel who said that,

> 'What was protected under Article 25 (right to practice and propagate any religion) was the religious faith and not a practice which may run counter to public order, health or morality. Polygamy was not integral part of religion and monogamy was a reform within the power of the state under Article 25.'

The ruling actually came against a government employee who was fired for misconduct after it was found that he had a second marriage in spite of being already married. The judgment was supported by the fact that no religion is bigger than Indian laws and polygamy isn't an important practice in any religion in India.

Adoption

Another issue which has been affecting both women and men equally within the community is the issue of adoption of children. Any move for an all-India Adoption Bill has always been thwarted by Muslim orthodox elements. The argument presented against the uniform adoption bill by the Muslim orthodox community in 1972 was:

a) Islam, as a religion, does not allow adoption. Any bill of this sort would allow Muslims to disobey the Qur'anic injunctions against adoption.
b) The proposed law would throw the Islamic law of inheritance out of gear. Once an adoption was made, succession and marriage (prohibited degree of relationship) would be affected. It was a thin attempt to foist Hindu law on Muslims.
c) Dissenting members pointed out that the draft bill was a Hindu religious concept in spirit, which was being foisted upon the Muslims.
d) Opponents argued that Muslim children were well looked after by their relatives if they were orphaned. Moreover, the adoption bill was no answer to the plight of abandoned children.[35]

Also, during the period, Jamaat-e-Islami sent a memorandum to the government complaining that:

'An exclusively Hindu religious custom is being elevated to the status of a general law which will certainly make inroads in and erode the social structure of other communities for whom there is otherwise no provision of such a provision.'

However, during the same period there were certain Muslim intellectuals who found nothing wrong in the enactment of the

Adoption Bill. For instance Daniel Latiffi suggested the two Qur'anic rules that (i) an adoptive father should have the liberty of marrying his adopted son's divorced wife and (ii) the adoptee should retain his natural father's name, should both be given specific protection in the Adoption Bill in its application to Muslims.[36]

However, according to scholars like Tariq Moddood, there was no need of adapting the Bill to the law of Islam. In his opinion, if the rules of Islamic law did not allow adoption, those rules could remain in force without any disturbance. If adoption was a sin in Islam, no Muslim had any need to commit it. But to a Muslim who, knowing that traditionally Islam did not allow adoption, wanted to adopt a child the secular state could not deny the benefit of the Bill when enacted. Muslims should have no grievance if a secular law permitting and regulating adoption, but not making it obligatory, is enacted and made available to those Indians who wish, in their discretion, to make use of its provisions.[37]

Tahir Mahmood says, 'Even if it is accepted that Islamic law prohibits adoption, how can the Muslims prevent enactment of a secular law of adoption which will be applicable only to those who wish to adopt a child? If Islamic law does not permit adoption, the Muslims need not make use of the Indian adoption law. The law will certainly not impose on any person a duty to adopt.... If Islam does not recognise a social or economic concept, the state cannot compel every Muslim to keep away from it. If that were possible, our banking laws should not be available to any Muslim, since Islam does prohibit interest on money.... The demand that a special saving clause exempting the entire Muslim community from its application be inserted in the Bill cannot be accepted'.

Also, it is notable that the Muslim Republic of Tunisia enacted in 1958 a modern law of adoption, the provisions of which were very similar to those of the Indian Adoption Bill, 1972. However, neither these reports from Muslim countries nor the other arguments succeded in changing dominant Muslim opinion in India which was absolutely against the enactment of the Adoption

Bill, 1972. Thus, during the short-lived Janata regime at the centre, the Adoption of Children Bill, 1972 was withdrawn from the legislature by the government on the plea that certain sections of Indians (Muslims and Parsis) were dead opposed to it.

In December 1980 a new adoption bill was introduced in Parliament, substantially on the lines of the earlier bill of 1972 on the same subject. Its application clause, however provided that when enacted, the Bill would not apply to persons governed by the Muslim personal law. This meant total exemption of the Muslim community members from the purview of the bill and reflected the victory of dominant Muslim opinion in this country which has always regarded adoption as a concept foreign to Islamic tradition.[38]

Apart from the above cultural opposition within Islam and the visible opposition to an all-India Adoption Bill, the law under which minorities can adopt is itself discriminatory and archaic in nature. One of the main reasons for this massive chasm is that at present, in India only the Hindus, Buddhists, Jains and Sikhs can adopt under the Hindu Adoptions and Maintenance Act, 1956 while adoption amongst Muslims and other non-Muslims in India is regulated by the Guardian and Wards Act,1890 (GAWA).

The non-Hindus are, therefore, forced to take recourse to the Guardians and Wards Act, 1890 under the option of 'guardianship' for any case of adoption. This has immediate repercussions on two planes: Firstly, this absence of law is widely understood to be a significant reason for the low number of adoptions in India. Secondly, even those who invoke GAWA, notwithstanding such disability, are actually deprived from their right to 'family' since there are various discrepancies in legal as well practical ways in the relation between a 'parent' and an 'adopted' child on one hand and between a 'guardian' and a 'ward' on the other hand.

Under GAWA, the relationship between the adoptive parents and the adopted child is that of guardian and ward respectively and of not parent and child. Unlike the Hindu Adoptions and Maintenance Act 1956, adoption under GAWA is not irrevocable and does not confer status of the biological child on the adopted child.[39]

In a landmark judgment in 2014, the Supreme Court has ruled that any person can adopt a child under the Juvenile Justice (Care and Protection of Children) Act 2000, irrespective of the religion he or she follows and even if the personal laws of the particular religion does not permit it. The JJ Act 2000 is a secular law enabling any person, irrespective of the religion he professes, to take a child in adoption. It is akin to the Special Marriage Act 1954, which enables any person living in India to get married under that Act, irrespective of the religion s/he follows.

'Personal beliefs and faiths, though must be honoured, cannot dictate the operation of the provisions of an enabling statute', ruled a bench headed by Chief Justice P Sathasivam. Terming the JJ Act a 'small step towards formation of a uniform civil code', the court said: A person is always free to adopt or choose not to do so and, instead, he follows dictates of the personal law. To us, the JJ Act is a small step in reaching the goal enshrined by Article 44 of the Constitution which prescribes a uniform civil code.[40]

The All-India Muslim Personal Law Board had registered its protest against the PIL, terming it a covert attempt to slip in a uniform code by the backdoor which would infringe on the Sharia law. 'We have our own personal law and no step should be taken to covertly formulate a uniform adoption code without taking into account our stand on the issue', the AIMPLB had said before the apex court.[41]

Given the discriminatory aspects of the law of adoption for minorities in India, Shabnam Hashmi, a prominent activist and director of Anhad had filed a writ petition under Article 32 of the Constitution, for recognition of the right of all children to adoption under right to life and equality, under Articles 14 and 21 of of the Constitution of India and to issue guidelines to the respondents to permit adoption by parents and of children belonging to all religions and sex, as against mere Guardianship. She sought a Writ of Mandamus to the respondents to enact a special enabling law for adoption which can be availed of by any person irrespective of his/her religion for adoption of child of any religion /sex. Hashmi is familiar with the entire issue, having herself, along with her husband Gauhar Raza, taken a girl child from 'Palna', a recognised adoption agency, under the Guardians and Wards Act, 1890 as the joint guardians of the child.

The Petitioner and her husband were constrained to take the child under the said Act since they both are non-Hindus and thus do not enjoy the right to adopt under the Indian law. The child, Seher Hashmi, has otherwise received all the love and care by the petitioner and her said husband, absolutely like their older biological child, Sahir Raza. Seher has, however, legally remained a 'ward' and is thus deprived of the legal status and privileges of an adopted child.[43]

In 2005, the family received a rude shock when Seher was denied the benefit of being included as a family member in the 'Service Book' of Gauhar Raza, a scientist working with the Government of India. The application was rejected on the ground that Seher is only a 'ward' and not a 'child' of the couple and hence she is not entitled to the benefits as a family member. This incident is only an instance that highlights the deeper problems underlying this issue which, in the absence of any legal framework for adoption by and of non-Hindus, forces them to resort to the Guardians and Wards Act.

According to Shabnam Hashmi, there has been reluctance on the part of government to bring about reform within these adoption laws. This is because the government only recognises the voices of orthodox sections within any community. And the orthodox sections within the Muslim community have been reluctant to bring about changes in the personal laws.[44] This has resulted in a stalemate.[45]

Hashmi suggested the need to enact a law which would be optional, and while not impinging on the religious sentiments of any faith, would provide a legal option of adoption for all persons to take advantage of, irrespective of the religion of the adoptive parents or of the adopted child, without violating their religious sanctions on the issue in any manner. Similar to the model of the Special Marriage Act, such a law would have no compulsive force requiring anyone to act contrary to his religious tenets; it would be merely an enabling legislation and should anyone feel that it was contrary to his religion, to adopt under such an Act, s/he would be free not to adopt.[46]

The right to adopt a child—till 2014 restricted to Hindus, Buddhists and Jains—now extends to Muslims, Christians, Jews, Parsis and all other communities, thanks to the Sathasivam judgment in the apex court.

Models of Reform for Indian Muslims

There have been several responses emanating from within the Muslim community to reconcile women's rights with cultural rights. Some scholars have felt the need for change has to come from within the community and others have felt the need is for the change to come through external sources. Division in the response lies between those who feel the need for change to be initiated by the state and others who feel that there should be no interference from the state and the change should come from within the community. Major suggestions on how to bring about these reforms are:

Internal Reform

Internal reformists feel that reform should come from within the community and there should be no interference from the state.[47] They feel that existing personal laws should be reformed to make them gender just. Scholars like Ashghar Ali Engineer favour reforms in a pluralistic country like India rather than a Uniform Civil Code.

No one in India, political leaders or individuals, have ever concentrated their efforts towards defining the Uniform Civil Code. All we know is that some common laws covering issues relating to marriage, succession and property is called Uniform Civil Code but what these laws would be is anyone's guess.

The patriarchal interpretation of Islam should be removed. Qur'an is full of rights-based discourses for women and not duty-based dictates. Qur'an is also very careful with matters like *talaq* with specific injunctions to a contrary effect. Several changes have come within the Muslim community as a result of relentless work by Muslim women's organisations and Muslim intellectuals. They have also raised the need for Muslim institutions to become more representative of diversity within the Muslim community. Even within the orthodox sections, there is a realisation that men need to be discouraged from making use of these sinful practices. So, there is some kind of consensus among various sections that there has to be a control on such practices within the community. Several mehods have been suggested to bring about change in Indian Muslim communities.

Re-reading Religious Texts, Takhayur & Ijtihad

Takhayur

> For instance, reforms can be brought about by reading Tahir Mahmood's *Statutes of Personal Law in Islamic Countries (1995).* The author reports that, 'unification of personal law has been achieved in the Muslim world by assuming that all or most of the different schools of Islamic jurisprudence are equally valid and acceptable, and by applying to them the principle of eclectic choice (*takhayur*). The choice has been exercised in different countries under the legislative, executive or judicial powers of the state, often through juristic aid and advice.

Professor Esposito, writing about the reformist methodology used to formulate the rules embodied in Egyptian Law No. 25 of 1929, notes that, '[w]hereas *takhayur* traditionally was restricted to selection of the dominant opinion of another law school, the reformers extended it to the adoption of an individual jurist's opinion. There are several issues on which one or the other Sharia school is more favourable than others. For instance, triple divorce in one sitting is not valid in the Ahl-e-Hadith whereas it is allowed in both Hanafi as well as Shafi schools.[48] Thus, this provision from Ahl-e-Hadith could be incorporated to abolish triple divorce in one sitting. Such compilation will greatly ease Muslim women's position in India.

All Muslim countries are making changes in Sharia law relating to women or even applying direct Qur'anic provisions or even attempting *ijtihad* in other matters. It is only in India that the 'personal law', as it is known in India, is considered untouchable. Thus, there is a total stagnation in Sharia laws in India and women continue to suffer.

Ijtihad

> Many modern Islamic scholars like Jamaludin Afghani, Muhammad Abdahu, Syed Ahmed Khan, Mohammad Iqbal, Maulana Chirag Ali, Maulavi Mumtaz Ali Khan have emphasised on intellectual assertion (ijtihad) after stagnation began to affect Islamic theological thinking due to political and social reasons. According to them, one must resort to ijtihad within the Islamic framework to solve new problems including issues of women's rights and entitlements.

However, the orthodox ulema argue that the gates of ijtihad were closed long ago and also that there are no qualified persons to practice the theory of ijtihad. They feel that great *imam*s and some of their followers had the requisite qualification and none today have these qualifications. Thus the debate raging within the Islamic world is for or against ijtihad.

According to Engineer, if the Islamic world has to understand the dynamic spirit of the Qur'an, they will have to enact changes in the Sharia and accord women an equal status. It is important to note that values like justice and compassion cannot be applied independent of the age and time. According to him the medieval period's understanding of justice was very different from what it is today. The AIMPLB's entire functioning is more reactive than proactive, Engineer says. They defend *riwayat* (tradition) rather than use ijtihad.

The conservative ulema point out that though ijtihad is an accepted principle in Islam, one intending to resort to ijtihad should have thorough knowledge of the Qur'an and the Sunnah and also of what is known as *usul al-fiqh,* ie. the principles of jurisprudence. They feel no one, including themselves, have these qualifications. However, this is not true. There are many among the ulema as well as the modern scholars of Islam, who are qualified to do ijtihad. It is rather fear of consequences or conservatism, rather than lack of qualification, which deter them from undertaking ijtihad.[49]

Also, there are internal struggles for controlling institutions which have become impediments to reform. If one *alim* shows the inclination to accept the need for ijtihad, his rivals denounce him as 'heretic' and seize control of the institution from him. A member of the Muslim Personal Law Board in India has gone on record to say, it is fear of rivals rather than lack of perception for certain badly-needed changes, which is the main impediment.[50]

Engineer notes, one has to bear in mind that at least in India—and in several other Islamic countries too—the people who choose career as 'ulama' come from poorer and backward classes who have no other choice. The children from middle and upper classes go for professional education like engineering, medical or management courses. They can afford to do so. It is the parents from poorer classes who perforce send their children to religious institutions as not only education in those institutions is free, but also, they get free boarding and lodging. These children grow up with backward outlooks, not knowing much about other developments in the world.[51] Moreover, religion becomes a power in their hands with which they rule millions of backward, poor and illiterate masses and also, in many cases, believing educated people who do not care to study religion by themselves. These sociological aspects of any religious community have to be borne in mind while trying to understand its belief-systems.

In a fast-changing world, recourse to ijtihad is a must and Islam is among those religions which approves of healthy change and allows its believers to not only grapple with the changes taking place around them, but also to strive to re-apply Islamic principles of jurisprudence. As far as ijtihad is concerned, it should be made absolutely clear that no one can change principles and values. These are most fundamental to religious teachings. Ijtihad could be done only in re-application of these values and principles in changed circumstances.

Re-codification of Muslim Personal Law

Codification of Muslim Personal Law has been suggested by several scholars as a possible strategy to bring about reform within the Indian Muslim community.

Citing the experience of enacting the Dissolution of Muslim Marriage Act, 1939, several scholars have pointed out that it would be possible to create a broad forum of legal scholars and ulema to lay the ground for eventual codification.[52] Tahir Mahmood suggested the need for an Indian Muslim Law, based on an eclectic selection of principle from the various schools of Sharia as a solution to all contemporary problems of Muslim laws in this country.[53]

In India, the Muslim Personal Law Board has a few years ago produced, in the name of 'codification', yet another textbook on the Hanafi law without taking into account any provision of the other schools of Islamic law prevalent in India—the Shafi, the Isna Ashari and the Ismaili, as also the stand of the Ahl-e-Hadith—on certain important matters. If the Board ever agrees to undertake an exercise towards preparing a draft-code, it will have to realise that a collection of the rules of any particular school of Muslim law, however dominant it may be locally, cannot qualify to be called *Code of Muslim Law in India*.[54]

Such codes, according to Mahmood, have been enacted in many Muslim countries. Among the non-Muslim nations, while the Philippines enacted a code of Muslim law long ago, South Africa is now preparing a similar code with the help of Indian scholars. A similar exercise could be taken up in India as well. In absence of a proper code, Muslim Law is suffering from all sorts of ailments. The multiplicity of juristic opinion within Islam, the insistence of various contemporary Muslim groups of to strictly adhere to particular juristic opinions of ancient times, freedom of any individual today to 'interpret' the religious law and, above all, the self-assumed obligation of people in general to 'enforce' its dictates as understood by them, have together turned Muslim Law into a Babel.[55]

The true egalitarian principles of Islamic laws are lying buried under heaps of age-long misinterpretations and widely prevailing misconceptions, scholars say. These have to be dug out and must replace the present distorted view of the laws.

Muslim women's unfettered freedom of choosing a life-partner by their free will, negotiating the terms of a proposed alliance, maintaining their independent identity and rights during marriage, walking out of an irretrievably broken marriage without any hassles, and enjoying unrestricted ownership of all property that comes to their hands by inheritance or otherwise, are some of the salient features of Islamic law. The current set of personal laws is not properly codified, which is why they are not easily comprehensible and there are ambiguities galore. In India, this is one of the reasons for their abuse by those with vested interests. Hence, codification of the entire gamut of Muslim personal laws should be given high priority.[56]

Other scholars have pointed out that AIMPLB should take the initiative to codify the Muslim Personal Law in the spirit of the Islamic Sharia. The ulema and well-known Muslim lawyers should draft a comprehensive bill in this respect, but well within Sharia framework, and give it to the government to enact it through Parliament.[57] The Islamic scholars should formulate *actual* Sharia laws. In free India's context, the colonial Anglo-Mohammedan Law should be completely discarded. The Sharia law should be formulated in accordance with social circumstances and requirements.[58]

However, codification can be initiated only through an institutional framework. The setting up of such institutions can be facilitated by the state. Alternatively, if the intervention by the state is viewed as an encroachment upon the autonomous space of minorities, the concerned community will first have to create an institutional structure for reform and then begin dialogue with the different segments of the community to work out a consensus.[59]

Need for Piecemeal Reform

According to Flavia Agnes, the need would be to work towards piecemeal reform of the practice which violate the provisions of the Constitution on a priority basis. Small beginning needs to be made by moving towards codification of the entire corpus of Muslim Personal Law. As triple talaq has been the most controversial issue, the practice needs to be declared un-Islamic, she says.[60]

An Uniform Civil Code is not best idea to reconcile cultural diversity with gender equality. At best, one could think in terms of an optional civil code. 'We need to think of devising ways of reconciling gender justice with legal recognition of the identities of multiple cultural groups', she opines. So, instead of a Uniform Civil Code, the need is to work towards separate gender-just personal laws for the different communities[61] Especially after the Shah Bano controversy and then the destruction of the Babri Masjid and the violence that followed, many women's groups in India are veering round to this position, aware that supporting a Uniform Civil Code at this juncture would only play into the hands of the Hindutva brigade.

These gender just personal laws have to emerge from the grassroots in a gradual manner in order to gain the acceptance of the different communities. They cannot be forcibly imposed or legislated from above. And as these different gender-just personal laws for the different communities evolve slowly, it will lead to *uniform principles*, although *not uniform laws*.[62]

Exit Option

The exit system means that women and men have a fundamental right to move out or disassociate from the system they are linked with. It means that if practices of any group are unacceptable to its members, they should have the option to move out or leave the group. The Indian Muslim community, and especially the Muslim women, have made good use of the exit system. The establishment of four boards, formation of various nikahnamas, and establishment of the all-women mosque point to its success.

The Model Nikahnama

Most *nikahnamas* prepared by local qazis or elders gave women a raw deal in cases where the marriage was called off. Reformists and women's groups have put pressure on the AIMPLB to design a uniform code for marriages in the community and, more important, abolish the practice of triple talaq. The issue was debated for almost a decade and the AIMPLB repeatedly assured the country that a model nikahnama would be issued. So, when its executive committee promised in December 2004 that it would reform the existing system, Muslim women across the country hoped that finally justice would come their way.[63] It was released in Bhopal on 1 May 2005 at the 18th general council meeting of the AIMPLB.

The *Model Nikahnama* is supposed to be a sort of standard marriage contract for the Indian Muslim community. The model nikahnama is broadly split into three parts: The Nikahnama (marriage contract), the *Hidayatnama* (guidelines for marriage under Sharia law) and the *Qarar* (declaration to abide by Sharia law). It essentially provides specific guidelines for a couple on how they should behave in the event of a dispute between them and how the issue should be resolved within the ambit of the Sharia law.

Emphasis is placed on using arbitrators and mediators to resolve a discord. Should that fail, the couple must approach the Dar-ul-Qaza, the Sharia court. Both parties are discouraged from approaching the country's law courts.

The model nikahnama says that the *mehr* (bride money given at the time of marriage) should be given in tangible assets. But it adds a rider that it would be all right if only half the amount is paid at the time of the marriage.[64] The document denounces dowry. It does not permit a man to marry his wife's sisters or aunts. And should the man want to take a second wife, the nikahnama suggests, he secure written consent from his first wife. However, none of this is enforceable.

Under the Hidayatnama, the document puts out a set of chauvinistic guidelines for women, including the necessity of a wife to be 'obedient' to her husband.

The model nikahnama has a few progressive features. For instance, it attempts to put in place a strict method of mediation and arbitration if a couple chooses to divorce. It has fixed *a time frame of four months* for the arbitrators/mediators to arrive at a decision, thereby not allowing the case to drag on indefinitely. It requires written records of all marriages and their copies to be given to the bride and the groom. These could be proof, should there be any dispute over facts. The document makes it mandatory for parents or guardians of couples to be present during the marriage, thereby preventing forced marriages.[65]

At the height of the triple talaq debate, an AIMPLB committee member even opined that the Board could not in one blow abolish the triple talaq system. Besides, the issue would get politicised and eventually block the process of reform. The AIMPLB believes the 'one-sitting declaration of triple talaq' will eventually vanish by slowly working on making the community aware of its ills. The member said, the Board wanted to declare a severe punishment for men who adopt the practice. Adding to the AIMPLB's problems were attempts by some sections of Muslims to opt out of it and create their own body. This, in turn, made it difficult for the Board to announce any major decision.

Although the AIMPLB has been unwilling to take a hardline position on triple talaq, it addresses the controversial issue, something it had been shying away from for years. The model nikahnama says talaq declared in one sitting will not be acknowledged. The document states: In the event the bridegroom proceeds to divorce the bride, he shall not pronounce talaq thrice consecutively to his wife, and even if he does, it will not be valid and binding upon the bride. The bridegroom agrees that he will pronounce talaq once each, at the interval of one month, and the divorce will be considered to be valid only if he gives such notes as provided under the tenets of the Holy Qur'an and provisions of the Mohamedan law to the arbitrators/mediators or Dar-ul-Qaza.

The model nikahnama was expected to give Muslim women more rights in marriage but has turned out to be a disappointment.[66] In the nikahnama, the AIMPLB put out a weak statement saying, 'triple talaq is avoidable'. The nikahnama does not provide any safeguards against men leaving their wives without sufficient maintenance. It has completely ignored areas such as marriage of minors and polygamy. Although the model nikahnama does put together some guidelines, its greatest fault is that it makes none of these mandatory.[67] Thus, unfortunately, not only is the model nikahnama completely inadequate, but it has proved that the AIMPLB does not have the courage to take a radically progressive step in favour of women.

Outraged at the AIMPLB's lack of willingness for reform, women's organisations across the country announced that they will not accept the model nikahnama and will formulate a new one. They exited from the present AIMPLB and formed their own Board, the All India Women's Muslim Personal Law Board and came up with their own nikahnama. In Mumbai, several women's groups issued a joint statement that said: The nikahnama released by the AIMPLB is one more proof of their misogyny and confirms the fact that they exist in a time warp with no notions of gender justice or women's equality.

The organisations took objection to the following guidelines: that a wife should be 'obedient' to her husband, that she required her husband's permission to step out of her marital home, that she should safeguard her 'honour' and 'respectability' when the 'need' arises, and that she should be 'allowed' to visit her parents and relatives.

The Mumbai group's nikahnama emphasised the need for the Tawfeez-e-Talaq clause, which gave a woman the right to divorce her husband if he marries again without her consent.[68] It stipulated that if the husband violated the nikahnama or pronounced talaq three times in one sitting, he was liable to pay double the mehr. Obviously, this was unacceptable to the AIMPLB. According to Islamic scholar Uzma Naheed, the Tawfeez-e-Talaq right was given to Muslim women a hundred years ago and the idea of doubling the mehr is found in the teachings of the Maliki school of jurisprudence (a school of religious law in Sunni Islam). Hence both clauses were very much within the framework of Sharia law and Islam. The group's demand for *khoola* (the right of a woman to ask for divorce) too was rejected. 'It has taken the AIMPLB so long to get a model nikahnama ready. To institute such radical clauses would be asking for too much', said SQR Ilyas, a member of the AIMPLB's executive committee.[69]

Meanwhile, political groups such as the All India Democratic Women's Association (AIDWA) appreciated the AIMPLB initiative in starting the reform process and for taking a small step in the right direction. The AIMPLB has at least 'started the process of discussions, change, codification and reform in Muslim Personal Laws', said an AIDWA statement. But AIDWA added that the model nikahnama fell short of democratic demands made by reformists. It said it was unfortunate that the AIMPLB had not banned polygamy and not addressed the issue of child marriage.[70]

The Four New Boards

Over the years, there has been a growing dissatisfaction with the apex body representing Muslim interest in India ie. AIMPLB. Therefore, not only women, several other groups too have moved out of the system to form new law boards. The three new boards are: The All-India Shia Personal Law Board (AISPLB), the All-India Muslim Personal Law Board Jabid (AIMPLBJ of the Barelvi sect) and the All-India Muslim Women's Personal Law Board.

The AIMWB was formed in Feburary 2005 to address the under-representation of Muslim women in the AIMPLB, calling the All-India Muslim Personal Law Board 'irresponsible and cruel' towards women. Shaista Amber, president of the board, pointed out that 'Despite prattling about working for the rights of the women, the men-dominated boards took no account of the voice of women'. Accusing men of dominating the affairs of the various personal law boards and holding them responsible for the bulk of the problems being faced by the Muslim women, she said, when women do not get justice from the Dar-ul-Qaza or the Sharia courts they have to knock at the doors of family courts.[71] 'We will try to form a Dar-ul-Qaza ourselves, which will deal with the cases of women', said the secretary, Parveen Abdi.

Talking about the functions of the new board, Amber said the new board would fight against the division of Islam into different sects, namely Sunni, Shia, Barelvis, Deobandis etc.[72] For this, the women's board would launch an extensive campaign against the patriarchal designs of the existing boards and enlighten women of the 'real spirit of Islam'. Abdi added that they would also try to educate the Muslim women about issues like triple talaq, mehr and family planning.[73]

The Shias who formed the Shia Personal Law Board (SPLB) in January 2005 alleged that the AIMPLB has reduced them to *a minority within the minority*, and therefore the need to form a separate law board. The community had been compelled to take this step on account of the injustice meted out to the Shias in the political, social and government spheres. The SMPLB called for the creation of separate Shia Waqf Boards in all States on the pattern of the ones that already exist in Uttar Pradesh and Bihar. The demand challenges the domination of the boards by the numerically larger Sunni Muslim community. The SMPLB also demand proportional representation for the community in all government, quasi-government Muslim welfare institutions.

A group of Shia women too in Feburary 2005 formed a personal law panel close on the heels of the formation of three new Muslim outfits, independent of the All India Muslim Personal Law Board (AIMPLB). They too cited as the reason for the formation of the panel 'an unfair deal at the hands of AIMPLB'.[74] Talat Rizvi, secretary of the outfit, said: 'We are compelled to form a separate board for women because the newly-formed Shia law board failed to give a single representation to women from the community.' According to her, the AIMPLB never cared to have a single Shia woman as a member, right from its inception in 1972, 'though Shia women had always been active in taking up the cause of Muslim women from time to time.' Rizvi hoped that the new board would not only go a long way in creating greater awareness among Shia women about their rights as enshrined in the Sharia and also help in their educational pursuits.[75]

Tauqir Raza Khan, grandson of the founder of the Barelvi sect, Ahmad Raza Khan of Bareli, announced the setting up of its own All-India Muslim Personal Law Board (Jadeed) in December 2004. He said the Shias and Deobandis were not welcome to be its members. Raza Khan claimed that the Barelvis were under-represented in the AIMPBL.

First Women's Jamaat and a Women's Mosque

Another case of exit is the case of an all-women's mosque set up in Pudukkottai, Tamil Nadu by Muslim women.

The first women's jamaat in the world lead to the first women's mosque in history. The Muslim Women's Jamaat Committee

(MWJC) is the first of its kind in the world. It was established on 18 Feburary 2004. The MWJC has been able to resolve many cases of dowry harassment, divorce and other matters of concern to local women. It has been fighting for women to receive decent settlements.[76]

Tamil Nadu has a unique system where jamaats, affiliated to the local mosque, sit in judgement on the domestic affairs of the community. A jamaat is essentially a citizen's council, but in Tamil Nadu it functions as a powerful dispute-settlement authority. These jamaat committees, however, have no women on board; nor do they allow women to represent their own cases. When a battered, harassed woman approaches the local police for help, she is asked to obey the local jamaat. A mosque-jamaat axis is a power centre that controls the community. The local police conveniently express helplessness to intervene in local disputes.[77]

The Mosque was established in recognition of the fact that having a women's place of worship would help women. It was also a result of realisation that a jamaat (community elders at the mosque who adjudicate on family matters) of women would be more sympathetic to women's cause.

Daud Sharifa, an unlikely feminist in India's traditionally male-dominated southern heartland, caused a storm by leading the movement for the women's mosque. Her NGO, STEPS leads this jamaat. In India, a majority of mosques do not allow women to pray. Muslim women have to pray in buildings adjoining mosques; in some mosques there are separate prayer enclosures.

Also, in Indian mosques, there are all-male jamaats which are elected bodies of Muslim theologians. Muslim feminists felt the need for women to be part of a mosque congregation. According to these feminists, the idea of a women's mosque was motivated by the rising number of complaints from local Muslim women against what they saw as partisan rulings by the all-male jamaats. In Pudukkottai, the regular local mosque jamaat had already received hundreds of petition from women against jamaat rulings in matters of dowry, divorce and domestic violence. Yet, every day, more than 15 petitions relating to marital disputes came to the NGO, many sent by other jamaats in the region. This led to STEPS forming its own jamaat. In its first year, this women's council resolved 55 cases of family disputes.[78]

What these women have been trying to show is that while there might be a few good men and a few good jamaats, the system is stacked against women. The clear call is that men-dominated jamaats should accept women within their fold.[79] Male-only jamaats and waqf boards have the power to decide many personal and marriage-related disputes in India's Muslim community.[80] Daud Sharifa says, the Qur'an does not stop women from praying in mosques; only society does. She points out that Muslim women are doubly burdened as a woman and that too from the minority community. A minority community woman does not get assistance from the government and its law enforcement and rights machinery, nor from welfare agencies. Her mosque functions as a space where women can meet, relax and share their problems. It serves as a home for destitute women and children.[81]

The symbolic project of actually building a women's mosque begins to seem somewhat secondary to what might be her main goal: building a broad-based, national movement to support the rights of Muslim women.

Deliberation and Dialogue

Conflict between culture and women's rights can be resolved through deliberation and dialogue. Some scholars believe there exists no deliberation within the Muslim community, only debates are more prominent within the different sects.[82] Others believe that dialogue exists between different schools. While there are internal differences, attempts have been made to bridge internal differences.

Role of State

Need for Secular Laws: Reverse Optionality

As against arguments for internal reforms or reinterpretation of classical texts, several Muslim Scholars and women's groups have felt the need for secular laws to replace the current personal laws. According to them, laws, in fact, should not be based on religion.[83] They are committed to *right to chosen political affiliation* that rests neither on biological differences nor on belonging by birth. These feminist Muslim groups, women's organisations and Muslim scholars have felt the need to ensure that common gender-just laws are established as the right of every individual.[84]

Reverse optionality rests on reversing the current order as existing in India—-that is, against the current scheme of communities being governed by their communities' personal laws. Here the need would be for all citizens to be governed by secular gender-friendly laws and personal laws become optional for citizens. This approach is against the previous two approaches to reform, that is, codification and internal reform.

According to the advocates of reverse optionality, codification of personal laws itself cannot resolve the problem of gender inequality in culturally diverse societies.[85] This is because even previously, when codification was brought about, it eroded some of the customary variations and diversities within communities. In other words, as a principle of plurality, it has so far been in danger of canceling itself out by advocating homogeneity within communities.

And as far as reform from within is concerned, it involves adopting the role of interlocutor within a community or arguing for a radical reinterpretation of religious texts. The historical process of reforms of all personal laws have been limited and did not abolish patriarchal privileges. Current attempts at reform flounder against the entrenched patriarchal and institutional power of religious leaders; they are setting limits on who can be the agents of reforms.

As a result, proposals for reforms are either watered down or curtailed or are simply not enabling for the state.[86] Reverse optionality suggested by Muslim women's groups like *Awaaz-e-Niswaan*, the Forum against Oppression of Women and several scholars [87] is based on certain central principles:[88]

a) All citizens are guaranteed the common secular gender-just law, but can choose to opt for their personal laws.
b) These laws will be based on the principle of equal rights for women as well as on the principle of affirmative action wherever necessary.
c) These laws will be comprehensive, covering areas of marriage, compulsory registeration of marriages, divorce, inheritance, guardianship, rights of residence, rights to matrimonial property, domestic violence, equal wages and benefits.
d) Once the principle of reverse optionality is operationalised there would be, at a point in time, three categories of citizens:
    i) Citizens who opt for personal laws.
    ii) Citizens who continue to be governed by common gender just laws.
    iii) Citizens who are caught in a situation of conflict if one party has chosen personal laws.
e) In the case of a conflict, contest or unforeseen contradictions between secular law and personal law, the broad principle should be that secular law should prevail.
f) The decision to be governed by personal law should be revocable at moments of legal conflict. The principle of revocability is important because the decision to choose personal law can be forced on young women, particularly at sensitive moments (such as marriage) when they would find it difficult to express their own opinion.[89]

Unlike other approaches, this approach focuses on intervention of the state as an important ingredient to bring about change.[90]

Changes through Secular State Initiative

Many Muslim groups such as the Muslims for Secular Democracy believe that all existing personal laws, applicable to people of different religious communities, discriminate against women and therefore urgently need change.

In case of Muslims, the theological defense of triple talaq (instant divorce) and polygamy are unacceptable to the group. It is also a fact that in many Muslim countries, family laws have been revised in respect of minimum age of marriage, polygamy, divorce, maintenance. For example, in most Muslim-majority countries, including those that claim to be run on Islamic principles, instant divorce is prohibited. Similarly, polygamy is either prohibited or is permissible under specific circumstances and only after permission has been obtained from the courts and the existing wife. Thus, there can be no 'Islamic' justification for these practices to be permitted in India: they must be prohibited. 'Our objection is not to the concept of talaaq divorce, per se, but to the practice among some Muslim sects in India of instant divorce', such groups say.

According to these scholars it is simply not true that what goes in the name of 'Muslim Personal Law' in India are God-given laws that are immutable and all Muslims are obliged to follow them.

- In India itself, the Muslim Personal Law does not apply in Jammu and Kashmir (the only Muslim majority State in the country) or in Goa.
- As elaborated above, many Muslim countries have prohibited the practice of instant talaaq, and polygamy is either totally prohibited or permitted only under special circumstances.
- Millions of Muslims living in secular societies throughout the world enter into marital relations according to the laws of the country they live in. Yet, they don't cease to be Muslims

Secularism denotes the insistence on a clear separation between religion and politics, between matters of faith and affairs of the state. By secularism is meant clear rejection of the idea of a theocratic state in the modern world. Muslims for Secular Democracy have raised voice against conservative and regressive clergy within the Muslim community and other religious communities in India.

According to these activists, the AIMPBL since its inception has remained mute witness to injustices against women.

This group feels reform within any personal law and gender justice requires state initiative. According to Javed Anand, all kind of reform requires state or judicial intervention. State intervention has been visible through various progressive judgements delivered by High Courts and the Supreme Court of India.

Internal reform among Indian Muslims does not seem to be a very plausible option, says Anand. Muslim women and the whole community cannot wait endlessly to bring about changes within their personal laws. Unlike the Christian community, which brought about reform as a result of internal consensus, the same is not visible in the near future within the Muslim community and hence the need for state intervention, he adds.[91]

For Anand, the reverse optionality proposed by several women's groups also seems a not very promising proposal. This is because the proposal will have to go through a ratification process by legislature at the State and national levels. Most probably it will require a majority of two-third votes in both the Houses of Legislature. And the proposal is unlikely to gain the majority required in the legislatures at national and State levels.[92]

Given the fact that internal reform and reverse optionality are not feasible options, activism on the part of all community members appear to be the answer to the statusquoist and regressive position of AIMPLB, Anand says. Liberal Muslim activism as well as state intervention will be able to bring about changes within Muslim Personal Law, he thinks.[93]

A Common Civil Code

Many scholars within the Muslim community have insisted on the need for a common civil code for all citizens of the country. However, it is to be pointed out here that their conception of a common civil code is very different from the rightist notion of a Uniform Civil Code.

Foremost among these have been scholars like Tariq Modood who feels a common family code need not be an adaptation of the Hindu system, as some assume when passionately pleading for the adoption of a uniform law by the Indian Muslims. It should be a synthesis of all that is good in India's diverse personal laws, an eclectic, not an exotic product, a picking and choosing from many systems so as to suit the so-Indian ethos and to express the genius of Indian culture and at the same time be in accordance with the spirit of the times.[94]

A common civil code, according to Modood, should be entirely different from Hindu personal law and will be partly based on the cream extracted from all systems of personal laws prevailing in the country. It is wrong to assume that Islamic conception will have no place in it. According to him, contractual concept of marriage, its solemnisation without ceremonies, facility of its dissolution in special circumstances, and women's property rights—all of which will be incorporated in the common civil code—are the ideals for which the Islamic jurisprudence stands.[95]

Many decades ago, Justice MC Chagla expressed the opinion that religion-based personal laws had no place in a secular society like India and all personal laws of India, including the Islamic laws, should as early as possible be replaced by a secular and common law.[96]

Similarly,Hamid Dalwai demanded an immediate implementation of the directive of Article 44.[97] Two great Indian scholars of Islamic law, Asaf AA Fyzee and Badruddin Tyabji, had no objection in accepting a secular and common civil code applicable to all Indians. However,all of them were conscious of tremendous difficulties to be faced in the enactment and enforcement of such a code. They therefore suggested that the enforcement of a UCC be postponed for a fairly long period during which Muslims should be trained to accept change in traditional family law.

Anand and Muslims for Secular Democracy support any endeavour by the state to bring about a uniform civil code. Endeavour, in their view, can only mean encouragement of nationwide discussion and deliberation on the issue based on tentative draft(s) that can give citizens some idea of what a uniform civil code is going to look like.[98]

Changes within the Muslim Community

Role of State, Community and Personal Law

The state's attitude towards the reform of Muslim personal law and the rights of Muslim women was determined in 1949 by the political consideration of governing a multicultural society and the imperatives of national unity and political stability.[99] The Indian executive and Parliament did not seriously contemplate changes in Muslim law since decolonisation.

Reflecting this neglect, not one of the 182 official Law Commissions of the post-colonial period assessed the functioning of the various Muslim laws or considered possible changes in Muslim law.[100] As a result, the executive introduced the only national-level legislative changes in Muslim law after decolonisation, the Muslim Women (Protection of Rights on Divorce) Act 1986, MWPRDA, without considerable prior consideration in the relevant policy. The state justified the Muslim Women Act as being consistent with its policy of protection of the rights of religious minorities. According to the state, in matters of personal law reform, the wishes of community leaders had to be respected. Thus, although the issue was actually one of women's rights, the state, together with the ulema, portrayed the issue as one of protection of minority rights.

The state accepted the ulema as the true representatives of the Muslim community and Muslim women and the Muslim community was seen by the state as monolithic and undifferentiated. To several scholars, by accepting the fundamentalist perception that the identity of the social and religious community was in danger, the state marginalised women's interests and their call for change in Indian Muslim family law. By recasting the issue as one of community and religious rights, the state accommodated fundamentalism at the expense of Muslim women's rights.[101]

However, what I would like to point out is that there has been a difference in the manner in which different branches of the state have reacted to the particular issue. *The executive and legislature have generally played a reactionary role as far as Muslim women's rights are concerned.* The state as embodied in the executive and the legislature has been quick to counteract the judiciary's progressive impulse as is evidenced by the reaction to the Shah Bano ruling. They have upheld the right of Muslim community in contrast to that of the Muslim women. On the other hand, the judiciary has upheld the right of Muslim women in several instances. They have interpreted several acts in favour of Muslim women.

Issues such as triple talaq, polygamy have led to the negative stereotyping of the Muslim community. After the Shah Bano case ruling was negated by the executive, the Muslim community came to be seen as a regressive community averse to any kind of reform. It came to be represented as a women-unfriendly community.

Here I would like to make two points which would lay the ground for my arguing against the stereotyping of the community. Firstly, lot of work has been done by liberal Muslims in India in favour of legal reform. They have been raising their voice against regressive practices followed within the community.

Secondly, because of internal pressures from women's groups and liberal Muslims, as well as an understanding for the need for reform developing within themselves, even the orthodox sections[102] of the community in India have lately taken some initiative to bring about reform within the community.

Changes have come about through two sources. One is the *internal source* and other is the *external source*. Internal source includes the move for change being introduced by various sections, ie. the women's movements, liberals and the clerics. The external sources which I would like to cite as reason for change within the Muslim community are the several High Court and Supreme Court rulings in India.

Changes through External Sources

The Courts in India

The Supreme Court and the State High Courts in India have through several progressive judgments brought about positive changes in lives of Muslim women. Despite stiff opposition, Indian courts have introduced a variety of changes in Muslim law, especially since the mid 1970s.[103] These judgments have been in the nature of either:

a) Encouraging or discouraging certain practices through their judgment, eg. in case of polygamy, or
b) Interpretation of certain provisions of Muslim personal law, eg. in case of liberal interpretation of the maintenance provision for women.

If we were to look at the practice of polygamy amongst Muslims in India, the approach of the Indian judiciary has not been to stop the practice absolutely, but is ordained to encourage and appreciate monogamy and to discourage and allow polygamy in exceptional cases. The Allahabad High Court in the landmark case of *Aziz v Asghari*[104] declared the practice of polygamy as 'highly undesirable' because it degrades the first wife in society and held that importing of a second wife into the household ordinarily means a stinging insult to the first. It leads to the asking of awkward questions, the raising of unsympathetic eyebrows and the pointing of derisive fingers at the first wife. The onus was placed on Muslim bigamists to prove that their bigamy was not injurious to their aggrieved wives.[105] In order to discourage the practice, in the *Aziz v Mt. Naro* case, the judiciary held that, 'a condition in the Nikahnama that the husband should not marry a second wife in the presence of his first wife and further if he does so, the first marriage would stand dissolved, is not contrary to the principle of Muslim law'.

Also, the courts upheld that it was not correct to say that a Muslim husband has a vested right to marry more than one wife and to have four wives at a time. In the *Abdul Rahim v Padma* case, the court held that, 'so far as polygamy is concerned, the provision of Muslim law is only permissive or only optional in nature and not obligatory. It only lays down a ceiling on wives, and does not lay down that every Mohammedan should have four wives as a matter of right'.[106]

In 1985, a victim of triple talaq and polygamy withdrew a petition in a Maharashtra court, sensing the mood of the country. In 2002, a writ petition under Article 32 was filed in the SC by Shahnaz Sheikh,[107] challenging the practice of polygamy as unconstitutional and violative of Article 25 of the Indian Constitution. The petitioner submited that the practice of polygamy prevalent among the Muslims in India is contrary to law, unconstitutional and unenforceable in as much as it offers a right of marrying any number of spouses to the husband without offering a corresponding right to the wife and is, therefore, discriminatory only on the basis of sex against the Muslim. It is, therefore, also violative of Article 15 of the Constitution of India.

The petitioner further said that the practice of polygamy forces the Muslim wife to share her matrimonial bed with other wives of her husband, while such practice does not exist among Hindus, Christians and other religious group in India.[108] The petitioner said that she and other Muslim women are discriminated against only on the basis of religion.

The practitioner submitted that the practice of polygamy is not indispensable to the practice of Muslim religion, and contended that by striking down this practice, rights of other Muslims under Article 26 of the constitution are not affected adversely.

Sheikh was threatened by physical death if she did not detract her complaint from the Supreme Court and did not agree to return to the exclusively Muslim jurisdiction. Amrita Chhachhi explains:

> Shehnaz Sheikh's case brings out poignantly the dilemma of Muslim women in the context of communalism and fundamentalism. After the petition was filed, she faced death threats and had to go into hiding. Muslim fundamentalist organisations put up posters against her and accused her of

> being sponsored by Hindus. Subsequently, she discovered that in fact, her lawyer was a member of the RSS (Hindu fundamentalist party) and was pushing her to go ahead, after she began to rethink future action.[109]

As far as the right to unilateral divorce is concerned, the courts, in several pronouncements, have held that the Muslim male's unilateral right is limited and has to go through a certain legal procedure. Justice Krishna Iyer in the *A Yusuf Rowther* case[110] held that: It is a popular fallacy that the Muslim male enjoys, under Qur'anic law, unbridled authority to liquidate the marriage. The Holy Qur'an expressly forbids a man to seek pretexts for divorcing his wife, so long as she remains faithful and obedient to him, '*if they (namely women) obey you then do not seek a way against them....*' the book says.

In the *Marrium* case,[111] the court held that: A divorce pronounced thrice in one breath by a Muslim husband would have no effect in law, if it was given without deliberation and without any intention of effecting an irrevocable divorce, such divorce is a form of *talaq-e-ehsaan* and thus is revocable by the husband before the iddat expires.

In the *Ziauddin Ahmad* case,[112] the court held that under Islamic law, a divorce is not valid unless, there is a reasonable cause for it, and it has been preceded by an (unsuccessful) attempt at reconciliation by two arbiters representing the husband and the wife, as required by the Qur'an.

In the *Ahmedabad Women's Action Group* (AWAG) case[113] too, a writ petition was filed to declare Muslim Personal Law, which enables a Muslim male to give unilateral talaq to his wife without her consent and without resort to judicial process of courts, as void, offending Articles 13, 14 and 15 of the Constitution. However, the Court refused to entertain the writ petition because the issue involved State policies. The court was of the opinion that the remedy could not be provided by the judicial process and instead, must be sought elsewhere. At the same time, the court tried to introduce some safeguards into the talaq process. The court stated that talaq, in order to be effective, has to be pronounced.

In the *Shamim Ara* case,[114] a mere plea taken in a written statement of a divorce having been pronounced sometime in the past was held to not be treated as effectuating a talaq. Instead, a talaq had to be 'pronounced', that is, it had to be proclaimed, uttered formally and articulated. Therefore, the court introduced a condition precedent for the effectiveness of a divorce.

The pro-women stand of the modern judiciary in India deserves appreciation, it has not only interpreted laws in their true meanings but has checked also the practice of an unbridled and arbitrary right of divorce of the husbands. Some courts have even held that under Muslim law, it is mandatory for the husband to prove that there were attempts at reconciliation or arbitration prior to the pronouncement of divorce. This is an extremely valuable trend. It is the judiciary that laid down this trend.[115]

In the *Daniel Latiffi* case, the Supreme Court judgment in 2001 elucidated on the general principles of talaq as laid down in Islamic law. While a divorce by a husband is talaq either in the oral or written form, he cannot at his free will resort to any of the modes at any time without assigning reasons.

Two arbitrators, one from either side, have to be appointed to bring about a settlement between the parties, the court ruled. Only if the discord persisted at an irreparable level could the husband have the right to resort to talaq. 'Talaq must be for a reasonable cause and be preceded by attempts at reconciliation between the husband and the wife by the arbitrators, one from the wife's family and the other husband's. If the attempts failed, talaq may be effected', the judgment held.[116]

Regarding the prescribed procedure for talaq, it ruled that: the pronouncement of talaq... has to necessarily satisfy all these conditions of pronouncing the talaq at a particular time and such a talaq must be valid and effective. It is not that on his own sweet will the husband has the unqualified prerogative to exercise this right to pronounce talaq.

Many of the references to Islamic law were drawn from the *Compendium of Islamic Laws,* a publication brought out by the All India Muslim Personal Law Board. The judgment has generally been welcomed. Anees Ahmed, an advocate in the Supreme Court, said that the landmark judgment established the legal requirement of providing divorce by the husband on the anvil of the Indian Evidence Act, 1872. It ensures transparency in matrimonial transactions and was expected to go a long way in ensuring that there was some restraint on husbands rendering reckless talaqs. For married Muslim men, there has been no requirement to go to court and it was done totally at the whim and caprice of the husband so long, to give talaq without involving the wife.[117]

Sheba Farooqi, as the general secretary of the National Federation of Indian Women in 2007, said that a campaign to register all marriages and divorces was under way and some governments had responded positively to that.[118] Anees Ahmed welcomed the campaign as it ensured that all marriages and divorces were registered with either a religious body or with a secular (state) institution, such as the Registrar of Marriages and Divorces. This would enable the wife to prove that her husband had actually divorced her, and she could claim maintenance and alimony according to the law. Otherwise, divorce rights of Muslim women involved protracted litigation, after filing a petition in a civil court to obtain a decree of divorce under the Dissolution of Marriage under Muslim Act, 1939.[119]

Syeda Hamid has also noted that in a large number of cases, talaq was being pronounced not in accordance with the injunctions of Islam. According to her, the ruling in the Daniel Latifi case was as historic as the judgment in the Shah Bano case, which had placed some obligations on the husband to pay maintenance to his divorced wife.[120]

However, most progressive judgments have come in terms of the courts' interpretation of the Muslim Women Act of 1986. The MWA can be termed as one of the most controversial legislation of our times. The Act symbolises the loss of secular values in public policy.

The Act deprives Muslim women of the right granted under a secular provision, Sec. 125 of the CrPC (law on maintenance) on the basis of religion alone and thus violates the constitutional mandate of equality. [Under the CrPC the ceiling of Rs 500 a month as the maximum amount payable as maintenance to all the claimants together—wife, divorced wife, children and parents—remained in force until 2001, when it was removed.]

Yet the Supreme Court, for example, has applied MWA 1986 from the very beginning generously. Case after case was decided under its provisions to grant quick relief to divorced Muslim women. The Muslim Women Act attempts—albeit not wholly successfully—to codify the Muslim law on divorced women's remedies. The judiciary applied a seemingly innocuous looking clause to pronounce judgements, which provided greater scope for protection against destitution. Section 3(1) of the Act stipulates:

> Notwithstanding anything contained in any other law for the time being in force, a divorced women shall be entitled to
>
> a) a reasonable and fair provision and maintenance to be made and paid to her within the iddat period by her former husband;
>
> b) The above clause, along with the preamble:
>
> An Act to protect the rights of Muslim women who have been divorced by or have obtained divorce from their husbands and to provide for matters connected therewith or incidental thereto provided sufficient scope for a positive and pro-women intervention.

The SC used a MWA provision to grant quick relief to divorced women in the form of exorbitant one-time payments. This, the courts were awarding within the framework of Islamic principles, and it seemed to be a better safeguard against destitution than the meager sums which women were entitled to under Sec. 125 of the CrPC.

The most significant issue which has emerged out of the enactment revolves around the stipulation of 'a fair and reasonable provision'. Drawing on the Islamic concept of *mataaon bil ma'aroofe* (fair and reasonable provision), several High Courts have also opened a new portal for the protection of divorced Muslim women.[121] In several judgements, the courts upheld the view that a divorced Muslim woman is entitled to 'a fair and reasonable provision' in addition to maintenance during iddat period.[122]

The courts have ruled that even when a wife has some source of income or even when she has remarried, the right under Sec.3 of the MWA is not extinguished. In the *Surfaira* case, for example, the concerned woman was awarded maintenance amount during iddat period, mehr dues and fair and reasonable provision by the court.[123] Another judgment upheld the woman's right to Rs 300,000 as fair and reasonable provision and also awarded Rs 7,500 as maintenance during the iddat period.[124]

The 1986 Act created a new liability and provided women with a statutory remedy of approaching the Waqf board or jamaat or the Muslim council for maintenance. If after the divorce, the woman was unable to maintain herself, the Waqf board was entrusted with the liability of providing her maintenance. This provision met with a lot of cynicism as the Waqf boards, through the length and breadth of the country, are in doldrums and hence are not in a position to provide maintenance to destitute women. However, the Supreme Court in its judgements has upheld the Muslim women's claims against the waqf boards. The court commented that it is up to the waqf board to prove that the woman is able to maintain herself or her relatives are in a position to maintain her. In certain rulings, the court held that the waqf boards are liable to meet the demands of Muslim women who have no support from their families.[125]

Conclusion

If we were to analyse the various suggested means to bring about reform within the Muslim community, one would realise that amongst several intellectuals and Muslim citizens, internal reform though difficult, seems to be the best possible suggestion to bring about changes within the community.

But this is also because it is the most non-controversial and easy suggestion for them to recommend. Exit and, to a small extent, dialogue and discussion and debates have also brought about reform and changes in the Muslim community.

Any multicultural polity should not be afraid of innovative ideas to bring about changes. Among the outstanding has been the reverse optionality suggested by several intellectuals. However, its advocates need to garner numbers in their favour to get the proposal through. By far the most controversial suggestion for bringing about reform amongst Muslim community is the enactment of a Uniform Civil Code. This would again require a nationwide consensus to be achieved on a draft document on UCC which has been arrived at after deliberation between different community members.

Problems faced by multicultural societies cannot just be resolved by giving the standard liberal argument as has been used in India in context of the Muslim community. What is needed is a more complex response to resolve the issue of cultural diversity and gender equality in the context of the Muslim community in India.

A plain argument for internal reform is too simplistic. As experience shows, reforms have been brought about by state intervention despite all claims to the contrary made by the internal reformists or the orthodox sections within the Muslim community. To bring about change in a multicultural polity like India's, innovative institutions whether from within the community or from outside is a pre-requisite. Just holding on to the argument that internal reform or deliberation could resolve the problem within the Muslim community, as suggested by several multiculturalists, is not sufficient to bring about changes within the Muslim community in India.

Experience has shown that internal reforms have been very difficult for Indian Muslims. A consensus between different sections of the Muslim community is immensely difficult to achieve. It has not happened in so many years. Changes, if any, have been very slow. Muslim groups found even the model nikahnama insufficient to address the problems faced by Muslim women in India.

Deliberations have also not paid much dividends as far as the Muslim community is concerned. Though this model has been used as a method, as seen in the case of the AIMPLB code book, because of the lack of representative nature of the AIMPLB, new groups have come up today to represent those sections which feel that their voices are neglected and not heard by the Board.

Among the new developments within the Muslim community has been the establishment of new institutions and mechanisms by liberal Muslim groups to get their voices heard within the community and by the state. This has resulted in weakening the AIMPLB's claim of being the sole representative of the Indian Muslim community.

New institutions and mechanisms, whether initiated by the state or by the community, are therefore, essential to bring about long-term changes within the community. These could be either borrowed from other Muslim countries, interpreted form the Qur'an or innovated as per Indian situations.

Church Laws in Modern India

CHRISTIAN PERSONAL law has been discriminatory against women in matters of divorce, maintenance, succession, adoption etc. This discriminatory structure had been part of the British Empire's structure of governance. For example, The Indian Divorce Act (1899) is discriminatory against women as it provides for adultery as the sole marital offence which—as far as a wife is concerned—had to be coupled with either cruelties such as desertion, incest or bestiality for any redressal. This colonial law is the platform on which divorce laws of all religious communities in India stand, with each religious group's own set of modifications.

This unegalitarian structure of the law was carried forward in the post-independence period. The Indian Divorce Act and the Indian Successions Act continued to be discriminatory. There was inability to bring about changes at par with the parent law in Britain. For example, in 1973, the British law was amended and provides for 'no fault divorce' or 'divorce by mutual consent'. A group of Protestant women led by the Joint Women's Programme took the matter to the church. This women's group, along with the church worked for several years, firstly to bring about consensus within the community to bring change, and then to get the state to legislate upon the agreed changes in the then existing law. The state, on its part, suggested reform in the form of Law Commission recommendations and judicial pronouncements.

Together, the JWP, the church and the state created a movement for changes in the archaic divorce law and after twenty years of activism and several drafts, the first amendment to the Marriage & Divorce Act was passed by the legislature in 2001.[1]

However, Section 10A (1) of the Divorce Act, added through this 2001 amendment, continues to be discriminatory in case of Christians, in regard to domicile and separation period. Section 10A (1) says that a Christian couple seeking divorce should be living separately for a period of 'two years or more'.

After it emerged that Christian separation rules differed from the Hindus' and others, the Act underwent further revision in 2012. As many as twenty-four States have supported a proposal to halve the separation period for Christian couples, seeking divorce by mutual consent. Yet the Bill could not be approved in the 2018 Budget session although the Supreme Court in 2016 questioned the existing law, and had urged the Centre to make necessary amendments. 'Should Christians stay separated for minimum two years when the period prescribed for others is one year? It does not make sense to us. It is a pure question of law and you (that is, the government) should have acted on your own', a bench of justices Vikramjit Sen and AM Sapre had observed.

Reasons for Stalemate in Christian Law

Curiously, during the period 1935-55, when the three religious communities, Hindus, Muslims and Parsis went through a process of reshaping their laws along the lines of the Anglo-Saxon matrimonial principle, there was no similar attempt being made to modernise the Christian family law.

Flavia Agnes says three reasons could have probably caused this stalemate during the pre-independence period.[2]

Firstly, the Christian religion was viewed as the religion of the colonial masters. Before independence, none of the nationalistic leaders felt the need for any reform through nationalistic intervention.

Secondly, absence of a Christian political leaders of repute within the nationalist movement perhaps resulted in the invisibility of issues concerning indigenous Christians.

Thirdly, the Indian Divorce Act of 1869, modeled on the English statute of 1857, was so structured so as to automatically incorporate the developments in English matrimonial statutes within its scheme. A full bench ruling of the Madras High Court in 1936 pronounced the need for Indian courts to keep pace with the upgradation of the parent law. Hence the necessity for statutory reform may not have arisen.

Now we need to look at reasons for there being no reforms in the Christian personal laws even in the post-independence period.

a) From being the religion of the colonial masters during the colonial phase, Christianity in India became the religion of an insignificant minority.
b) A significant development of the post-independent era reform was that the dominant protestant ideology with which the Christian community in British India was governed during the colonial rule was replaced by the ascendency of the Roman Catholic Church. Among all the constituents of churches in India, the Roman Catholic ideology became the most powerful politically. The Roman Catholic Church became a significant contender for representing the values and aspirations of Christians in India as opposed to the liberal protestant ideology of British India.

Jyotsana Chatterjee points out that[3] this was largely because Protestant leadership came from north-India and was not as literate as the Catholic leadership of the south.[4] Catholics schools, colleges were active institutions. Christian leadership was thus provided by Catholics, who were from south India. The state too recognised Catholic leadership more than the Protestant leadership.[5]

The Catholic Church in India is a conservative church, with conservative views on issues like divorce, adoption, succession etc. The Catholic Church has rigid stand on indissolubility of marriage etc.[6]

c) Thirdly, while the superstructure of the British-era statute remained intact, political developments drastically affected the infrastructure. The Act, meant for colonial rulers, now became applicable primarily to native Christians.

The progressive developments in the English matrimonial law could no longer be borrowed by matrimonial courts of a newly independent nation, in case of litigation in India under this Act. Devoid of any dynamism, the Act got fossilised at the level of 19th century Puritanism.[7]

So paradoxically, the only primary inheritor of the British Matrimonial Causes Act, the Indian Christians, were denied access to progressive developments in the divorce law in other Christian-majority countries.

Any attempt at tracing the developments within the Christian personal laws is far more complex than that of other religious communities. This is largely due to the fact that Christians were governed by statutes which revolutionarised the scheme of personal laws in India and set parameters of reform for all communities. Yet, these very same laws proved detrimental for the Christians themselves in India.

While other communities have made some attempt to keep abreast with the changing trends in matrimonial laws in the western world, for Indian Christians, these very laws have remained static for more than a century. Christian women, especially, have to bear the brunt of all these archaic laws.

Problems faced by Christian Women

I will focus on the problems which women face due to archaic provisions of marriage and divorce laws, succession laws and adoption laws.

Section 10 of the IDA

Section 10 of Indian Divorce Act, which deals with the grounds for divorce amongst Christians in India, was blatantly discriminatory against Christian women.[8] Section 10 of the IDA, 1869 discriminates against women because it prescribes different requirement for men and women for obtaining divorce. 'This discriminatory provision was tailor-made for the colonial Christian officers in India, to deny easy divorce to their Indian wives', says Chatterjee. Designed primarily to protect the interests of British personnel in India, the law affords *adultery only* as a ground for divorce for the man.[9] On the other hand, the grounds for divorce for a women are so difficult and complex to prove that divorcing a husband is virtually impossible for a woman. This safeguarded the marital rights of English men who came to India and married Indian women, who served as sexual outlets for the English male, while they left their English wives behind. On completing their term in India, many an Englishmen returned to his English wife, deserting the Indian wife. The latter had no recourse to divorce under the Act, as *neither adultery nor bigamy* alone constituted a ground for divorce for her.[10]

The plight of Christian women tied through a matrimonial bond to a violent or absentee husband became the focus of recommendations of the Law Commission of India. Time and again, emphasis was laid on the need to remove defects in the law on matters related to marriage and divorce within the Christian community.

The matter becomes clear if one compares the position regarding the two sexes under Section 10. The ground for divorce available to the Christian husband is expressed simply as adultery—

no other fact needs to be proven by a husband. But the ground for divorce available to the wife is expressed in very narrow terms in this section.

The section requires that the adultery committed by the husband must have been a) incestuous or b) accompanied by bigamy or c) accompanied by marriage with another woman or d) coupled with such cruelty as would itself have entitled a women to a divorce or e) coupled with desertion without reasonable excuse for at least two years.

Thus the woman was placed in much more unfavourable position than the man, since she is required to prove, besides adultery, one or other of the additional facts enumerated above. These provisions of Sec 10 appear to be violative of Article 14 of free India's Constitution. The Constitution says, *the state must not deny to any person equality before the law or the equal protection of the laws within the territory of India.*

Section 10 also violates Article 15 (1) of the constitution under which, *the state shall not discriminate against any citizen on ground of religion, race, caste, the place of birth or any of them.* Therefore there is an urgent need to remove the discrimination that is writ large in Sec10 of the IDA, 1869 and to introduce equal treatment of the sexes.[11]

Laws of Succession

Another area of discrimination faced by Christian women, especially from Kerela, was that while Christians in India were generally governed by the Indian Succession Act 1925, Christians in Kerela were governed under the Travancore and Cochin Christian Succession Acts, the TCSA and the CCSA.

Under the Travancore Christian Succession Act, the right of the daughter to parental property was limited to a quarter of the share of the son or Rupees 5000, whichever is less. Under the Cochin Christian Succession Act, the share of daughter was one-third of the son or Rupees 5000, whichever is less.

Despite the enactment of the Hindu Succession Act of 1956 which improved the situation of Hindu women and granted daughters' and wives' share in the parental property (but not in the ancestral property), Christians women continued to be governed by the discriminatory provisions of the *uncodified Hindu law*, which denied the daughter a share in the parental property.

Following the merger of Travancore and Cochin with the Indian union in 1949, this region came to form what was termed as Part B States in 1951.[12] This meant that certain Acts that were in existence in the rest of India were now applicable to Travancore and Cochin. One such Act was the Indian Successions Act 1925, which should have logically repealed the TCSA and CCSA of 1916. However, judgments on some cases relating to Christian property rights that came up after April 1951 in the Travancore-Cochin and Madras High Courts upheld the TCSA 1916 as the valid law among the Christians of Kerala (*Kurian Augusty vs Devassy Alley*, AIR, 1957, Tra-Coc).[13]

Thus, even ten years after independence from British rule, in 1957, the Cochin and Travancore High Courts affirmed that Christians in the region are not governed by the Indian Succession Act and the discriminatory statutes enacted by the princely States continued to apply to them.

In another twist in women's rights, in 1974, a single judge of the Madras High Court ruled that the Travancore Succession Act stood repealed after independence, and Christians in the region are not governed either by progressive provisions of the Indian Succession Act or by the Hindu Succession Act but by the *uncodified Hindu customary law* and under this law, the son is the sole heir to the father's property to the exclusion of the daughters.

The controversy was finally resolved in a ruling given by the Supreme Court in Mary Roy's case.[14] Roy challenged the Constitutional validity of Sections 24 and 28 of the CSA as they are discriminatory against Christian women. In the 1986 *Mary Roy vs State of Kerala* case, the Supreme Court declared that the

Christians in the former State of Travancore are governed by the provisions in Chapter 11 of Part V of the Indian Succession Act 1925, as extension of Part B States (Laws) Act 1951. As a result, Christians all over India were brought under the provisions of Section 37 of the 1925 Act, which provides that the property of the intestate will be distributed equally among the children after deducting the one-third share for the widow. The court struck down the discriminatory provisions on a technicality and thus, brought the Christians of Kerala under the purview of ISA 1925.

By giving Christian women equal inheritance rights, the apex court had not only questioned the exclusivity of the culture which the Christians laid claim to but also removed the authority of the dominant section over the individual and inferiorised sections within the community.

While the repeal was welcome and overdue, the court restrained itself from examining the provision under the constitutional mandate of equality and non-discrimination on the ground of sex under Articles 14 and 15 of the Constitution, which could have set the precedent for examining gender discrimination under other personal laws.[15]

Dowry and Church Pasaram

The Travancore Christian Succession Act raised another issue—the issue of Dowry. Under the TCSA, women were eligible to receive one-fourth the sons' share or Rupees 5000, whichever was less as *Stri dhanam* and did not inherit paternal property.

Discrimination against women was again the issue when the Central government sought to introduce the nation-wide Dowry Prohibitation Act in the 1960s. Religious leaders as well as many legal experts raised the slogan of minority rights violation within the Christian community and were quick to oppose the application of the Act on the Christians of Kerela.

For the church it meant a loss of 'pasaram'—the practice of giving 2 per cent to 4 per cent of the dowry (*stri dhanam* given by the bride's family to the groom's family) to the church.

The arguments raised against this was that within the Christian community, dowry was the daughter's share in paternal property which was only held in trust by the groom's family. This amount, according to the customs of the community, was returned to the bride's family in the event of her death without any child or in the event of a divorce. The stress was on the *uniqueness of the dowry system* among Kerala Christians which shared no similarities with practices in northern India.[16]

There were voices of dissent within the community against dowry. The Youth Christian Council for Action, a Protestant youth group, had as far back as the 1940s wanted an equal share in property to replace the practice of dowry. The head of the Mar Thoma church, Juhanon Mar Thoma Metropolitan (Mar Thoma XVIII, 1894-1976) who headed this church from 1949, had expressed a similar demand in his letter to the then Chief Minister of Kerala in 1976. The priest had called the Travancore Christian Succession Act 'a definite insult to women'.

Despite the existence of alternate views, when the Dowry Prohibition Act was introduced in 1961, churches were quick to remove the dowry amount column from church records. This meant that large sums of money continued to exchange hands as did the practice of receiving pasaram. In effect, Christian women were denied even the security of records for evidence of dowry or share received. This situation was aggravated by the practice of making the bride and the groom sign legal documents on the occasion of the marriage, declaring that the bride did not have any further interest in her father's property.[17]

It is not only women but all sections which are affected by the archaic and unreformed nature of Christian personal laws. If we look at the Adoption laws or Section 118 of the Indian Succession Act, it reveals discrimination against the Christian community as a whole.[18]

Adoption

The Christians in India have been under a general law—the Guardian and Ward Act of 1890—which says that a Christian couple wanting to adopt a child can only be its *legal guardians* and *not legal parents*. Nor can the adopted child claim the privileges of a legal child from its adopted parents. At present, only the Hindus have a separate adoption law and the Indian Muslims have gone to court against being considered just 'guardians' of their adopted children.

An amendment in the colonial law is urgently required to give the Christians in India an equal opportunity to adopt children and bring them up as good citizens.[19] What acts as a deterrent for a Christian couple to legally adopt a child is the *very definition of Hindu* in the law. It says that anyone who is not a Muslim or Christian is deemed to be Hindu and s/he can adopt any child and bring her/him up in her/his culture and tradition.[20]

Such a definition suffers from multiple deficiencies.

First of all, it is quite ironical to define the identity of certain citizens of the country primarily based on their religious affiliation. And that too by way of exclusion. The problem has been, how to ascertain religion of a child?[21]

Secondly, all those who are not Muslim and Christians are not necessarily Hindus. Such an unqualified claim is contrary to social reality of India. For India is a home to the Zoroastrians, Jains, Buddhists, Bahais, Jews and scores of animists who do not subscribe to the Hindu ethos and traditions and to club all of them under the umbrella term Hindu is not only assumption, but it contravenes their distinctive identities.[22]

Thirdly. Article 14 of the Constitution guarantees equality in opportunity to all its citizens, irrespective of caste, creed and culture. In matters of adoption by different communities, there is a clear case of discrimination against the Christian community as they are still outside the purview of adopting children legally.

Fourthly, The Constitution of India also guarantees freedom to all citizens to profess, practice, and propagate their religious beliefs and there should be no discrimination on the basis of one's religion. The archaic adoption law violates this.[23]

Such discriminatory laws are not only a violation of the constitutional rights of Christians but are also depriving thousands of innocent children who wait in orphanages for a chance to belong to a family where they can blossom as healthy human beings.[24]

Scholars have repeatedly pointed out that the problem arises because there is no single Indian Adoption Act in keeping with modern times and situations. Discrimination is not only against Christians but against all Indians. Religion-based laws on adoption are undesirable. They will not help orphans and foundlings. They will only complicate the issue. What India, therefore, needs is a single adoption law for all Indians.[25]

The Catholic Bishops' Council of India, CBCI, has recommended introduction of a Christian Adoption Bill in Parliament to speed up the formalities for adoption among the Christian community in India. They have also forwarded a draft of such a Bill to the Law Department.

However, the Central government's talks with the States on a common Adoption Law have not led to any significant breakthrough. This is because the States point out that a Christian can only adopt a Christian.[26] This, to several Christian groups, is a ridiculous position as no new-born child can give information about his/her religion. The current restrictive adoption laws can lead towards increase in incidences of trafficking and also Indian orphans being adopted by foreigners, says Jyotsna Chatterjee. According to her, the need absolutely is for a common adoption law. But a new and uniform law will not be easy as minority communities may see this as a move towards a Uniform Civil Code throughout the country, she notes.[27]

Endowment for Charity & Religious Purposes

Section 118 of the ISA, titled, 'Bequest to Religious or Charitable Uses' states that: No man having a nephew or niece or any nearer relative shall have power to bequeath any property to religious or charitable uses, except by a will executed not less than twelve months before his death, and deposited within six months from its execution in some place provided by law for the safe custody of the will of living persons.

The underlying principle contained in Section 118 of the Indian Succession Act indisputably was to prevent persons from making ill-considered death-bed bequest under religious influence.[28]

A division Bench of the Kerala High Court in the case of *Preman vs Union of India* in 1998 stated that Article 118 discriminates against a Christian vis-à-vis non-Christians, discriminates against testamentary disposition by a Christian vis-à-vis non-testamentary disposition, discriminates against religious and charitable use of property vis-à-vis all other uses including not so desirable purposes, discriminates against the Christian who has a nephew, niece or nearest relative vis-à-vis a Christian who has no relative at all, and discriminates against a Christian who dies within twelve months of execution of the will. The court pointed out that the dead have no control over death.

Even after the Kerala High Court judgement, India's Parliament did not legislate to remove the discrimination.

After the Kerala HC ruling, in 1998, a Christian priest, John Vellamathom, took the matter to the Supreme Court and challenged the violation of personal freedoms on the ground that since the original statute upon which this stipulation was based had been repealed in England, there could not be any reasonable justification for retaining the same in the Indian statute book.

As the Division Bench of the Kerala High Court had already struck down this discriminative provision in 1998, the task before the Supreme Court was a simple and easy one. Ruling on the Constitutional validity of Section118 of the Indian Succession Act, the Supreme Court said in the John Vellamathom case that:[29]

> A charitable disposition of property for the benefit of the public in the advancement of religion, knowledge, commerce, health, safety or any other object beneficial to mankind has specifically been acknowledged not only in different religious texts but

> also in different statutes.... Charitable purpose includes relief to poor, education, medical relief, advancement of objects of public utility etc.... Charitable purposes are philanthropic and since a person's freedom to dispose of property for such purposes has nothing to do with religious influence, the impugned provision treating bequests for both religious and charitable purposes is discriminatory and violative of Article 14 of the Constitution. Assuming that the purpose of Section 118 of the Act is to prevent bequest of property under religious influence, there is no justification in restricting testamentary disposition of property for charitable purpose. 'Once it is held that the underlying purpose for enacting the said provision was merely to thwart influence exercised by people professing religion resulting in death-bed disposition, having regard to the fact that such a contingency has adequately been taken care of in other provisions under the Act, the purpose and object of the Act must be held to be non-existent.'

Based on this reasoning, the Supreme Court in 2003 struck down Sec 118 of the Indian Succession Act as anomalous, discriminatory and violative of Articles 14, 15, 25 and 26 of the Constitution. The Judges in the Vellamathom case held that there cannot be *unusual burden* on Christian testators alone when all other testators making similar bequests for similar charities and similar religious purposes are not subjected to such procedure.

While striking down the provision, the court also relied upon the Declaration on the Right to Development adopted by the World Conference on Human Rights. It is in this context that the court explained Article 25 of the Indian Constitution:

> Article 25 provides freedom of 'profession', meaning thereby the right of the believer to state his creed in public and freedom of practice, meaning his right to give it expression in forms of private and public worships. A disposition towards making gift for charitable or religious purpose may be a pious act of a person but the same cannot be said to be an integral part of any religion. It is not the case of the petitioners that the religion of

> Christianity commands gift for charitable or religious purpose compulsory or the same is regarded as such by the community following Christianity. Disposition of property for religious and charitable purpose is recommended in all the religions, but the same cannot be said to be an integral part of it. If a person professing Christian religion does not show any inclination of disposition towards charitable or religious purposes, he does not cease to be a Christian. Even certain practices adopted by the persons professing a particular religion may not have anything to do with the religion itself. Article 25 merely protects the freedom to practice rituals and ceremonies etc. which are only the integral parts of the religion. Article 25 of the Constitution of India will, therefore, not have any application in the instant case.[30]

Chief Justice Khare also went on to stress the need for implementation of Article 44. Article 44 provides that the state shall endeavour to secure for the citizens a uniform civil code throughout the territory of India. The apex court noted:

> The aforesaid provision is based on the premise that there is no necessary connection between religious and personal law in a civilized society. Article 25 of the Constitution confers freedom of conscience and free profession, practice and propagation of religion. The aforesaid two provisions viz. Articles 25 and 44 show that the former guarantees religious freedom whereas the latter divests religion from social relations and personal law. It is no matter of doubt that marriage, succession and the like matters of a secular character cannot be brought within the guarantee enshrined under Articles 25 and 26 of the Constitution. It is a matter of regret that Article 44 of the Constitution has not been given effect to. Parliament is still to take steps for framing a common civil code in the country. A common civil code will help the cause of national integration by removing the contradictions based on ideologies.

But what needs to be brought out here is that the question before the court was not of gender justice or national integration, but that of personal freedom of a Christian Priest. Contrary to popular belief, through this Petition, the Petitioner-Priest sought to protect his right of religious freedom and the right to follow the dictates of one's religion. And yet, this judgment became popularly known as the one in favour of the Hindu rightwing's anti-minority demand for a Uniform Civil Code.

Media interpreted the judgment as one of anti-minority and pro-UCC rather than a judgment in defense of personal freedoms and cultural plurality. The newspapers were flooded with reports and editorials on UCC with quotes from Muslim religious leadership and Muslim intelligentsia on the one end and women's rights activists at the other, while many scholars felt that the judgment itself was of relevance neither to the Muslim identity nor women's rights.[31]

Several groups welcomed the judgment as pro-UCC. Still others considered it to be a pro-women judgment. Christian groups in Kerala gave a cautiously positive response to the apex court judgment. Several Christian groups in Kerala did not want a code implemented with retrospective effect, because it could mean that married women in the community can ask for a share of the property in earlier cases of property denial through provisions of the succession act.[32]

Annulment of Christian Marriage

There is a lot of confusion regarding Christian divorce. Just civil divorce won't help. Need is for annulment in church as well. Church does not easily agree to civil annulment only and civil law does not agree to church annulment only. So, this causes a lot of distress to not just women but also men.

Unequal Church

There is no equality in church.[33] It is equally patriarchal, like most religions. Women cannot become priests, especially in the Catholic Church. Power lies with the priests, men. There, however, has been a gender policy in the Catholic Church, made public in 2010.

In India, however, this policy is yet to be implemented. Structures which facilitate collaborative partnership between women and men as well as the clergy and laity were taken note of and it was said, these need improvement.

In 1992, the Catholic Bishops' Conference India General Assembly stated, 'with a sense of sorrow we must admit that the women feel discriminated against, even in the Church'.

> In the decision-making and the consultative structures like the Parish Pastoral Council, Diocesan Pastoral Council, Diocesan Finance Committee which are canonically advocated structures in the Church, the presence of women is inadequate. In spite of the great contribution of lay women in spheres of education, health care, etc. their potentials are yet to be sufficiently tapped in the administrative and executive roles, as well as theological, liturgical, pastoral and missionary apostolates of the Church. Lack of development and articulation of a spirituality rooted in women's experiences and insights into God, Mission, the Sacraments and the Scriptures have impoverished the Church. The interiority of women and the capacity to endure suffering are the areas that are not adequately capitalised in the building up of the Kingdom.[34]

The CBCI recommended that churches

1. Provide opportunities for theologically-trained women to contribute as pastoral workers, researchers, faith formators, professors in theology and spiritual counsellors.
2. Offer at least 35% (moving towards an ideal of 50%) representation of women as office-bearers and members on parish and diocesan pastoral councils, and finance committees and in the ecclesial bodies at the local and national levels.
3. Affirm the pastoral work of women–lay and religious–as catechists, lectors, and animators of Basic/Small Christian communities, counsellors, liturgists and community workers through the recognition of these as ministries.

4. Work towards a commitment for the uplift of the tribal, Dalit and disadvantaged women, including their education and opportunities for employment in Church institutions.
5. Take concerted efforts to address the needs of migrants and domestic workers and keep fighting against the trafficking of women and children.
6. Help women emotionally and legally through the canonical processes of separation of bed and board and annulment.

What these recommendations highlighted, of course, was that women have no say even in affairs that affect them in the personal sphere. That so far, the Church as an institution, is wide open to men. They can be priests, monks, deacons, acolytes etc. All roles that are denied to women. Even being an 'official' Lector is denied to women.

Although several documents issued during and after the Vatican Council II (1962-63) meet spoke about the equality of women and men, after sixty years, a lot still remains to be done to make the shift from subordination to partnership in church and society. A survey on awareness of the gender policy adopted in India in 2010 showed that gender awareness in the churches here remained at low levels.

While only 16 per cent of the 1,000 parish council members surveyed from 99 dioceses – two thirds of them graduates – had read the Gender Policy of the Catholic Church, 44 per cent of them had not even heard about the policy (data revealed at the Indian Church Conference 2014).

Sexual abuse in Church

In India, church-related sexual abuse cases are fewer than reported in the west. At the end of the deliberations of the Indian Church Conference's second consultation, it was unanimously decided to draft a policy and evolve a code of ethics to curb sexual violence of women within the church by both preventive and punitive measures. Accordingly, a group was chosen to draft the policy.

'Gender awareness is far below our expectations', said Holy Spirit Missionary Sister Julie George, a practicing lawyer and director of Streevani (Voice of Women), as she released the survey report on the role of women in the Catholic churches in India.

According to Professor Christopher Raj,[35] very few women are ordained in the Catholic churches in India. Younger women are thought to be unclean because of their menstrual cycle and thus women priests are generally of an older age. Priesthood is accepted now largely because women are seen as mothers.

Professor Raj says, more women are represented in the protestant churches in India and the Catholics need to learn from Christians of other denominations. Only a beginning has been made in this direction.

Initiative for Reforms

Reforms against several provisions of the existing personal laws in India was suggested by women's groups, Protestant groups and Catholic groups. Several Law Commissions and judicial pronouncements also advocated for the need for reforms in Christian personal laws.

Law Commissions

The need to revise the archaic Christian laws has been engaging the attention of the Central government since the 1950s. Government of India, considering the need to reform such laws, made a reference to the Law Commission of India in 1958, requesting it to revise the laws relating to marriage and divorce among Christians in India.

Accordingly, the committee prepared a draft bill and circulated it for comment to the State governments and other interested bodies and persons including several churches and other Christian organisations. After considering the comments received and the oral evidence recorded, the Law Commission submitted its *15th Report* on law relating to marriage and divorce amongst Christians in India to the government in 1960.

The Law Commission suggested comprehensive amendments to the act in a bill titled, *The Christian Marriage and Matrimonial Causes Bill 1960,* submitted along with its 15th report, whereby both husband and wife were given the right to seek dissolution of marriage on almost all grounds mentioned in the Special Marriage Act 1954, including on the ground of adultery (unconditionally), cruelty and desertion as per Clause 30 of the draft Bill. In Clause 31, the Law Commission also recommended that a provision be made for the grant of divorce after a decree for judicial separation, when cohabitation had not been resumed.

On receipt of the 15th Report, the government finalised a bill on the lines suggested by the Law Commission and again referred the matter to the Law Commission for its views after inviting opinion from the public.[36] Accordingly, the Law Commission after ascertaining public opinion submitted *the 22nd Report* and reiterated its views with regard to the Christian Marriage and Matrimonial Bill. The Bill was introduced in Parliament but lapsed on the dissolution of the Lok Sabha.[37]

Both the 15th and 22nd reports were prepared after soliciting the views of the Christian churches and the Christian community for liberalising the law of divorce. However, the status quo continued with its attendant hardships to Christian women as Parliament had no time to pass this Bill.

Consequently, in 1983, the Law Commission suo moto took note of the urgent need to amend the unjust discriminatory provision in Section 10 of the IDA and gave its *90th Report* on the grounds of divorce amongst Christians in India.

The 90th Law Commission recommended that it is most urgently necessary that Sec 10 of the IDA, 1869 be revised to remove the elements of discrimination. Adultery as a ground of divorce should be made available to the Christian wife also (without the need to prove any other aggravating or concomitant circumstances, as at present). Opportunity should also be taken to make available to the husband a divorce followed by second marriage (a ground which is at present available only to wife).

The Commission also stated that, 'We regard such an amendment as a constitutional imperative. In our view, if the section is to stand the test of the constitutional mandate of equality before the law and equal protection of laws in context of avoiding discrimination between the sexes, then the amendment is necessary. If Parliament does not remove the discrimination, the courts in exercise of their jurisdiction to remedy violation of fundamental rights, are bound, someday, to declare the section as void'.[38]

The Law Commission's *164th Report* recommended: That Parliament enact a comprehensive law governing marriage, divorce and other allied aspects of the Christians in India. The draft bill enclosed with the 15th report of the Law Commission, the draft CMMC Bill 1961, as modified by the 22nd report of the Law Commission and the draft Christian Marriage Bill, 1994, referred to herein above, should serve as a basis of such a law.[39]

It said, the Law Commission further recommends that, 'in any event, paragraphs 1 to 5 of Section 17 and Section 20 of IDA, 1869 be deleted forthwith'. It emphasised on the need *to do away with the provision of a Christian couple to secure dissolution of marriage, to be confirmed by three judges of a High Court.*

A decree for the dissolution of marriage among the Hindus, Buddhist, Sikhs and Jains under the Hindu Marriage Act 1955, among the Parsis under the Parsi Marriage and Divorce Act 1936, among the Muslims under the dissolution of Muslim Marriage Act 1939 are made by the district courts and under the last mentioned act, even by courts of lower rank and all decrees operate with the fullest efficacy without any confirmation from the High Courts, the Law Commission pointed out. Only for Christians in India, such 3-judge confirmation was needed.

'It is difficult to appreciate the retention of the provisions of Section 17 of the Divorce Act providing that the Christian couples have to—even after obtaining a decree for dissolution from the district court—may be after a long-drawn and strenuous litigation, still wait for confirmation thereof from the High Court before those decrees can be complete and binding',[40] the law panel added.

The Law Commission further emphasised the fact that, 'the provisions contained in Sec 17 and 20 of the IDA are only procedural in nature and there is absolutely no possibility of any member of the Christian community objecting to amendment suggested herein. Section 10 of the Act also needs to be amended suitably so that the female spouses are not discriminated vis-à-vis male spouses in obtaining divorce'.[41]

Judicial Pronouncements

Courts have struck down several discriminatory provisions of Christian personal laws. It would be pertinent here to look at some of these judgements. The courts pointed out IDA Sec 10, 17 and 20 to be discriminatory against women and as violation of Articles 14, 15 and 21 of the Constitution of India in several of their rulings.

IDA 1869 Constitutionally Invalid and Archaic

In *Swapna vs Sadananda Ghosh* case,[42] the court held: If the husband is entitled to dissolution on the ground of adultery simpliciter on the part of the wife, but the wife is not so entitled unless some other matrimonial fault is also found to be superadded, then it is difficult to understand as to why this provision shall not be *held to be discriminatory on the ground of sex alone* and thus to be ultra vires. Article 15 of the Constitution countermands any discrimination on such ground. In *Mary Sonia v. Union of India*, a full bench of a High Court had struck down the discriminatory words in Section 10 IDA.

In the *Youth Welfare Federation vs Union of India* case,[43] a full bench of the Andhra Pradesh High Court held that Sec 10 of the IDA is *inconsistent with Article 14 of the Constitution*, being discriminatory against wife, 'who is subjected to more onerous grounds to obtain divorce than the husband...'

A special bench of the same court in the case of *N Sarada Mani vs G Alexander*[44] again reiterated the view of the full bench as under:

> ...we are of the opinion that the grounds which are available to the wife (*sic* husband) under Sec 10 should also be made available to the husband (*sic* wife) in a petition filed by him (*sic* her) seeking divorce and parliament should immediately take note of the discrimination writ large between the grounds available to the wife and the husband in a petition for divorce. It is for parliament to take note of this anomaly and fill in the void by suitable legislation. A pre-Constitution discrimination by the provision in section 10 of IDA,1869, it is rightly held by the full bench in Youth Welfare Federation case, cannot survive the test of equality between men and women as envisaged under Articles14 and 15 of the Constitution of India.

A special Bench of the Kerala High Court in the case of *EJ Ammini vs Union of India*[45] held that Section 10 is violative of Articles 14, 15 and 21. The court observed that:

> Life of a Christian wife who is compelled to live against her will, though in name only as the wife of a man who hates her, has cruelly treated her and deserted her putting an end to the marital relationship irreversibly, will be a sub-human life without dignity and personal liberty. It will be a humiliating and oppressed life without the freedom to remarry and enjoy life in the normal course. *It will be a life without the freedom to uphold the dignity of the individual in all respects* as ensured by the constitution in the preamble and in Article 21.

'The impugned provisions... are highly harsh and oppressive and as such arbitrary and violative of Article 14.... If in the case of spouses belonging to all other religions and even among Christians under certain circumstances (those who get married under SMA, 1954 or the Foreign Marriage Act, 1969) dissolution of marriage is permissible on the grounds of desertion and/or cruelty without proving adultery, it will be too harsh, unfair and unjust not to allow such a right of dissolution to Christians governed by the Act alone', the court said.

The court also invalidated Section 10 on the ground of *violation of Article 15 as it discriminated against Christian spouses on the basis of religion.* The rationale was that cruelty and desertion are available as grounds for dissolution of marriage to spouses of all religions except Christian spouses. Having found Section 10 unconstitutional, the court applied the rule of severability and severed the words incestuous and adultery as coupled in Section 10 IDA and declared that Section 10 would remain operative without those words. The court adopted this technique to retain provisions of divorce for Christian wives on the grounds of adultery, desertion and cruelty.

Subsequently the Bombay High Court in the case of Pragati *Varghese vs Cyril George Varghese*[46] followed the lead given by the Kerala High Court in recognising adultery, cruelty and desertion as grounds for divorce in a landmark judgement.

Need to amend Sections 17 and 20 of IDA

The general practice appears to be that Christian parties seeking dissolution of marriage under this act generally approach the district court but that court can grant only the *decree nisi*, which has to be confirmed by a bench of not less than three judges of the High Court.

On account of the heavy load of work in all the High Courts in the country, constitution of a three-judge bench to hear the confirmation matters under this Act takes a long time, indeed several years. Parties who have obtained a *decree nisi* of dissolution from the district court have to wait interminably till a special bench of three judges is constituted.

The personal laws governing the Hindus and Muslims do not contain any provision for confirmation by a special bench of three judges.

The aforesaid provision for confirmation by a special bench of three judges of the High Court has been uniformly criticised by almost all the High Courts in the country. They suggest that the relevant provisions be amended to bring them on par with the corresponding provisions in other personal laws.

Judicial Instruction to Parliament

A Full Bench hearing the *Mary Sonia vs Union of India* case[47] made the following pertinent observation: That despite the recommendations of the Law Commission in its 90th Report for making amendment to Sec10 of the IDA, no final decision has been taken in the matter.

> *The direction issued was to take a decision within six months from the date of a receipt of a copy of the order dated 13.12. 1990.* In spite of such a preemptory direction, the Central government has not even cared to inform this court about the decision, if any, taken in the matter. It is after taking note of, if we may say so, the totally intransigent attitude adopted by the central government in the matter of taking a final decision regarding the amendment of the law on the point which was recommended by successive law commissions of India at least from 1961 onwards and the various courts in India through their observations and directions including the positive direction in this case, that we have decided to consider the matter on merits and to grant reliefs prayed for, assuming the role of the reformer to the extent legally permissible as an attempt to bridge the gap between the personal laws.

Change in Christian Personal law

In India, the Christian community is a fragmented community and any attempt to bring them under one umbrella is a Herculean task.[48] Lot of ground work went into readying the amendment bills for passage by Parliament.[49] Earlier, divorce cases were rare. But now, with increase in divorce cases, the need for change in the customary divorce laws have been acutely felt.[50] Earlier, Christians went to the priest. But now the situation is different. People would rather choose legal resolution.[51]

In 1962, the government constituted a joint committee and solicited suggestions from the Christian community in an attempt to amend the Indian Divorce Act, 1869. A bill entitled the Matrimonial Causes Bill, 1962 was presented to Parliament. But the bill was never enacted and lapsed in 1971.

A new chapter in the history of change in the Indian Divorce Act was opened in 1981 by Archbishop Kenneth Philips. At a meeting with the members of the Ecclesiastical Tribunal at the Archbishop's house in 1982, the sexist bias in the IDA was unequivocally condemned and it was unanimously agreed that the act should be amended to eliminate the anomalies in it.

Subsequently in 1983, the Society for Protection of Fundamental Rights, Bombay and the All India Christian Forum presented a memorandum to the Law Ministry in condemnation of separate personal laws and the need for the government to legislate upon a uniform civil code.[52] Several groups came together to get the changes passed.[53] Under the leadership of Jyotsana Chatterjee, director of JWP, the movement for reform within Christian personal law started with the coming together of various churches, women's groups and the state to bring about reform within Christian personal laws.[54] Both Protestants and Catholics came together.[55]

In February 1986, members of various women's fellowships of churches in Delhi, representing the opinion of a wide cross-section of the Christian community, presented a memorandum to the Prime Minister of India.[56] It seemed that without the approval of the religious hierarchy, the government would not respond. So JWP, a branch of the Christian (Protestant) Institute for the Study of Religion and Society, with the backing of the Church of North India, (CNI) drafted a bill titled, the 'Christian Marriage and Matrimonial Causes Bill, 1988 (CMMC)', which was sent to the representatives of various churches. Two more bills were also drafted at this time, ie. the Indian Succession Bill, 1988 and the Indian Christian Adoption Bill, 1988.[57]

Catholic Opposition to the 1988 Bill

Catholics were opposed to certain provision of the Divorce Bill. The priest's canon, lawyers and all the representatives of the Catholic churches accepted all the provisions of the bill except the grounds for divorce, including mutual consent. At their request, all Catholics were exempted from this section.

It was also at this juncture that the Catholic churches appealed to the government to recognise its power to annul a marriage, but this plea went unheeded. To comply with the churches' demand would endow religion with greater powers and diminish the power of the state.

Likewise, the churches acceptance of civil decrees would mean throwing its religious hold to the winds and acknowledging the state as the arbiter in crucial issues like marriage and divorce, which are viewed by the courts from a legal rather than from a religious or moral perspective. Both parties were uncompromising, and the deadlock continued. Catholics wanted marriage to be recognised as a sacrament and not contract.[58]

Opinion was, however, slowly building for the Indian churches to recognise the need for change. Women's groups pointed out to church authorities the need for gender justice in marriage legislation, which provides a decent maintenance for women and children, most often the sufferers in marital break-up.

Opinion among Groups on the Bills

A clear line of thinking began to develop amongst enlightened Catholics in the 1980s. Spiritual leadership in the church is supposed to be attuned to what is called *the sense of the faithful*, which mean that church leaders must be aware of and sensitive to the views of its members, which have been arrived at after mature reflection in honesty and faithfulness to the gospel message of truth, equality and justice.

The Catholic Church has various levels of consultative councils of lay people and numerous lay organisations which engage Catholics in a dynamic reflection on their faith as related to contemporary events and in a wide-ranging social outreach.[59] By contacting these organisations, the average Catholic in the pew can express their opinion of the CMMC, as well as seek a solution to the awkward situation of reconciling church teaching against divorce with the reality of increasing numbers of marriage failures.

Civil Effects of Sacramental Marriage

A clear consensus has emerged from the people that the church must make a clear distinction between its religious teachings on marriage as a sacrament and the recognition of marriage as a civil contract. Indeed, church law has accepted this distinction in acceding to the civil registration of its marriages.[60]

Thus, the Catholic Church as a religious body in India has every right to safeguard its belief and teaching on the insolubility of marriage.[61] At the same time, its own law respects the freedom of conscience of those Catholics who decided to avail the facilities granted by the civil law for divorce. They also conced that their views should not stand in the way of reform for other groups or churches who do not come under the purview of their laws.[62]

Precedent of Civil Law Option in Goa

An interesting precedent noted in the Union Territories of Goa, Daman and Diu drew the attention of the Catholic Bishops' Coference India. According to a law enacted by the Portuguese government in 1911, Hindus, Muslims and Christians must at least one month prior to the religious celebration of their marriage, register their marriage civilly, with due notice. All the religious communities were thus equally recognised by the state. The state gave recognition to marriage as a civil contract, while giving all the religious communities the options of a religious marriage.

Provisions for marriage were equal for both sexes. This offered relief to Catholics that in case a church annulment of the marriage was unattainable, a civil divorce could be a solution. The Catholic

Church has not refused to accept this law, promulgated by the government. On the contrary, a provision exists to grant civil dissolution to marriages that have been annulled by the church, by a simple notification without a second tortuous round in the civil courts.

In free India, the Union territories of Goa, Daman and Diu have at their own request been exempted from the purview of the CMMC Bill 1990, since the UCC already exists in these places.

This has been acceded to by the Catholic Bishop of Goa, Daman and Diu. In countries such as France, Germany, Spain, Portugal, Switzerland and the Scandinavian countries, a similar system of civil registration of marriage first and religious ceremony later, if so wished, has been accepted by the Catholic Church.[63]

Real Life Incidences

Despite the deeply held values of the Indian Christian community, expressed in their nuptial vows that marriage is *till death do us part*, and the belief of Roman Catholics that marriage is indissoluble and sacramental, the reality of frequent marriage break-up from the 1980s is reflected in church statistics. For instance, in 1993-94 about 3,000 marriages were celebrated in the archdiocese of Bombay.[64] About ten per cent of these went for annulments, while about three to five per cent found their own solution to a sour marriage. Similar statistics indicating serious problems were discovered in Kerala, Madras, Bangalore and Pune. The discrepancy in the laws, church positions and reality show up by the fact that the church cannot insist that maintenance be provided for the woman and her children, as the objective of annulment is to show that the consent is defective, and no marriage ever existed. The children, however, are legitimate.[65]

Qualified Assent to 1994 Bill

The impetus for reform accelerated from the early 1990s and finally the CBCI, the apex body of 14 million Catholics in India, which includes those belonging to the *Latin rite*, the *Syro-Malabar rite* and the *Syro-Malankara rite*, gave a qualified assent to the Christian Marriage Act 1994 but did not directly propose a bill to the government of India. It took the position that would not directly propose a bill with grounds for divorce, but it would not object to anyone else proposing such a bill. It also promised to actively work for refinement of the final draft by proposing its own canon lawyers to be members of the final draft committee.[66]

Together the Protestants and Roman Catholics represent ninety per cent of the 21 million Christians in India.[67] A certain fraternal unity was also maintained with the NCCI, which includes the Church of North India and Church of South India, the Maranatha churches and the Lutheran churches. Such a unanimity is not arrived at without considerable struggle, painstaking efforts and determination.[68]

The consensus bill also proposed changes in the Indian Succession Act, 1925 and drafted a new Christian Adoption Bill, 1994. The purpose of this bill was to give the Christians an amended law, which provided for equitable conditions for adopting for Christians along with Hindus and all others. The draft retained the portions that were positive.[69]

One of the positive aspects of the Indian Christian Marriage Act 1872, was that it permitted couples, one of whom need not be a Christian, to be married by the church. This was retained in the 1994 Bill, as in the present context, mixed marriages were becoming common because of the small size of the Christian community and also because the church did not force the non-Christian party to convert.[70]

At a conference organised by CNI at Delhi, which was attended by representatives of the Law Commission and Minorities Commission, a broad consensus among the various churches was arrived at.[71]

The Catholic church supported the recommendation to repeal the IDA, the provision of automatic recognition of church annulments by civil courts as in Goa, but instead of a new Bill providing for divorce, suggested a via media that provisions of the Special Marriage Act 1954 should apply to all marriages solemnised under ICMA.[72] This was a tactical move which would save the church embarrassment that may be caused even by a tacit acquiescence to a bill liberalising divorce. The rigid stand of the Catholic clergy was resented by the Catholic laity. Several Catholic organisations such as the All India Council of Christian Women (AICCW), the All India Catholic Union (AICU); Satyashodhak, Bombay, the United Christian Women's Association (Prerna), Pune, Justice and Peace Commission, Bombay, etc. extended their support to the proposed bill.[73]

Following this, a broad forum titled 'Ecumenical Committee for Changes in Christian Personal Law' was formed, consisting of representatives of various churches as well as secular organisations. The Committee finalised three draft bills dealing with (i) marriage, divorce, custody, maintenance and right to matrimonial property; (ii) succession; and (iii) adoption. The CBCI, the 27-member Churches of North India and some other independent churches of West Asian traditions extended their support to the draft bills.[74]

Government's Reluctance to bring Reform

It took more than twenty years to reform the marriage laws for the Christians in India. Add to it the state's reluctance to bring about changes which delayed the whole process of reform. Despite sustained and systematic efforts to bring changes, the government did not introduce the 1994 Bills in Parliament.[75] The state appeared to want to stay away from providing Christians any relief in their personal laws.

When a question regarding the status of these Bills was raised in Parliament in 1997, the then government gave an evasive reply to the effect that JWP, a women's organisation, had submitted certain draft legislations relating to marriage, divorce, adoption, maintenance and succession. Since the policy of the government was not to interfere with the personal laws of the minority communities, unless the necessary initiative came from the community concerned, it would not be possible to bring in reform, the then government said.

The government also assured the House that the matter was being referred to the Minorities' Commission.[76] These comments undermined the decade-long efforts initiated by Christian community leaders and women's organisations to arrive at a consensus within the community to present a united front to the government. With this statement, the government threw the ball back to the religious hierarchy to reaffirm its commitment to reforming the existing laws and women's concerns were once again made subject to the vagaries of the religious dogmas. This was a cause of concern for the community, as the response of the religious clergy to this new challenge could be highly unpredictable.[77]

The Bills, which had been endorsed by the National Council of Churches in India and the CBCI, were then resubmitted to the government through the Minorities Commission on 27 October 1997. But while the community was awaiting eagerly for the presentation of the Bills to the Parliament, the government lost its majority and mid-term polls were declared. The political developments again delayed the process of reform.[78]

The last round of deliberation saw the consolidated bill on marriage and divorce being shelved and two separate bills titled, The Christian Marriage Bill and The Indian Divorce Bill being submitted instead. In these two Bills, the provisions of matrimonial remedies have been brought on par with the Hindu Marriage Act and the Special Marriage Act with the additional provision for property or joint matrimonial property.

The Christian Marriage Act, 2000

When the government did not respond despite several requests, the Christian Marriage Bill 1997 was forwarded by the CBCI and NCCI to the government, with the same proposals. From 1997 to April 2000, there was no action on part of the government, even though Section 10 of the IDA was struck down in several High Courts of the country. This demonstrated the amount of government apathy to issues that concerned provision of justice to women and to Christans.[79]

Finally, in April 2000, the then Law Minister, along with church leaders and women activists of the Christian community agreed on a comprehensive bill that was gender just. Thus, it was during Arun Jaitely's tenure that the long-awaited changes to Christian personal laws came about. In the new amendments, divorce and marriage acts are at par with the Hindu acts.[80]

The problem with the Christian Marriage Act, 2000 is that it is still governed by the Divorce Act of 1869. This act, for mutual consent divorce, requires a two-year separation in front of the court. This is a lot of time for couples who want a divorce. The waiting period can be very painful for both parties. The need is to reduce the time period for Indian Christians and make separation time same as for couples of other faiths.

As far as grounds for divorce are concerned, loss of compatibility needs to be considered as a provision for divorce. UK has reformed its divorce laws, but the archaic colonial law is still followed in India, though the Hindu law now is more liberal than the Christian law. The Christians in India have to follow the annulment time in the SMA, which is six months and the case dies if for some reason, mostly financial settlement, the husband or wife withdraws the plea.

There has been much progress in the community in Kerala too, where Christian women are more in number and so more affected by regressive laws.

In September 2017, for the first time in the history of churches in Kerala, a joint movement of independent progressive women from various churches including the Catholic, Protestant and Eastern churches set up the Kerala unit of the Indian Christian Women's Movement (ICWM). The organisers said, the forum will attempt to bring together an ecumenical group of Christian women under the banner 'Women's Lives Matter'. The purpose is not creating another organisation in society, they declared but to form a consensus across boundaries in order to change unjust beliefs, practices and structures that perpetuate patriarchy and gender discrimination.

Gender Policy of the Church in India

Sister Julie George, Director of Streevani, Pune brought the Catholic Bishops' Conference India document on 'Gender Policy of the Catholic Church in India' into limelight and stresses the need for its implementation in order to create a gender just church and society. It is due to the rise of women's movements in India in the last four decades that a paradigm shift in the public sphere has been brought about. The official Church has responded to the signs of the times by issuing a statement in the form of a policy document unveiled at the 2010 Catholic Bishops' Conference of India in which160 Dioceses with 3 ritual bodies participated.

George notes how women are agents of social transformation. Women are the portal through which all people come to this world, the irony is that often they become ritually outsiders when they give birth, when they menstruate and when they tend to the dying and this happens knowingly or unknowingly even in the church, she points out.

She argues, even if women are not formally ordained or included in the hierarchy, they are naturally attuned to the divine. Women can be accepted as the recipients of the *Gift of the Spirit* and valued as prophetesses standing outside the power system.

According to the *Stree Shakti* publication,[81] Pope Francis has advocated working harder, 'to develop a profound theology of women'. While several interpretations can be put to what exactly he meant, there is a formidable body of writing by women about their experience of God; from the early Christian martyrs, women mystics and great doctors of the church, to the famous contemporary feminist theologians of the present day. 'The fact is that women live the Gospel in their lives and not within the formalised power structure. It is an overwhelming experience to view how the very concept of theology has been deepened by these examples of women's writing and lived experiences over the years' George notes.

Theology has been stretched to include different literary genres and different forms of life expression. Theology has authorised women to bring in their feminine genius and allowed women to share their poignant experiences and present a comprehensive picture of women's rights in the church. 'Women found ways to write theology, as books and articles, hymns and poems, all testimonies of their refusal to surrender the Word in their endeavour to transform traditions of exclusion', she adds.

Angela Nijssen in her article, 'Participation of women in the life of seven Christian communities' and towards a feminine theology, fittingly advocates a 'different theology of women', one which needs to correct the distortions of women's image of previous theologies which underlined the discriminating cultural attitudes towards women.

Pearl Drego, the author, who has amazingly gathered the voices of women's movements, as well as those of women theologians, academicians, women with special charismas and women from the margins, says that, 'If we see feminist theology as not only theologising on women's dignity, identity, status, from biblical, spiritual, and ecclesial perspectives but as rooted in lived contextual realities, and viewed from sociological, anthropological, political, linguistic and other interpretations; as emerging from the struggles of women for justice on the ground and the struggles of women as part of larger movements for political, social, marital and personal independence, then its canvas expands in manifold ways, keeping it both soul-filled and pragmatic'.

Drego notes that feminist theologising in India emerged through women's resistance against oppression and deprivation, 'through reflection in faith on these struggles and through women's responses and critique of Church documents and statements on women'.

> By studying scripture passages related to women and critiquing Papal pronouncements as well as declarations of bishops, Indian, Asian and Western, women's local study groups and national conferences produced documents on women's condition in Church and society. 'The experience and wisdom of women are conducive for the growth and transformation of the Church and society.'
>
> — (Gender Policy of the Catholic Church of India, 2010)

Such statements and discussions continued to grow in response to national events that included women, as well as to reactions against atrocities on women. The contributions of women leaders and thinkers and a host of seminars of theologians, both men and women, added to the array of ideas, visions and prescriptions for saving women from oppression and for their advancement at all levels. The discussions heard women's voices raised and a document emerged 'out of collective reflection, debate and discussion, analysis of scripture, church documents, Christian media, women's writings and speeches, legal and canon law issues, new claims, analysis of violence and structural subjugation are included in this enterprise', the policy document said.

Right of Women in the Church

While the Christian community has been able to reform some of the provisions of its personal laws by formal endorsement of the Christian Bill in the year 2000, overall it has not been a easy process to bring about reforms within the community. It took several years of Women's, Protestant and Catholic group initiatives, several judicial pronouncements and four law commission recommendations to bring about changes within the Christian community.[82]

Reforming these archaic provisions meant that so many individuals and groups had to gain mastery over the scriptures, negotiate with competing schools of thought within the community and effect compromises within the contending churches.[83] In addition, they had to constantly remind and persuade the state, particularly the Law Ministry, to take necessary action even after a consensus had been reached within a community.[84] Though the government frequently proclaimed that consensus had to come from within the community to bring about any change, the community on the other hand complained that despite consensus coming from within the community way back in the 1980s, the Indian Christian community had to wait for twenty years to bring about the desired changes.[85]

Feminist theology emerged as Christian women began affirming their action plans and academic research through the reinterpretation of the scripture, including the reviews of Paul's injunctions to women, study of women in the Old and New Testament, Biblical views of male and female, the issues of equality in the Church, male imagery of God, ordination and ministries, marriage and canon law. In India too, global trends were followed. All these subjects became hot topics of discussion not only for women theologians but also for Church leaders and scholars in general. Christian women gradually made these issues their own and began contributing to mainstream theology. Some argued for 'women's space' to claim their identity, some stayed within the Christian arena of discourse with their vision of new ecclesial communities, others used Mary Daly's post-Christian scenario.

In India, women of the Catholic religious orders showed both character and charisma in their starting of a host of institutions to educate and elevate, but it was only in the late 1980s that sisters were sent to study theology, liturgy, sacraments, scripture, Christology, ecclesiology etc. Women also became even more active on the liturgical and catechetical front. However, in Protestant churches, women's education in theology had begun earlier and several went abroad to train. The United Theological College in Bangalore was where many were trained.

One of the first women to be ordained deacon was Rev Elizabeth Paul who was born in Tamil Nadu in 1927. She was educated in Chennai and held the position of Dorothy Cadbury fellow at Selly Oak College, Birmingham. On her return to India, she studied theology as an external student of the Serampore University. In 1987, the first women of the Church of South India to be ordained were Rev Nirmala Vasanthakumar, Rev Florence Deenadayalan and Rev Elizabeth Paul.

Even though the emergence of Catholic Indian feminist theology showed and still shows evidence of a strong impress from feminist trends around the world, it is basically steeped in local traditions and in Indian women's movements, while at the same time absorbing trends from Protestant churches within the country. The Catholic feminist theology in India accompanies the journey of Indian women, (not just of Indian Christian women) in their struggle for identity, dignity, respect, partnership, freedom of opportunity, redressal of grievances, preservation of basic human rights etc. Feminist sociology and anthropology, feminist literature, feminist counselling, feminist liturgies, feminist architecture, are important feeders for the material of Indian feminist theologies.

Aruna Gnanadason gives examples of how the phase of Protestant Christianity in India, which began in 1906 'played a crucial role in improving the status of Indian women', though in later decades, the work of education and health was unfortunately focussed on the elite. Quoting Mary Daly and the Orthodox Sister Elizabeth Behr Sigel, she argues for the inclusion of women and derides 'tokenism' by which 'women are often coopted into male-dominated committees and councils to project an image of openness'.

Gnanadason shows that while there are powerful women's organisations in the Church of North India and the Church of South India, in the Mar Thoma Church and the Methodist Church, women are not concerned about taking part in decision-making, even when it comes to ordination—a matter which 'is discussed and voted on in a 96 per cent male-dominated Synod!' Bishops don't seem to understand the work done at the village level. 'The Sisters are overloaded with teaching work, social work, and work in the parish church. Sisters are few in number but the work assigned is too much.... Sisters have to get organised to speak up.... Serving the poor needs humility and self-cleansing of a male-dominated church', she says.

The scene in India was different in the 1960s as regards critiques and challenges, when the first calls for reform in the personal laws became loud. Few Catholic women took theological training seriously then. The Protestant church was better, but the situation was still bleak as regards women theologising. According to a survey done by the Council of Christian Education of the Methodist Church in Southern Asia: The United Theological College, Bangalore reported 11 women were registered in the academic year 1974-75, while the Bishops College, Calcutta and Serampore College had no women students. The Leonard Theological College had seven women in the Seminary and 12 in the Women's School. The North India Theological College had two women for the Bachelor of Theology degree and 12 for other studies, all the women being wives of those studying in the School of Theology.

The 28th Plenary Assembly of the CBCI, which was the space in which gender issues were discussed, said, gender sensitivity is not a women's question. It is a human question and a spiritual question. 'Therefore, Church authorities should invest in women's group formation at various levels. Dioceses should train and empower women for canonical and judiciary undertakings, marriage and family counselling, priestly formation and lay-leadership training. Appointing women formators, women spiritual directors and consulters along with men, in seminaries and houses of formation to give a human, both feminine and masculine, expression to priestly/religious formation for the mission is the need of the hour', the Bishops' Conference said.

Conclusion

As we draw from the Christian experience, one can see that in multicultural polities like India, changes within minority community require certain ingredients. Changes came within the Christian community not only as a result of consensus between different denominations, but also as a result of states recognition of the law commission recommendations. Noteworthy is also the fact that these changes would not have been possible had the courts in India not repeatedly struck down discriminatory provisions, had women activists and other groups not put pressure and had not several Law Commissions made elaborate suggestions for need for comprehensive amendments to the Indian Divorce Act 1872.

The new Act thus came into force though the deliberative democratic process. State was only an external facilitator. However, despite the new Bill introduced after consensus, more suggestions for the Bill have come forth from organisations like JWP and Majlis.[86]

While there are several groups of Catholic women with feminist agendas and actions, they have their specific regional, language, congregational, academic and other identities. Catholic feminists are still in the process of forming a visible entity.

Protestant women have often been ahead of Catholic feminists. Liberal and mainstream Protestantism has, in fact, for some time been more supportive overall of equal rights, status, and opportunities for women than Catholicism, Eastern Orthodoxy, Islam, Buddhism, Daoism, Shintoism and most other major world religions—a fact that has frequently been made evident in gender empowerment reports and statistics. Protestants' liberal interpretations and/or rejection of misogynist and androcentric teachings and rules in the Bible have been facilitated by the Protestant tenet that the individual Christian has the right and ability to interpret the scriptures, and by the fact that the Bible does not portray Jesus making any negative statements about women or establishing special rules for them. Such significant gains have not generally been seen among the female adherents of fundamentalist and conservative Protestant groups, groups that insist on a literal reading of the Christian Bible and promote restrictive gender roles within the Church and family.

There is, and has been, a spectrum of women theological writers and speakers, with different perspectives, frameworks, attitudes and ideologies, women theologians from the north and south, from the tribal belt, Dalit communities and mountain heights, from groups that have lived decades of Christianity and from groups whose grandparents or parents were recently baptised. A variety of contexts have shaped the many genres of feminist approaches prevalent in India today.

While it may take some more time to bring feminist unity amidst the diversity, the lack of consensus has not stopped scores of feminist groups and thousands of women the world over from taking decisive action in Church structures and activities. While it is true that we belong today to a global intellectual and academic network, and that for a topic like feminist theology Indians are bound to be conditioned by the immensely popular literature published abroad, there is a value in reading, respecting and remembering the women, especially the Catholic women, who have overcome patriarchy, worked incessantly for women, conceptualised their feminist theology within their studies or struggles, and published works on the same. Participation of women in Church administration and liturgy have taken on new dimensions of urgency in feminist theory and praxis, upholding the struggles for justice by all peoples on all continents, at all stages of history.

Feminist theology has, therefore, taken a position that is both critical and reformist, aiming at changes in the way women are perceived, in the way women perceive themselves, and changes in the cultural and religious slogans and attitudes that keep women confined, inarticulate and unseen. In the words of Pope Francis, we 'Say No to the inequality that spawns violence'.

Sikhs: Women and Cultural Diversity

WHEN THE British cabinet mission came to India to negotiate Indian independence in 1945, three parties were recognised on the Indian side—Muslim, Sikhs and Others. As a result, Muslims succeeded in arguing for creation of Pakistan.

The Sikhs, however, chose to throw in their lot with the Hindus of India on the assurances from Congress leaders for a federal structure with an autonomous State in which Sikhs would enjoy a glow of freedom. It was promised that no constitution would be adopted unless it was acceptable to Sikhs. Unfortunately, this assurance was forgotten, and the Constitution Assembly adopted a constitution with all authority vesting in the union government. Half the land of the Sikhs was given to Pakistan, and large populations of Sikhs and Punjabi Hindus were driven east from their ancestral residences.

The Sikh members refused to sign the draft of the constitution. But their protests were ignored, and the constitution was adopted in 1950, when India became a republic.

During reorganisation of States in 1956, while homogeneous States were created for all major Indian languages, Sikhs were told that creation of a Punjbi suba would not be considered. It was only after prolonged agitation that the present truncated State of Punjab was created in 1966, with very much reduced power in comparison to other States. The Hindu Punjabis were given the State of Haryana and the Sikhs, the Indian Punjab. Neither, however, has a capital city, the two States share the newly built city of Chandigarh as their State capital.

Besides territory and control of natural resources, the Sikhs even lost their identity and name in independent India. Under Article 25 of the Constitution, the Sikhs were clubbed with Hindus and deemed to be much like the Buddhists and Jains. When personal laws were enacted for Hindus in 1955 and 1956, these were made applicable to Sikhs even without consulting them.

Thus, the Sikhs did not have their own personal laws. Therefore, all the discriminatory aspects of the Hindu personal laws were automatically followed within Sikh culture, legally. Several cultural practices which were against women were also adapted by the Sikhs. Let us look at some Indian cultural practices which are now followed within the Sikh religion. Sikh scholars, however, point out that such practices are part of the *Sikh culture* and *not Sikh religion.*

Inheritance process for sons and daughters are highly unequal among Sikhs as the culture has been borrowed from Hindus. Even though India's laws have changed, the son is commonly the heir because the daughter is expected to benefit an inheritance from her husband's family. Many Sikh scholars feel that this may be totally against Guru Nanak's teachings and is not intrinsic to Sikh religion.

A major indication of this inferiority of the female has resulted in the huge problem of infanticide in Punjab, where girls are not valued. The babies are aborted just because they are girls. In 2018, the male/female ratio in Punjab is 895 which is much lower than the national ratio of 940 (This follows from the 2011 Census data). The ratio of men and women in Punjab is so out of balance that it makes sociologists wonder where all the men will find wives in the future.

Due to female infanticide there is polygamy in Punjab. Evils like female foeticide, dowry deaths, honor killings and domestic violence exist in the Sikh community today, as a result. The boy child of the family is treated better than the girl child in terms of education and property.

On the issue of child marriage, Sikh cultural practices are better than others. Rarely are brides given in marriage when children, Sikhs, even those who espouse child marriage, extended the time of consummation until it is not harmful to the girl's health.

Within marriages, however, there are the issues of physical and sexual abuse by husbands and marital families. Much of this is kept secret, Sikh women's groups admit that often, women in families, though they know of the abuse, do not come forward to help the victim of abuse. Sometimes, punishment for the victim woman can be rape by male family or community members.

There remains great controversy about women doing Seva in Darbar Sahib. Today, most Sikh women hesitate to participate publicly in local Gurdwaras. They do have the right to perform all spiritual duties, but few women manage Gurdwara affairs, take the *hukam*, organise events, give sermons or as *Panj Pyare*s (five people especially chosen by the religious body) lead a Nagar Kirtan. To an outsider, it definitely looks like a male-dominated religion and society and that equality between men and women in Sikhism is a mere rhetoric. The SGPC (Shiromani Gurudwara Prabhandak Committee, the religious governing body for Sikhs) has had to pass a stricture so that girl children are not considered below male children.

Seva in Harmandir Sahib

Scholars often ask how a religion that has a core belief in gender equality can justify not allowing Sikh women to play the Gurbani Kirtan in Harmandir Sahib or ban women from doing certain *sevas* which are 'reserved' for only men. If this was some small random Gurdwara somewhere, one might just write it off as a minor aberration. However, when this is the practice at the Harmandir Sahib, which is one of the most visible and visited place of worship for Sikhs, one would expect that the managers of the Sikh temple would do what is right.

The Panj Piaray

Women can't be in the Panj Piaray.[1] Khalsa has no gender and the *Panj Piaray* is any five (5) *Sikhs* of the Guru, not any five men of the Guru. This is such a clear indication of how deep the issue of gender inequality is in the Sikh communities and how communities rationalise cultural practices to suit themselves and their own understanding.

Here a blogger is quoted verbatim:

> When I last went with my family to Harmandir Sahib in Amritsar, after *Asa Di Var* they were giving the *panj piaray* prasad, and I held my cupped hands up to receive it. The sevadar gave me parsad. My wife, who was right next to me, innocently had her hands raised and cupped ready to receive the Guru's prasad, but the sevadhar would not give it to her because she was a woman. I then took half of my parsad and gave it to her. The sevadhar and another person then tried to scold me that I couldn't do that.

The Sikh religious community is still very much a man's world, particularly in the area of family, community and religious life. Interpretation of the *Adi Guru Granth Sahib* has been by and large by men, from their viewpoint. It is then not wrong to suggest that the Sikh women's agency has been ignored, displaced, dislocated and disavowed from the religio-asthetic matrix in the Gurdwara.

There is another kind of discourse that occurs behindclosed doors in the inner sanctums of the religious organising committees world-wide where very few women have ever voluntarily ventured or been invited. As Shauna Singh Baldwin said in her 1937 book, *What the Body Remembers,* 'Men only see women from the corners of their eyes'. Women in the inner sanctums of Gurdwara Committees are seen by the male gatekeepers only as peripherally important, mostly relegated to work in the *langar* hall alongside other men, for whom all domains are open (Singh, 2003 [9]).

Can we even have Female Granthis?

Sikh women are often told they are not allowed to participate in certain aspects of religious life though there may be no scriptural precedence for the exclusion.

The pulpit (which is known as the *katha*) represents the confessional approach followed by religious preachers who instruct and nurture the understanding and religious participation of their communities. The podium, (which is called the *bolarey*) on the other hand, represents the approach to understanding various religious traditions as cross-cultural phenomena of human life by following historical, psychological, sociological, anthropological, textual, philosophical, ethical, and comparative methods.

For Sikhs, both the pulpit and the podium are all the purview of the Sikh male. Katha, *kirtan*, bolarey are well-established precincts of the Gurdwara. Women overwhelmingly do not see their questions, their ideas, their inquiry reflected in the katha or bolarey from the stage of the Gurdwaras.

It is a rare occasion when a woman speaks or performs the kirtan. Their view is that when men speak in the Gurdwaras, it is a hyper-masculine patriarchal message. As Cynthia Mahmood says, 'a key impetus for feminist Sikhs is that no longer is the woman the other, she must not be spoken for'. She describes *langar* hall participants telling her how women are silenced and not given the freedom to express their views. 'Until we recognise that framework, Sikh women have largely been disappearing from the history.'[2]

'Does a monotheistic religion such as Sikhism have to be androcentric? Since the Divine in Sikhism does not take a human form (neither male nor female), can we establish a feminine subjectivity, can we project the Divine according to our gender as men have always done according to theirs? Surely, we can, but the institution of the Gurudwara is not ready for this conversation', she opines.

In writing about the feminist philosophy of religion, Grace Jantzen (1999) says, 'At present, men construct not only the symbolic of the Divine, but also that of women's roles and relationships to the Divine: women are those who are called to be the suffering servants of humanity in the reproduction of the world, and are seen as saintly if they accept that position with humility and modesty.... But this forcing of women into the roles constructed for us by men is in the end a loss for both sexes (p. 15)'.

Then there is the matter of addressing the Divine through the feminine voice, allowed for the maintenance of and understanding of the primary masculine identity of God (Doris Jacobsh, 2003, p 27). There is the often-quoted verse in the *Adi Granth* where Guru Nanak's message about womanhood (mostly focused on the procreative part of a woman) seems to be used over and over again to encapsulate the Sikh view of gender equality.

However, the message of the verse misses the present generation of Sikh women by a wide margin. The verse says: 'We are conceived in the woman's womb and we grow in it. We are engaged to women and we wed them....' This common reference focuses on the functions related to motherhood/wifehood, partners for the sake of procreation or to fulfill the needs of men, while staying largely silent on any female agency.

Bard Balwand (of *Satta and Balwand Var* fame) is quoted to say that Khivi, the Guru's wife, is a noble woman, who gives soothing, leafy shade to all (www.srigranth.org). 'The dignity of females in Gurbani, its practical demonstration was initiated at Khadur Sahib. The *Mata* thus paved the way for complete independence (*puran azadi*).'

One Sikh feminist scholar points out that if one delves into Sikhism, 'we see an opening for my feminine identity. The Gurus, starting with Guru Nanak, not only placed value in my sex and gendered identity, but honored us with our ever-present Kaur title'.

The cultural, economic, political, and social backdrop is still patriarchy, no matter how one presents the egalitarian and feminist interpretations inherent in Sikh philosophy. Men were privileged, men were hyper-visible, and that tradition continues today in the majority of Sikh institutions (including the Gurdwaras) and communities, say other scholars.

Feminist Interpretations of Sikh Tenets

Recently, there has been scholarly focus on aspects of gender in the writings of Guru Gobind Singh and then through the eighteenth-century, notably by Nikki Guninder Kaur Singh, Doris R Jakobsh, and JS Grewal. Unlike the women's liberation movement, which tends to focus on religious aspects, Sikhism for women empowers them and requires equal responsibility in spiritual and temporal spheres while maintaining the integrity of family, these feminist scholars say.

It is significant that Sikhism accorded women complete equality with men in all sphere of life over 500 years ago. Women were recognised as spiritual equals of men. Asceticism and renunciation were not favoured by Guru Nanak. Marriage was thus seen as a sacred institution. The superior spiritual and philosophical attributes of women were recognised.

According to Nikki Singh, Guru Gobind Singh's treatment (not invocation) of Durga is suggestive of woman's power in society. Durga 'as a figure of myth' could provide inspiration for revitalising the society. She is independent and powerful. By affirming the female power, Guru Gobind Singh is said to have projected a positive image of women. All women are exalted through the mythical Durga. The recalling of Durga as Bhagauti imparts feminine identity to the sword which, in Nikki Singh's view, is a metaphor leading towards 'a recognition of the female principle'. The prayer at the end of the *Chandi Charitra*, which is believed to be a composition of Guru Gobind Singh, is to stand for the right cause and to die fighting till the end.

Moreover, the Sikh prayer (*ardas*) to date starts with the opening verse of the *Chandi di Var*. According to another scholar, Prabhjot Kaur, more than 500 years ago when almost all religious traditions had relegated women to the background, in some cases not allowing them even a glimpse of the scriptures—with the assumption that no woman had the capacity to have any direct experience with the Divine—Guru Nanak's message that only and *only* by becoming a woman, ie. by cultivating the spiritual qualities of a woman, can one have any spiritual experience is not only revolutionary but also totally out of sync with the fundamentalist religious temperament of his times.

While guiding on the path of spirituality, Guru Nanak exhorts man to become a woman, ie. he must acquire the qualities that are intrinsic to the nature of a woman if he wants to achieve higher level of spirituality. Guru Nanak exhorts the seeker to seek guidance from the bride who is embellished with the above-stated spiritual qualities of humility and undemanding generosity; the one who remains in a state of deep and intense love for the transcendent groom.

The bride in the Guru Granth Sahib sublimates the feminine love to the highest level. The love of a woman for her husband, which is denigrated as material, selfish and transitory in other religious traditions, forms the basis of sacred love for the supreme in the Sikh religious traditions. All Sikh Gurus were family men. Their wives were full partners in the onward march of the Sikh movement, yet they led their everyday lives like ordinary housewives.

Performance of everyday household duties has been given a respectable voice in the Granth Sahib. By her very nature, a woman wants her house to be well kept and aesthetically decorated. Beautifully embroidered clothes fascinate her. These traits of a women too have been duly recognised.[3]

The Gurus' aim of creating healthy social order could not be fulfilled with evils like dowry prevalent in the society of four hundred years ago. The Gurus hit on ostentatious display of dowry which emanated from a sense of false prestige. The third Guru pointed out that real dowry was not the material possessions but the inculcation of virtues, which was the permanent asset of a human being. Sikh code of conduct strictly prohibits the overburdening of the parents of the bride at the time of marriage.

The Sikh Gurus were pained to see the plight of the widows and their exploitation at the hands of people in the name of religion. They stood for the right of the widows to live as human beings after the death of the husbands. Sikh code of conduct explicitly states that a widow, if she so desires, has the right to get married again.

Says Prabhjot Kaur, as far as female infanticide is considered, in Sikhism (that is in the religion and religious code) a daughter enjoys equal status with the son. Guru Nanak openly chides those who attribute pollution to women because of menstruation and asserts that 'pollution lies in the heart and mind of persons and not in the cosmic process of birth'. Sikh Gurus, thus, do not approve of any superstition regarding who is polluted and who is not. For them, the only pollution is 'impurity of mind' which leads to unclean character that ultimately contaminates the whole society, leading to all the ills that the Gurus had to work against throughout their lives, to make life worth living for the common man.

As an autonomous human being, a woman is the pivot of the Sikh scripture. The Sikh Gurus, abiding in male bodies, gave voice to her authentic feelings and thought, making *her* voice the voice of the whole humanity and thus granting full human status to her. Sikh women, in contrast to women of other religion, could participate in public affairs at par with men in every field during the time of these Gurus. Not only that, they had the courage and the right to challenge the decisions taken by men if they deviated from the right path.

A woman's selfless love for the child, which is as pure in essence as the benevolent love of the Guru for the devotee, only elevates her to higher realm of spirituality. However, in the Sikh scripture, motherhood is only one aspect of womanhood. Her being childless or being a mother does not alter her status as an authentic person. She is a full human being in her own right, while the aspect of her personality which expresses itself in motherhood too finds a respectable status in Sikh scriptures. It is important to note that it is the selfless love of mother and not the ownership right of the father in patriarchal structures that find place in the Guru Granth Sahib.

The woman in Sikhism has an independent personality in her own right, who maintains her identity in every situation. She is not expected to change her name after marriage. She is a Kaur before and after marriage. She neither allows herself to be exploited nor does she suffer from any complex whatsoever.

In an age when the inferiority of women had been taken for granted and female infanticide, custom of *purdah* and *sati* were commonly practiced, the Gurus spoke against them in the voice of reason and sanity, Prabhjot Kaur points out. In the Guru Granth Sahib, the veil is compared to suppression.[4] Also widow remarriage was encouraged. Baptism by the Guru was and is open to all. When the Sikhs take *amrit*, they must all, regardless of sex, keep the same five Ks (the five items Guru Gobind Singh commanded his *khalsa* order to wear, carry on person). A Sikh woman has the right to become *granthi*, a lay preacher and *sevadar*.

The appointment of Bibi Jagir Kaur to the post of president in the Shiromani Gurudwara Prabhandak Committee, the most important religious body of Sikhs, in 1999 clearly indicates that women in Sikhism have full freedom to participate in religious worship and religious activities.

Unlike Hinduism, Sikhism upholds family life as the ideal. Sikhism recognises the futility of both sexual excesses and of celibacy and denial of sex. In the Guru Granth Sahib the gender relation is based on equality of the human being by birth. Accordingly, only God is male while all the rest are female.

Anand Karaj (the Sikh marriage ceremony) is followed by not just Sikhs but also Hindus. It is simple, easy, cheap, free from dowry, gives equal rights to women, one wife is advocated, and it is free from the binding of caste system.[5]

In the poetry of the Gurus, both female and male dimension run parallel. The Divine in Sikh religion is identified in both genders. Scriptural verses unleash multiple relationships with the Infinite. The first Guru defined the Divine as 'Itself mother and Itself father'. Rather than an exclusive monotheistic patriarchal God, the Gurus reached out to the Being—transcending every binary, every category in personal relations—and passionately embraced the one in numerous relationship. The womb in the Guru Granth Sahib is affirmed as the source of life. Attention is shifted from death and the other world to the very origins of the world. The maternal power with her paradigm of natality overturns the male ideal with death as its paradigm.[6] The Granth honours the maternal space as free from hegemonic designation of class, caste and name.

The Sikh Gurus were acutely aware of their oppressive patrilineal and patri-centred north Indian society in which the family, name, caste and profession came down through birth. So, the mother's pregnant body is envisioned as free from 'isms' and social hegemonies. The Guru Granth takes women's genealogy seriously and acknowledges mother's milk full of biological and spiritual nutrients. Even the recitation of Divine name is succulently experienced as milk in the mouth. The textuality of the Guru Granth lies in its physical sensuality—in drinking the Guru's words as though they were the mothers life-giving milk. The Gurus compare the intensity of saintly devotion to that of an infant's love for the mother's milk. They believed, it is when the Divine is genuinely imagined as mother that her positive characteristic begin to filter the mind and ignite respect for mothers, sisters, daughters and wives. Women are regarded as life and blood individuals who partake the qualities and powers of the Divine one. They are thanked for their creating and nurturing.

Doris Jakobsh does not talk about any relevance of Durga mythology for gender relations. She chooses to concentrate on the evidence of the *Pakhyan Charitra* in the *Dasam Granth* in support of her hypothesis that a novel construct of gender difference was developing in Sikhism: a masculine ethos was transformed into 'hyper-masculine' ethos. This is then taken to mean that the *Pakhyan Charitra* was respectable among Sikh men, and its tales integral to the construction of the relative position of women, which was the reverse of the male construct initiated by Guru Gobind Singh through the Khalsa order.

For Jakobsh, the women represented an anti-thesis of the warrior-saint. Jakobsh quotes selectively from the *Rahitnama* associated with *Chaupa Singh* to show that women were not included in the regular discipline outlined for the Khalsa; anyone who administered baptism of the double-edged sword to a woman was a defaulter and liable to penance. That the woman was forbidden to read the Granth Sahib in a general assembly of Sikhs.[7] Notions of impurity too came to be associated with women, and men who took orders from their women were regarded as sinful, licentious and stupid. A *Gursikh* should not trust a woman.

Consequently, a polarisation of sexes is supposed to have been brought about by the institution of the Khalsa (order of followers by Gobind Singh), and the woman became the opposite of the manliness of the warrior-saint. In short, the male was exalted and the female was denigrated.

However, this *Rahitnama* was neither the earliest nor the representative prescriptive test. The Gurus certainly conferred equal opportunity on both women and men, although it was equal opportunity of access to spiritual liberation.[8] It was not equality in the sense that women might do everything that might be open to men. A woman's place was in the home, sheltered there by the caring and devotion of an upright husband. Patriarchy had been deprived of its domineering aspects, but patriarchy was still intact (McLeod 1997, p. 243).[9] The *Rahitnama* literature of the eighteenth century, however, does not support the 'theology of difference' postulated by Jakobsh.

The controversy over women performing voluntary religious service at the Golden Temple erupted in February 2003 when two Sikh women from Britain were prevented from doing religious service there. In 2005, sixty-five year after first making the demand that they be allowed to take part in two rituals at the holiest of Sikh shrines—the Golden Temple, women were finally allowed to enter an arena so far dominated by males. The Gurudwara Prabhandak Committee decided that Sikh women be allowed to perform kirtan and palki seva on religious occasions.

But the fact is, women have not been granted real equality and liberty.

Urgent need for Personal Laws for Sikhs

While feminists in India question the need for personal laws for minorities and instead emphasise the need for a uniform civil code, several Sikh scholars feel that personal laws should be equitable for Sikh women. This is because to them, *Sikhism is a modern religion* which seeks equality between men and women.

We all know that the Indian Constitution's Article 25 (1) gives freedom of religion to all. It is this Article which sanctions special personal laws to each religious community. However, the Sikh community has been denied this privilege, so that all Hindu Acts related to the institution of family regulate the life of Sikhs, including that of women. In other words, the Sikhs do not have any legal status and are assumed to be Hindus. Therefore, the claim of the Indian Constitution of providing religious freedom to all cannot be sustained.[10]

Obviously, Hindu laws (under whose jurisdiction come the Sikhs) are based on the Hindu philosophy, which, in many ways, clashes with Sikh principles. Hindu laws are age-old laws framed centuries ago, whereas Sikh religion is the *most modern among religions* whose tenets are based on the concept of human rights and rationality. If law is an instrument of change, then a Sikh Personal Law based on the rational and scientific doctrines of Sikhism can make the dream of gender justice come true.[11]

Firstly, there is need to identify the areas which Sikh Personal Law should cover. This can be done by a detailed survey of all personal laws, especially the Hindu laws, to examine how these differ from the principles of Sikhism. All objectionable elements in the Hindu laws need to be eliminated. The next step should be to propose laws derived from the doctrine of the Sikh scriptures and the proud heritage of Sikh culture, history and tradition.

Personal laws cover several aspects, which are directly or indirectly related to women.

Marriage

The Sikh Marriage Act should take care of the following aspects:

Under Sikh Marriage Act, dowry should be strictly prohibited in any form.

The definition of dowry given in the Indian Dowry Prohibition Act (1961) needs to be revised, so that 'unlimited gifts' are included as part of dowry. There should also be a check on the quality and quantity of gifts given in consideration of marriage. According to the Indian Dowry Act of1961, 'Dowry is any property or valuable security given or agreed to be given either directly or indirectly by one party to the other party, or by parents of either party to the other, at or before or after the marriage, as consideration for marriage'. The Act, however, does not include gifts which are given unlimitedly.

There should be another clause in the Sikh Marriage Act to ban excessive expenditure in connection with marriage and related ceremonies. Any effort towards ostentatious display on such occasions should attract drastic punishment. The *Sikh Reht Maryada* issued by the Shiromani Gurdwara Prabandhak Committee prescribing norms of marriage, should also emphasise this.

In the Sikh Marriage Act, caste should not be given any importance. Any two people who are Sikhs without consideration of caste should be allowed to marry. According to the *Sikh Reht Maryada*, caste or status have no place in a Sikh marriage.

There should be provision for compulsory registration of marriage. Such evidence is specifically needed by women in order to claim inheritance rights and maintenance rights in the event of separation, or to sue for bigamy. Marriage merely by religious ceremony is relatively more difficult to prove in a court of law, especially if years have passed, the witnesses have died and the husband denies the legality of the marriage. This problem is faced by many Sikh women in India and abroad.

Scholars point out that under the Sikh Marriage Act, age of marriage should be increased. 'The Sikhs, being a progressive community, should encourage their daughters to be professionally qualified and economically independent before marriage'. Therefore, the age of marriage for a girl could be 21 years and that of boy 24 years.[12]

Divorce

Law for divorce should not be harsher for women, and it should be framed in such a manner that it does not harass any of the parties concerned. Religious conversion for the purpose of bigamous marriage should be banned.

Along with other grounds for divorce as per the Hindu Law, mutual incompatibility should be introduced as another ground for seeking divorce. It is possible for a legal battle to drag on for years through various courts of appeal with one party trying to prove desertion, cruelty, adultery and bigamy (as grounds for divorce) and the other party trying to disprove it. In the absence of this clause, parties tend to falsely accuse the other, whereas the truth could be that they just cannot get along with each other.

It, however, does not mean that divorce should be encouraged. The point is that law should make it easy for man and woman to separate, if there are no chances of reconciliation.

Bigamy

Bigamy should be considered a serious offence under Sikh Personal Law. Any woman residing with a man for a considerable period without being his blood relative, or vice versa, should be treated as a case of bigamy. This has been suggested in view of it being very difficult to prove bigamy.

When bigamy has been proved, the court should order arrest of the offender.

Under Hindu Law, in case of bigamy, it is only *the first wife* or her family who can prosecute the husband and *not the second wife*. This should not be the case while chalking out Sikh Personal Law, because it could be possible that the second wife herself has been cheated and might have got married without knowing that this was her husband's second marriage.

Similarly, *adultery* should be considered a serious matrimonial offence in Sikh Personal Law. It is not so under Hindu Law and cannot be used as a ground for divorce.

Female Infanticide, Child Marriage and Culture

Female infanticide in Punjab has skewered the male-female balance in Punjabi society, both among Hindus and Sikhs. The unbalance is such today that Punjab is said to be buying its brides from distant lands, culturally very different. It is the poor from other communities who now supply wives to Punjab, at a cost. In other words, brides are bought and sold.

As recalled earlier, on the issue of child marriage, Sikh cultural practices are better than other communities in India. Rarely are brides given in marriage when children. Within marriages, however, there are the issues of physical and sexual abuse by husbands and marital families.

Inheritance Rights

Sikhs are governed by the Hindu Succession Act in matters relating to inheritance of property, under which the woman does not have equal right to ancestral property. Inheritance process for sons and daughters are highly unequal among Sikhs, borrowed from Hindus.

Many action groups dealing with victims of matrimonial discord have found that lack of inheritance right to the woman has been a major cause of dowry. Dowry, in fact, is a way to disinherit women. Parents feel that this is the only time their daughters can get something from them. Thus, they try to be generous to daughters and spend lavishly on their marriages.

Under the Sikh Succession Act, a woman from birth itself should be equal partner in the ancestral property as well as self-acquired property. This is not only her just right, but also obviates the need of dowry.

Under Hindu law, woman has equal right in self-acquired property of father. However, there have been cases where a father deprives his daughter of her share in the property (self-acquired) by writing a will. The power to make unrestrained will is used to deprive daughters of their rights.

Any will which disinherits the daughter should be considered invalid under the Sikh Succession Act, because it has been observed that women generally do not challenge the father's will due to customary practices. If she does so, she spoils her relationship with her brothers.

Matrimonial Property

The need for a Sikh Women's Right to Matrimonial Property Act is obvious. The Sikh woman should be given equal right in matrimonial property. Matrimonial property is that which is acquired by both the parties to marriage during the subsistence of marriage.

The demand for joint ownership of property (both, in the name of husband and the wife) is just. Any succession act should include joint ownership of a dwelling house or agricultural land or other property.

As per Hindu law, a woman does not have equal right in the income, assets and property after divorce unless it is joint. Thus, Hindu law ignores the contribution in cash and kind made by a woman during the subsistence of marriage and deprives her of this right. Women's contribution in the house and family, although imperceptible and incapable of being evaluated in terms of money, entitles her to an equal share.

Therefore, all properties, moveable and immoveable, acquired after marriage, must be jointly owned by husband and wife. She should also be joint owner of the assets of the matrimonial home and any savings made. It should be made compulsory that all distribution and allotment of rural and urban land by the government should be done in the joint name of husband and wife. In case of separation, properties should be divided between the two in as just a manner as possible.

This kind of legislation can remove economic disparity between men and women, because economic dependence on the man leads to other kinds of inequalities that a woman is subjected to.

Care should be taken that under the Sikh Women's Right to Matrimonial Property Act, the woman should not merely acquire property, but should be allowed to control it and use it in any manner she wants.

Under this Act, provision should also be made for safeguarding the interest of woman against being deprived of her joint ownership, *especially in agricultural land where the land exceeds the ceiling. Her share should be protected, because often it is her share which is given over to the state.*

Right of Residence

During matrimonial discord, women are often thrown out of the house, and denied partition of the dwelling house of the husband's family. This points to the need to introduce the Sikh Women's Right to Residence Act.

Under this Act, in cases where the husband and wife share the residence owned by the husband, the wife should have the right of residence. Where husband is not an owner of any property and both share a rented accommodation or the rent is paid by the employer or if husband has a private job, the man should provide alternate accommodation to the wife.

The Act should direct women to approach the court for a right to restrain the husband and his relatives from entering the premise where she is living or direct the husband to provide a suitable accommodation.

As per Hindu law, there is denial of right of residence to married daughter in her father's house, when she is deserted by her husband. There should be provision for legal claim. Women's right to both ancestral and self-acquired property of father will take care of this aspect to some extent.

Sikh Adoption and Maintenance Act

This Act should remove the ceiling of Rs 500 as maintenance given to the wife in case of separation as per the Hindu law. Limit of Rs 500 as maximum amount of maintenance was fixed about fifty years ago which is totally inadequate to meet the present basic financial requirements.

While fixing the amount of maintenance for a Sikh woman, a man's future capacity to earn should also be taken into consideration, eg. his increments, Government Provident Fund etc. Other things to be taken care of while having the amount of maintenance fixed should be the standard of living of the couple during marital life and also his moveable and immoveable property, and not just his monthly income, because the party can have undisclosed and illegitimate sources of income as well. In case of salaried husband, to ensure that he pays maintenance, legislation should empower court to deduct the amount from husband's salary. In case of private job of the husband or work on daily wages, and also in case of the educated/employed women, different criteria to determine maintenance need to be worked out.

Maintenance should include not only food, shelter and clothing, but also other essential needs like medical treatment of the ex-wife and children and educational and recreational needs of the child according to father's living standard. The present provision of maintenance to child is up to the age of 18 years only, which deters his/her education, specially professional studies. Therefore, Sikh Adoption and Maintenance Act should raise this age limit suitably.

Since a husband's defense to a maintenance petition in most of the cases is that he does not earn and, therefore, cannot support his family, a case study of the party should be done. The burden of proof of establishing what is the husband's income, should be on the husband himself. Maintenance should be made retrospective. It should be payable from the time husband has refused to pay the wife any maintenance. It could be possible that she approaches the court long after she was subject to ill-treatment.

The procedure involved in determining and procuring maintenance should be completed within six months, because the legal procedure involves mental, physical and financial agony for both the parties, especially for the woman who is more often uneducated and unemployed.

Guardianship

Under Hindu Minority and Guardianship Act 1956, father is the natural guardian of the minor. Natural guardianship is the father's right. A child can be in the mother's custody up to five years after which father can claim the custody of the child. The Hindu law is based on the patriarchal values of descent/ inheritance through the male. Thus, the law does not recognise the woman as an equal partner to the marriage.

The Sikh Minority and Guardianship Act should make the mother a joint guardian of her children. Even the United Nations Declaration of Human Rights of the child stresses that a child of tender years shall not be separated from his mother. It is suggested that a child should be allowed to stay with the mother till the age of 14 or more. Other criteria of appointing a guardian may include the past conduct of the person towards the child and capacity of the person to look after the child. Moreover, paramount consideration should be given to the welfare of the child while drafting this Act.

Conclusion

Members of the Sikh community feel that in contrast to Hindu laws and an Uniform Civil Cde, the need is for a Sikh Personal Law within the ambit of the Indian socio-cultural system.

It is comparatively easier to enact laws than to ensure their effective application. The most important thing, therefore, is to internalise the Sikh ethics and practise them in day-to-day life.

The laws should be simple and clear. They should not be complicated and frightening. In order to make Sikh personal laws effective, all cases of violation of the law should be sorted out in a speedy manner, because it has been observed that due to lengthy and expensive proceedings, a woman fighting for her right gives up mid-way and the whole exercise goes futile.

Thus, a Sikh Personal Law should be designed in the interest of women and should work as a positive force to bring egalitarian order. Absence of gender bias in the Sikh Personal Law should be an example in itself for other communities.

The idea is to bring gender equality through significant pieces of legislation. Hence, women's organisations in Punjab, sensitive lawyers and judges, human rights activists, intellectuals and scholars, political parties (the Shromani Akali Dal and the SGPC) and other Sikh bodies ought to work together to formulate a model Sikh Personal Law in such a manner that the scales of justice are not weighed against women.

The Case of the Jain Community

THE JAINS are one of the most ancient communities in India. Unlike other minority communities such as the Parsis, Jews and Christians, the Jain community is Indian in every sense. The Jains are the indigenous inhabitants of this country and their mythological and historical personages are from India.

Their language for writing and speaking purpose is necessarily Indian. Their sacred temples and places of pilgrimage are located only in India. Jains never undertook religious expeditions on a large scale to foreign countries for conversion, they were like the Parsis in this matter. The Jains, therefore, have no religious connection with people outside India, unlike the Buddhists.

Jainism, traditionally known as Jaina dharma, belongs to the *śramāa* tradition and is one of the oldest Indian religions. Jainism is a religion of equality, devoted to recognising the rights of all living creatures, so not surprisingly, it accepts that women are able to play their part on the road to liberation.

The Jains, a small community, have through centuries succeeded in maintaining their distinctive socio-cultural and religious features. It is now acknowledged that Jainism is a distinct religion of India and is neither an offshoot of Buddhism, nor

Hinduism. For example, the Hindus regard marriage as a religious sacrament while Jains regard it as a civil contract. Among the Hindus adoption is a religious ceremony but this is not true of Jains. According to Jain law, a widow inherits the property of the dead husband, not so the Hindu woman.

Although Jainism is in many ways dedicated to equality, for some Jains a woman's very femaleness creates spiritual inequality. Jainism is male-centered at an institutional level. The ascetic lifestyle reflects the power hierarchy of Indian society at large, in which women are subordinate to men regardless of personal qualities, education or experience.

Law reflects the culture of a religion, borrowing laws from the scriptures. Thus, we will see how the Jain philosophy of women being inferior is also reflected in Jain law.

The laws on marriage, succession etc during the British period were discriminatory against women. It was only later that it came to be assimilated under the Hindu law which was clearly patriarchal. Thus, Jain culture is also discriminatory to women and there is need for reform within these laws through interpretations by courts.

Jains a Significant Minority

There are about 1.3 billion Jains in India today, spread through out the land. The women of this community are relatively well-educated.

Dissimilarities with Hindus

In Hinduism, salvation means merging of soul with universal soul or eternal stay in paradise. In Jainism, it is action-less and peaceful existence. In Vedic philosophy or *Sanatana Dharma*, salvation is giving up the sense of doership and realising the Self to be the same as Universe and God. In Jainism, salvation can be achieved only through self-effort and is considered to be the right of human beings.[1]

In Jainism, one definite path to attain liberation (*moksha*) is prescribed. The prescribed three-fold path consists of the three jewels of Jainism (Right Belief, Right Knowledge, Right Conduct). In Hinduism, no one definite path to salvation is prescribed.

According to Jain cosmology, the universe is eternal. In Hinduism, it is believed to be made by a creator. *Karma* is an invisible force in Hinduism, whereas it is a form of matter which can stick to the soul in Jainism.[2] In Hinduism, gods are worshipped for minor boons and are offered food etc. In Jainism, the *Tirthankara*s represent the true goal of all human beings. Their qualities are worshipped by the Jains.

The scriptures known as *Veda*s are regarded by Hindus as one of the foundations of Hinduism. Those who rejected the Vedas as the prime source of religious knowledge were labelled *nastika*. As a consequence, Jainism and Buddhism were categorised by Hindus as *nāstika darśana*.

The orthodox schools of Hinduism, such as *Vedanta, Mimamsa* and *Samkhya*, claim the *Sruti*s do not have any author and hence are supreme to other religious scriptures. This position was countered by the Jains who said that saying *Veda*s are authorless is equivalent to saying that anonymous poems are written by nobody. Jain scriptures, they believed, were of human origin, created and handed down through omniscient teachers, and hence claim greater worth.

According to the Jains, the origin of Vedas lies with Marichi, the son of Bharata Chakravarti, who was the son of the first Tirthankara, Rishabha. Jains maintain that these scriptures were later corrupted by the Brahmins. Jains point out that Hindus do not know their own scriptures since they are unaware of the names of the *tirthankara*s present in the Vedas.

Jains have had a long-standing debate with the Mimamsa school of Hinduism. Kumarila Bhatta, a proponent of the Mimamsa school, argued that the Vedas are the source of all knowledge and it is through them that humans can differentiate between right and wrong. Jain monks, such as Haribhadra, held that humans are already in possession of all the knowledge, which only needs to be illuminated or uncovered in order to gain the status of omniscience.

The practice of Vedic animal sacrifices was opposed by the Jains. Hemachandra, a Jain monk, cites passages from *Manusmriti*, the Hindu law book, to demonstrate how, in the light of false scriptures, Hindus have resorted to violence. Akalanka, another Jain monk, sarcastically notes that if killing can result in enlightenment, one should become a hunter or fisherman. The rejection of Hindu epics and scriptures were dominant in Jainism since very early times.[3]

The central Hindu scriptures and epics like the Vedas, *Mahabharata* and *Ramayana* are categorised as false scriptures in *Nandisutra*, one of the Svetambara canonical literature. Later, Jains adapted various Hindu epics in accordance with their own system. There were disputes between the Jains and the Hindus on the forms of these epics.

Within the doctrine of Jainism, the *tirthankara* holds the highest status. Hemachandra says that a *deva* (roughly a godly soul) is the one who has conquered his internal desires and passions. This requirement, according to him, was fulfilled only by the tirthankaras. The gods of the Hindus are attached to worldly pleasures such as women and weapon and hence cannot be regarded as necessary for spiritual upliftment.[4]

Marriage

Though the Jains and the Hindus regard marriage as obligatory for every person, there is a great difference in their outlook. Jains look at the problem from a purely social point of view. Hindus treat marriage from a religious point of view. Among the Hindus, marriage is made compulsory for every person because the birth of a son is said to enable one to obtain *moksha*. According to Hindus, there is an intimate connection between marriage and the ultimate object in life viz. moksha. As marriage has something to do with the emancipation of the soul, marriage and religion are very closely connected with one another in Hindu society.[5]

It is believed by Hindus that one's progeny is intimately connected with and instrumental to happiness, both in this world as well as hereafter. Moreover, the birth of a son is considered by Hindus to be especially contributory towards helping the father to execute his obligations due to the departed ancestors—one of the three debts or obligations which every Hindu is bound to discharge. Thus, a Hindu has to marry to beget a male child with a view to avoid eternal damnation in hell after his death. This is how the institution of marriage among Hindus loses its social character, gets mixed up with the religious behaviour of the people and becomes a religious act.

In the Jains, marriage is not treated as a religious duty but is considered as a purely social act. It is regarded more in the nature of a civil contract than a religious ceremony. Its object is to maintain the continuity of the human race and not to obtain salvation by securing male offsprings. Marriages are entered into for purely practical reasons. It is not ordained in Jain religion to marry for emancipation of the soul. Marriage is not concerned with life hereafter. When no offerings are to be made to the forefathers, the question of discharging obligations due to departed ancestors does not arise.

Jain scriptures do not lay down elaborate rules and regulations regarding marriage. Marriage is completely based on the local customs of the people designed to adjust the life of persons in this world, as it is not concerned with the happiness of persons hereafter.

If marriage among Jains would have been based on their *agamas* (ie. basic religious books), it would have been practically the same throughout many centuries and there would not have been great diversity of customs regarding various aspects of marriage throughout the country. Since marriage practices of the Jains differ to a considerable extent, it is clear that the institution of marriage is based on local customs and not on the holy scriptures.

From this, it need not be inferred that the Jain holy books do not refer to marriage at all. They do discuss the subject of marriage but in this respect, their basic stand is that a lawful wife is necessary for a man for the successful completion of his householder's life. They do not prescribe any rules regarding matters like her age, qualifications, *gotra*, caste, race etc. as these are based on local customs. Practically, there is very little relation between marriage customs and Jain scriptures.

In Jain scriptures, while narrating particular events, references are made and opinions given on the marriage customs connected with the events. But such opinions are not applicable for all places and times, since such opinions were given by taking into account the marriage customs prevailing at that time, in that place. This means that marriage customs referred to in the Jain sacred books are not binding on Jains for all time to come and they are free to devise their own customs according to local conditions.

Among Jains, there is only an indirect connection between marriage, like for any other custom, and religion.

For Jains, the ultimate object in life is the attainment of *moksha*, ie. liberation of soul from worldly bondage. The best way, according to Jainism, to achieve this aim is to perform right action along with right faith and right knowledge. Right action includes proper channelising of sexual practices with a view to lead a useful life which serves as a stepping stone for getting salvation. Moreover, religion depends for its existence on the number of its followers. The strength of the followers can be rightfully maintained through the procreation of legitimate children. Taking into account these considerations, it can be stated that the object of marriage in Jainism is twofold, viz. (1) to give a legitimate outlet to sexual desires so that the human being may rightly live a useful life, enjoying the fruits of *dharma*, *artha* and *kama*, and thus be entitled to attain the great object, *moksha*; and (2) to promote the cause of *dharma* (law) by generating righteous and chivalrous sons and daughters. It is a duty of the householder to be contented with his own life and to contrive for the continuance of the human race.

Diversity in Food & Clothing

The history of the Jain church is full of references to the various schisms that have taken place from time to time and some of these schisms contributed to the rise of sects and subsects in the Jain religion. These sectarian differences give rise to different cultural practices in terms of food and clothing, marriage and inheritance laws and practices that differ from community to community of Jains, depending on their regional affiliations.

It is now necessary to see what the exact difference between two sects within Jainisam is. Literally, the *Digambara* sect are naked while the *Svetambara* sect are white clad. Yet, there is very little difference between the two branches as regards the essentials of religious doctrine. For example, the most authoritative book of the Digambaras, *Tattvathadhigama* is also a standard book of the Svetamabaras. However, there are some major as well as minor tenets on which the two sects are opposed to one another.

The Digambaras believe that a monk who owns any property or wears clothes cannot attain salvation. The Svetamabars assert that the practice of complete nudity is not essential for liberation.

The Digambaras hold the view that women are not entitled to moksha in their lives. The Svetambaras believe that women can achieve *Nirvana*.

According to Digambaras, once a saint attains *Kevala Jnana* (omniscience), s/he needs no food but can sustain life without eating. This view is not acceptable to the Svetamabaras.

The Digambaras maintain that the embryo of Mahavira, the last Tirthankara, was not removed from the womb of Devananda, a Brahmin lady, to that of Trisala or Priyankarini, a Kshatriya lady. The Svetamabaras believe this to have happened.[6]

The Digambaras believe that the ancient sacred literature of the Jains disappeared completely and as such disown the canonical books of the Svetambaras.[7]

The Digambaras assert that Mahavira never married but according to the Svetambaras, Mahavira married Yashoda and had a daughter by name Anojja.

The Svetembaras consider Mallinatha, the 19th Tirthankara, as a female but Digambaras say that Mallinatha was a male.

According to the Digambaras, the Tirthankaras must be represented as nude and unadorned and with downcast eyes. This need not be so, according to the Svetambaras.[8]

The Many Subsects and Cultural Practices

The Svetambara and the Digambara sects are further divided into subsects. The Svetambara branch is divided into the Sthanakwasi, Murtipujak and Terapanthi subsects, and the Digambara into the Bisapanthi, Terapanthi and Taranpanthi. Murtipujak Jains are further divided into groups called Gacchas, the most important of which are the Tapa and Kharatara Gacchas. Minor subsects are the Gumanapanthis and Totaapanthis.

The Bisapanthi and Terapanthi Digambaras, for example, worship statues in temples, while the Taranpanthis worship scriptures. Among the Bisapanthi, women may anoint Jain images in temples, and there are no restrictions concerning green vegetables. The Terapanthi women are restricted from touching images of the Jinas and eating of green vegetables is restricted during certain times of the month.

The 20th century teacher of Jainism, Kanji Swami was deeply influenced by the *Samayasāra* of Kundakunda. He lectured on these teachings for forty-five years to comprehensively elaborate on the philosophy described by Kundakunda and other earlier teachers. Kundakunda's mystical doctrine was not exclusively Digambara, since he drew on Jain ideas which existed before the sectarian schism.

Kanji Swami believed Kundakunda's *Essence of the Doctrine* to be the essence of Jain teachings. This work is the most well-known of the second or third century mystic and is concerned with the real nature of the soul. Mundane doctrines such as on diets have been ignored by Kanji Swami. His emphasis on *nishcaya naya*, the higher level of truth over *vyavahara naya*, ordinary life, surpassed even Kundakunda.

Ritual and merit-making activities are largely irrelevant, Kanji Swami said, because they are linked to the passions. The practice of austerities and meditation cannot affect the soul, and polarities such as good and bad, fasting and non-fasting, are significant only at the worldly level in the realm of transmigration. The Kanji Swami Panth has always been a lay movement and ascetics have no special status. Sixty *brahmacharis*, lower-order ascetics, in the Kanji Swami Panth are mostly women that took vows of asceticism to keep away from rich clothes and jewellery.

Kanji Swami and Kundakundan, both saw ascetics as personifying the fundamental principles of Jainism, preventing and destroying karma and thus leading to self-knowledge and the soul. In the Kanji Swami Panth, the ascetics cover their mouth with strips of cloth while speaking, otherwise they keep them in their hands. They stay in temples or in the especially reserved buildings known as *upasrayas*. They collect food in their bowls from the *sravakas* or householders and eat at their places of stay.

The Sthanakvasi arose not directly from the Svetambaras but as reformers of an older reforming sect, viz. the Lonka sect of Jains. Though celibate, they are allowed to travel and own property. The original stock of the Svetambaras is known as murtipujaka Svetambaras, since they are worshippers of idols. They offer flowers, fruits, saffron etc. to their idols. The murtipujaka subsect is also known by terms like pujera (worshippers), deravasi (monastry residents), chaityavasi (temple residents) and mandiramargi (temple goers). The murtipujaka Svetambaras are found scattered all over India for business purposes in large urban centers, but a large number are concentrated in the State of Gujarat.

Many people of the Lonka sect joined this group and they took the name of Sthanakvasi, meaning those who do not have their religious activities in temples but carry on their religious duties in places known as *sthanakas* which are like prayer-halls.

The Terapantha sect observes a remarkable festival called *maryada mahotasava.* This distinctive festival is celebrated every year on the 7th day of the bright half of the month of *Magha* when all ascetics and lay disciples, male and female, meet together at one predetermined place and discuss the various problems of the Terapanthis.

The ritual of penance of the Terapanthis is considered to be very severe. The dresses of the Terapanthi monks and nuns are akin to that of the Sthanakvasi monks and nuns. But there is a difference in the length of of the piece of white cloth kept tied over the mouth, in case of the Muhapanthis. The Terapanthis are considered reformists as they emphasise on simplicity in religion. For example, the Terapanthis do not even construct monasteries for their monks, who inhabit a part of the house which the householders build for themselves. Their religious head, Acharya Tulsi, started the *Anuvrata Andolana*, that is the 'small vow movement' which attempts to utilise the spiritual doctrines of the Jain for moral uplift of the masses in India. The Terapanthis are still limited in number and even though they are noticed in different cities in India, they are concentrated mainly in Bikaner, Jodhpur and Mewar areas of Rajasthan.

Sadhus (monks) and *Sadhvis* (nuns) are people who have voluntarily given up their household lives and worldly affairs and have accepted the five major vows to uplift their souls on the spiritual path.

Class and Caste among Jains

The Jains are also divided into various castes through the rules of caste endogamy, but inter-caste relations are not very strictly followed within the community. The Jains also maintain the traditional affiliation to a certain line of monks.

Occupations involving less mobility such as those of merchants have been adopted by the community. The Jains own large business-houses connected with textiles, grains, machinery, chemical industry, the paper industry, newspapers, precious metals, jewellery and banking businesses and capital investment. Most of the middle-class Jain are accountants, bankers and craftsmen.

Vedic society was composed of four classes, ie. brahmna, rajanya, vaisaya and sudra. Jainism looked at society as classless and casteless. After Pasavantha and Mahavira, various Jain acharyas made no distinction whatsoever among people in the matter of following religion and said that the *varna* system, that is the division of society into varnas or classes, is based upon differences in professions. In their view, birth played no part in determining the class of particular person. They said, classes were not watertight compartments and each person had the complete freedom to observe any religious rites and practices along with others. The *brahmanahood* of the best ascetics as well as of ordinary people is considered on their actions and not on their birth in the brahmana class.

The existing caste system is a late development in Jain communities. The exact number of Jain castes is unknown, it is believed there are eighty-four castes among the Jains. There are Jain sections or divisions in several Hindu castes too. These are mainly occupational castes, some members of which happen to follow the Jain religion. The Gaurvas are similar to Brahmins in matters of religion and culture. They abstain from flesh and liquor and do not take food and water from any Hindu caste, including the Brahmins. They are mainly servants in village temple which though dedicated to Brahmanic gods, still have by their sides broken remaines of Jain images. In Uttar Pradesh, there are Jain sections among the Rajputs and the Unaya caste. The Agarwalas can be found among Hndus, Jains, Muslims, Sikhs and Buddhists.

Each caste forms a very small group. Since all of them are endogamous groups, many have necessarily to remain unmarried and as such the population is fast declining. There are 60 castes whose population is less than one hundred in number. There are seventeen castes which are on the verge of being wiped out. The population of Disavaka caste, according to the 1901 census was

1971, it fell to 355 in 1911 and by this time might have ceased to exist. The historical evidence of other castes exist.

Nevertheless, one must note that the Jain religion does not recognise castes in the community. No acharya biographies mention castes. It is also interesting to note that only a few castes like the Osavala, Humbada, Nema etc are common to both, the Digambaras and Svetambaras and the caste system among the Jains is a social and not religious institution. The attitude of Jains towards caste is that it is one of the social practices unconnected with religion, observed by people and it is not the religion's business to regulate the working of the caste system.

Naturally, the Jains evolved a caste system of their own which is more or less similar to the caste system found in Hindu society. This was bound to happen sooner or later because the Jains were surrounded on all sides by Hindus and as such, they could not escape from copying the most important characteristic of the Hindu society viz. the caste system.

Among Jains, even though there are several castes, no prominent position is assigned to any caste, not even to Jain Brahmins. As the highest rung of ladder is not fixed, naturally the question of arranging castes in order of social precedence does not arise. All castes are treated on an equal footing and no differentiation is accepted between castes as regards social prestige. However, among Jains, the castes which do not allow widow remarriage consider themselves as superior to those which allow and practice widow marriage. Also under the influence of the Hindu community, inter-dining is prohibited in several castes. Even now when caste feasts take place, members from other castes are generally not invited.

However, there is no restriction on social intercourse based on transmission of impurity by even the touch of a low caste person. This might possibly be due to the fact that majority of the Jains consider themselves as vaisyas and there are practically no sudras among Jains. But from ancient literature it appears that some groups of people were despised and isolated from the civilised castes of people. Amongst them are mentioned the peacock-tamers, acrobats, hunters, pole-dancers, fishermen, cobblers etc. These names suggest that the despised people were mainly flesheaters and as such they might have been isolated from the rest.

Just like the Hindus, even in Jainism there are several persons who have been debarred from practicing certain religious rites. In some castes, which have been divided into Visas and Dasas, at certain places the Dasas are not allowed even at present to worship in temples. The ascetics decline to take food from the hands of people who practice widow remarriage. According to the Digambara sects, the sudras cannot give food to Jain ascetics, they are not entitled to moksha, they cannot become ascetics of high order and they are possibly not allowed to worship. While Jain kings gave much more superiority to the Hindu Kshatriya caste, Brahmins also enjoyed certain privileges such as immunity from paying taxes and capital punishment.

Castes were often named after places of their origin. Members of a caste could follow any occupation unlike in the Hindu community. Overall, the Jain castes are not arranged in a hierarchical order of respectability, no restriction were put on social intercourse between different caste members and there was no lack of choice of occupation.

Discriminatory Practices against Women

Amongst Jains, marriage is a purely social act. Its object is to maintain the continuity of the human race and not to attain salvation. According to Jains, every person is to enter the marriage contract. Those persons who keep their grown-up daughters in their homes without getting them married fall from religion. Thus, child marriage within the Jains was the order of the day until a few years ago. Liberal feminists believe women suffer the most in a marriage set up by others. Women just perform sexual slavery for men. They, therefore, condemn such set up marriages, especially child marriages.

Nakedness

For the Digambaras, mendicants must be nude because it is a symbol of their perfect detachment from everything, whether material possession or moral defilement. This leads to the conviction that a woman can never go naked because of her physiology and the innate impurity caused by numerous microscopic beings in her body. Hence she is not considered able to reach emancipation as a woman and must be reborn as a man first. This may be one reason why there are fewer nuns than monks among the Digambara sect.[9]

In contrast, Svetambaras focus on a more internal approach. An individual must meet the requirements of 'right faith, right knowledge and right behaviour', which are the only necessary conditions for attaining the goal of salvation. If these 'three gems' are met, the individual's gender does not matter.

Ahimsa and Women

Digambaras also believe that women are inherently *himsic* (which is best translated as harmful). This comes partly from a belief that menstrual blood kills micro-organisms living in the female body. The killing of the micro-organisms is said to show that a female body is less 'non-violent' than a male body, although that idea doesn't have any scientific support and isn't found in modern Jain thinking.

Impurity

Some Jain texts say that menstrual blood is a sign of impurity. But the idea that women are spiritually impure because of menstruation is a rather odd basis for a Jain argument, since Jainism usually concerns itself with thinking, speaking, and acting rightly. There isn't any other area where Jainism says that involuntary bodily functions are a spiritual obstacle.

Attachment

Another argument is that because a woman's nature is to care for children and other dependents, she will find it much more difficult to break free from these earthly attachments, and unless she does this, she cannot achieve liberation.

Discriminating Scriptures

Historically, Jainism's attitude towards women has shared a view common amongst other Indian and Asian traditions, which see women as innately unequal to men. Yet, against long-established social attitudes in Asian countries, Jainism gives women a central role in its ethical and spiritual patterns.

The religion of Jains include women in their fourfold *sangha*; the religious order of Jain laymen, laywomen, monks and nuns.[10] The early Svetambara scriptures prevented pregnant women, young women or those who have a small child, to enter the ranks of a nun. Regardless, the number of nuns given in those texts were always double the number of monks. Parsva and Mahavira, two historical teachers of Jainism, had huge numbers of female devotees and ascetics.

The religious status of women is one of the chief differences between the two principal sects of Digambaras and Svetambaras. It is also a crucial issue in the history of Jainism.

The *Sutrakritanga* (the second *anga* or limb of the Jain canon) and the *Uttaradhyayana* (the second *Mulasutra* text) deal with a variety of subjects; both works are guides for young initiates, instructing them in true Jain doctrine, the correct path to the highest good, the principal duties of a monk, but, above all, the dangers that punctuate a monk's spiritual life. Lecture XXXII of the *Uttaradhyayana Sutra,* titled the 'Causes of Carelessness', recalls some of the sanctions we came across in *Acharanga Sutra*: A *sramana* engaged in penance, should not allow himself to watch the shape, beauty, coquetry, laughter, prattle, gestures and glances of women, nor retain a recollection of them in his mind.

Soon enough, feminine influence comes to be identified as one of the prime causes of carelessness—and the principal source of danger—in a monk's spiritual career. Attachment to women, decrees the *Uttaradhyayana Sutra*, is the most difficult to surmount and those who have achieved this will find it simple to sever their affections to other ties and pleasures. Forbearance and indifference to womanhood is the mark of a true monk—'those who possess the three *guptis* cannot be disturbed even by well-adorned goddesses'. The wholesome way for a monk is still to live alone, especially sheltered from the female presence because 'it is not safe for mice to live near the dwelling of a cat ....'

The threat to the monk's chastity and ascetic vows derives not merely from his own lack of control and continued attachment to the pleasures a woman affords, but from the cat-like predatory female who presents an unrelenting threat to his spiritual pursuits.

The *Sutrakritanga Sutra* devotes an entire chapter to the 'Knowledge of Women'. Its principal intent is to familiarise and caution the monks about the ways of the women. Part I is titled, 'How Women Tempt a Monk'. Here the monk is upgraded from the status of a mouse to that of a fearless single lion. The woman, though, remains the entrapper who ensnares the monk/lion with a piece of flesh. The 'flesh' here is not simply allegorical, for it is her physical flesh that tempts the ascetic and misleads him from his true path. Subsequent passages regard the monk variously as an antelope, a man who drinks poisoned milk, a pot filled with lac, and the woman as hunter, poison, thorn and fire (which causes the pot of lac to melt). A woman is defined simultaneously by stupidity and caprice: 'with clever pretences women make up to him, however foolish they be; they know how to contrive that some monks will become intimate with them'. Pretending to be pious, women will, the monks are warned, 'attempt to lure them' by beseeching them to accept a robe, an alms bowl, food or drink from them, or even by pleading with the monks to teach them the law of asceticism, as if they wish to give up their current way of life. However, a monk should never trust a woman because 'one man has in his heart [women], another in his words, and another still in his actions'.

Such views are also echoed by many contemporary *sadhvis* too. While narrating the story of a legendary monk, Sadhvi Prafullprabha, a Shvetambar nun, endorses the view that women are by nature fickle-minded and bearers of unbridled sexuality.

If, in the earlier texts, the nuns are effaced from discussions on celibacy, many post-canonical texts, such as *Brihatkalpasutra*, *Brihatkalpabhashya*, *Nishitha Churni* and *Avashyaka Niryukti*, developed specific rules for female mendicants in great detail. Writers have noted that while in its early phase Jainism, like other shramanic religions, defended an egalitarian outlook towards women, many of its later texts and commentaries developed a panoply of additionally stringent rules for female mendicants. These were geared towards maintaining a strict control over the nuns' conduct, especially their sexual conduct.

Brihatkalpasutra, for instance, forbids a *sadhvi* from venturing out of the upashraya on her own, unaccompanied, for the purpose of *gochari* (alms), food or toilet. It prescribes 11 kinds of clothes for the nun, and all of which must be worn while the nuns are travelling. It indicates the constant fear of sexual lapse so far as the female ascetics were concerned. These codes are, however, relatively mild when compared to the prescriptions of the *Brihatkalpabhashya.* This text prohibits the nuns from keeping in their possession or using all those fruits and vegetables, which had elongated or oblong shapes. Similarly, objects with handles and knobs were banned for nuns. These objects were taboo on account of their similarity in shape to the male organ. It was believed that the sight of these fruits and objects would stir sexual desires in nuns and that they could be deployed for gaining sexual pleasures. Further, nuns were strictly warned that they should repudiate any pleasure arising from the accidental touch of an animal and refrain from masturbation under all circumstances. Indeed, strict penalties have been stipulated for any infraction.

It was the opinion of the writers of these texts, that for many women, asceticism was a refuge from the problems of life and not driven by purely spiritual aspirations. These women could not, therefore, embrace a life of renunciation, nor follow the five *mahavratas* it entailed in any genuine manner. They continued to hanker after worldly pleasures, including sexual pleasure, necessitating a strict regime of control. There is a perceptible difference in the kind of strictures pertaining to celibacy that are issued to the male and female mendicants. The strictures to monks lie more in the domain of cautions and warnings – portents of the depths to which a monk may sink if he fails to solidly defend his vow of *brahmacharya*. His portrayal approximates that of a victim who needs to continuously guard his chastity from women.

According to the Svetambara's scriptures such as *Chhedasutra*, women were given lesser authority than their male counterparts. The reasons for this, in the commentaries, were that things which could endanger the vow of chasity should be avoided. Nalini Balbir writes that the belief that women are more fragile then men are all-pervading in these texts.

The Digambara sect of Jainism believes that women must be reborn as men in order to achieve liberation. Digambara texts like *Yuktiprabodha* say that women's genitals and breasts are sources of impurity and have many micro-organisims living in them. They believe that women cannot take higher vows of ascetic renunciation, because naked women would have two deep emotions: shame of being naked and fear of sexual assault which they might face.

Women have inferior skill in debating. Actually, women were not allowed to participate in debates, although Jainism provides evidence for women participating in debates in the *Uttamdhyayana Sutra*. Jaina debates were more than a measure of scholarship; they also involved the summoning of occult powers in order to defeat opponents, and such powerful public displays by women were highly problematic.

Kundakunda's *Sutraprabhat* is the first text known that refutes the validity of clothed mendicancy and denies women access to spiritual pursuits on account of the prohibition on female nudity.

Kundakunda lent scriptural weight to the argument against women's salvation.

Women's Celibacy Suspect

The complete absence of nuns in these scriptures is quite conspicuous. Should we assume that the early Jain texts believed that nuns were capable of exercising self-restraint or were asexual beings, not requiring the same degree of discipline that was being enjoined upon the monks? Or should we draw a different conclusion: that notwithstanding the ostensible equal attention to both nuns and monks in laying down the rules governing their conduct, Jain texts were still unable to fully abandon the norms of the surrounding culture, which characterised renunciation as exclusively male.

Brenda Falk, in her study of the Buddhist nun orders attributes the decline of female orders in Buddhism to precisely this reason. She has argued that Buddhism was unable to shake off the patriarchal norms of Hinduism, even while offering a radically different ideology of women's spiritual entitlements. It appears that Jainism too, despite recognising women as equal components of the Jain spiritual world, both as *shravika*s and *sadhvi*s, could not wrench free from the tendency to portray renunciation as an essentially male pursuit. Thus, we see many of its monastic codes almost unknowingly erase the presence of its female practitioners, with their role then reduced to being mere impediments in the path of this essentially male quest for salvation.

One direct consequence of characterising the feminine as inherently sexual—inimical rather than amenable to the path of renunciation—was that even those women who were engaged in the pursuit of liberation were invested with a sexual agency. Their ability to renounce sex and remain steadfast to the vow of celibacy was rendered suspect.

Women differ morally from men in that they cannot commit the extremely impure acts that men can; consequently, women cannot be born into the lowest hell. Jaina cosmology posits three realms: various hells, the earth, and various heavens. The hells and heavens are multi-layered: the lowest hell is for the worst acts and the highest heaven for the purest acts. The argument follows that since women's moral nature prevents them from being born in the lowest hell, therefore, as an act of cosmic balance, their moral nature prevents them from being born in the highest heaven. In other words, being more temperate morally than men is perceived as a limitation—if they cannot be as bad they cannot be as good.

Conclusion

One striking difference in the way that Hindu and Jain renunciant discourses treat the gender question is that the latter offers to women the ideal of *swadharma* (self-focused religiosity) in addition to the overriding ideal of *stree dharma*, which is then seized upon by Jain female ascetics to undermine the negative portrayals of womanhood and to ward off the cultural expectations of marriage and motherhood.

Catherine Clementin-Ojha writes that outside of this solitary ideal of *stree dharma*, a woman appears only as 'a taunting demon ... who threaten[s] to lure well-intentioned but susceptible yogis to the fires of hellish delusion'. For Jainism, we may say, that though such virulent characterisations were never absent, the presence of a simultaneous positive acknowledgement of women's spiritual capacities enabled female spiritual aspirants to disregard or downplay the disparaging references and cultural models. An investigation of the Jain texts reveals how the images and ideals of heterodox traditions may overlap or digress from those purveyed by dominant Hindu normative codes.

The Terāpanthin subsect has a special category of nuns called the *samāi*, which is officially free from certain rules restricting their movements and they can visit institutions in India or abroad to pursue academic research.The inferior status of nuns compared to monks depends on the order of Jainism they belong to. Examples of prominent nuns as influential teachers, propagators of the faith, writers and so on have been, and still are, numerous. Women lead the key Jain religious activities surrounding food, especially fasting, and often have principal roles in the performance of worship, particularly singing hymns. Jain women are also often the keenest participants in religious festivals.

Despite the vital importance of female activity in Jain religious life and the high proportion of female mendicants, nuns must defer to male colleagues. Frequently, senior nuns have limited authority and are not allowed to preach like monks. This is partly connected to the main philosophical distinction between the Digambaras and Svetambaras. The sectarian dispute over whether the 19th Jina, Malli, was male or female symbolises disagreements about female liberation. Individual monastic orders have both men and women members. Female groups as a whole are generally supervised by men members and leading nuns are appointed by monks.

Among the Digambaras, where the place of women is always more inferior than among other Jain orders, a nun is initiated by a monk and traditionally becomes a member of a male mendicant's 'lineage'. In some cases, a Digambara nun may be an independent group leader and initiate her own disciples, female or even males. Nuns have their own religious titles—gurūi, gāini, pravartini—which refer to their function as group leader. One exceptional case is that of the nun Candanā, who was appointed acharya. This title was bestowed on her by Amar Muni, the creator of the Veerayatan centre in Bihar.

For the Digambaras clothes indicate a clinging to possessions and the mendicant must be free of all such things. Both sects deny women nudity, but the Svetambaras still allow women to become mendicants and, therefore, have access to salvation. Significantly, Svetambara monks are not nude either, which for the Digambaras means they are not mendicants, so by arguing in favour of clothed nuns, the Svetambaras are also arguing for clothed monks. This has been a significant factor in the debate about women. Since this whole debate has been in the hands of men, in a sense the Svetambaras have been arguing for themselves, not just for women.

A woman's inferior social position reflects her inferior spiritual position. The Svetambara sect, however, disagrees with this position, and even today the majority of Svetambara monastics are female. Thus, it has been the Svetambara sect which has been more liberal about entering of women in Jain religion. This is larglely related to salvation for women. The principles of non-violence and Ahimsa can be very helpful for emancipation of women. New denominations like the Sthankavasi, the Terapanth and the Kanjipanth are among the more egalitarian sects. Certain key religious leaders have also been instrumental in bringing the reformatory spirit in Jainism.

In the context of deciding if a set of independent personal laws should be granted to the Jains of India or a Uniform Civil Code should be given to the community, the fact is till the time discriminatory practices in a culture don't disappear, even law cannot do much. So, reinterpretation of Jain holy texts and belief in the constitution of the country can possibly offer a way out.

Granting of minority status to the Jain community may be a step in the right direction to understand diversity in cultural and legal sphere in 21st century India.

Do we need Buddhist Personal Laws?

PATRIARCHY, THE context of society since Buddha's time, continues to influence and shape contemporary Buddhism in India. It is the fundamentalism within Buddhism that has a voice. Buddha's original teachings over 2,500 years ago did not discriminate against women. After achieving enlightenment, the Buddha began to admit people to his Order, based on their own choice so that they could devote their lives to the Path of Enlightenment he discovered. The oldest stories about Buddha do not exhibit gender bias, rather speak of his first disciples being women.

The most consistent and ubiquitous feature of gender-based discrimination in Buddhist-majority and former Buddhist-majority countries today is the prevalence of negative attitudes toward women, which mimic those found in Buddhist scriptures of times after the Buddha. A number of studies and statistics have also established an overall pattern of relatively low female empowerment. The unbalanced male-to-female population ratios in several countries, which have resulted from female-specific abortion and high female mortality rates (an imbalance of as much as 12 to 15 per cent in some areas), are also said to be the cause of social problems that affect women and men alike: increased anti-social behaviour, crime, violence, prostitution, and civil unrest.[1]

It is only when the Buddha established an Order that male-domination crept into what can be called early Buddhism. In a few years, so rowdy did the Order become that Suddhodhana, the Buddha's father, made a request that, 'in future no boy be admitted to the Order without the permission of his parents'. (Gombrich 177.) The Buddha granted the request and accordingly made a *Vinaya* rule to prohibit the admission of boys into the Order without the consent of their parents (Vin I 82–83; Horner 4: 104). This rule was against the very behaviour that the Buddha had himself undertaken against his own father's wishes. Ernst Gombrich notes: 'In doing so, he (the Buddha), in fact, corrects himself for he decides that what he did to his own father, and what he has just repeated with his own son, should never again be inflicted on any parent.'

According to Gombrich, unlike most of the other Vinaya rules which were prescribed due to an unwise act of a disciple monk or nun, the culprit here was the Buddha himself. If Gombrich is correct, we should wonder why the Buddha never insisted that a married man wishing to renounce should seek his wife's permission in addition to that of his parents? A son going forth into a monastic order might break the hearts of non-consenting parents, a husband going forth might ruin the life of his wife for good, especially in those times when women had to live in marital households, with very few rights of their own. The Buddha never bothered to say that the wives' permission ought to be sought to recruit their husbands, possibly simply because he knew that the wives of would-be monks in his time were hardly empowered to harm the Order. In those times, even if it were a queen who lost her husband without her consent to the Order, she was powerless against the Order unless she got support from her in-laws. And if her in-laws had already given consent to their son for his renunciation, there would be little chance that they would help her against the Order.

Gombrich's assertion appears even more odd because the Buddha did insist that married women should seek the permission of both the parents and the husband to go forth (Vin IV 335; Horner 3) into the monastic Order. Does it mean that the Buddha did have a bias against women who wished to enter the Order? And what about the case of young children who lost their parents to the Order?

According to longstanding Buddhist tradition, women have pursued the ordained life since Buddhism's beginning in the 5th century BCE.[2] The Buddha certainly could not afford to clash with society. This yearning of women is epitomised in the figure of Mahapajapati Gotami, the historical Buddha's aunt and foster mother, who is believed to be first Buddhist nun (*bhikkhuni*).

As the scriptures recount, the Buddha initially refuses Mahapajapati's request that women be allowed to enter the *Sangha* (Order, monastery). With steadfast resolve, Mahapajapati and her following of 500 women cut off their hair, don saffron robes and walk 150 miles to Vesali (Vaishali) where the Buddha is teaching. Ananda (the Buddha's chief desciple) sees the aspirants and, moved by their pitiful appearance, he approaches the Buddha and intercedes on their behalf. Ultimately, on the grounds that women are as capable as men of attaining Enlightenment, Mahapajapati and her retinue are admitted into the Sangha.

What the Texts Say

Despite its small size, the *Therigatha* is a very significant document in the study of early Buddhism as well as the earliest-known collection of women's literature. The *Therigatha* contains passages reaffirming the view that women are the equal of men in terms of spiritual attainment, as well as verses that address issues of particular interest to women in ancient South Asian society. The *Therigatha,* often translated as *Verses of the Elder Nuns* (from Pali where their is the feminine elder nun and gatha means verses), date from a three hundred year period, with some dated as early as the late 6th century BCE.

While relevant sources suggest that the community of fully ordained nuns (Bhikkhuni Sangha) was established five years after the community of monks (Bhikkhu Sangha), recent scholarship reveals internal inconsistencies in the account of the foundation of the order of nuns, including chronological discrepancies.

Some Buddhist texts say that Buddha was born as a princess in his previous life, while parallel sources negate this.

No discriminatory actions or teachings can be found in the *Tripitika*, the Buddhist bible. However, because the Buddha's teachings were passed down orally only through male teachers after his death, and were only recorded 400 years later, Buddhism today is filtered, formed and designed through patriarchy. It is apparent in the belief system about women and men in some later-day religious texts and ceremonies, as well as in the hierarchical and patriarchal structure of Buddhist institutions in all three major schools of Buddhism.

The *Theravada Vinaya* reports fewer direct meetings between Mahapajapati Gotami and the Buddha than other *Vinaya*s. In the *Nandakovada Sutta* the Buddha does not even speak to her, whereas in parallel versions of this discourse transmitted by other schools, he personally imparts her teachings. Such distancing takes place not only in relation to Mahapajapati Gotami. The nun protagonist of the *Cūavedalla Sutta* does not have any direct contact with the Buddha, whereas in the parallel version she personally speaks to him.

In *Dhammadinna* there is a legend where a woman remains a woman and is ordained by the Buddha, evidently becoming a nun. So she does not have to be transformed into a male body to achieve salvation.

The *Pali Vinaya* reports rulings promulgated by the Buddha when a bhikkhu reportedly changed into a female and a bhikkhūi became a male. Unlike the *Dhammapada* commentary, this *Vinaya* does not give a value judgment for these two cases. Instead, both are simply reported as a matter of fact, without a distinction between the case of a male changing to a female or vice versa. That is, in the canonical account there is no indication that for the bhikkhu to become a female is the result of *bad karma*, or that for a bhikkhuni to change into a male is the result of *good karma*. Bee Scherer speaks of a 'basically non-judgmental reaction of the Buddha', noting, 'this initial pragmatic approach towards gender-crossing is later modified in the authoritative commentary...to the *vinaya*' where the commentarial stance is evidence for 'an underlying assumption on gender inequality'.

To reason with King Pasenadi of Kosala, the early texts say, the Blessed One uttered these stanzas: A woman may be better than a man, ruler of the people. She may be wise and virtuous. A good wife who reveres her mother-in-law. A man born from her may be a hero and a king. The son of such a fortunate woman may well govern the kingdom.

The above discourse presents a re-evaluation of the notion, apparently shared by the king, that the birth of a female is unfortunate. The phrasing of the stanzas seems to reflect an attempt to adjust this re-evaluation to the frame of mind of the king. Hence they conclude with the glorious vision—for a king—of a heroic future king who governs the kingdom. This, of course, does not imply that from an early Buddhist viewpoint, women are only good for bearing sons, but is simply a reflection of the narrative context.

CHINESE TEXTS

Chizen Akanuma's reference work for identifying parallels (1929) does not list any parallel for the 'Discourse on the Daughter'. Nevertheless, elsewhere in the Chinese *agamas*, material can be found that also considers female birth in a positive light. Although there is evidence for a more negative attitude towards women emerging in commentarial literature, the two specimens translated above from the *Ekottarika* agama express a rather different attitude. The perspective afforded in these texts appears to be rather that female birth is a valuable asset, as it affords an opportunity for Bhadda Kaccana and Bhadda Kapilani (two nuns) to walk the path to liberation.

Women who want to live as disciples of the Buddha have not always been encouraged or supported, however. But there are some who overcame the adversity. For example, the Chinese Chan (Zen) tradition remembers women who became masters, respected by men as well as women (see *Women Ancestors of Zen*).

A passage in the *Mahaparinibbana Sutta* also shows that the bhikkhunis were considered integral to the Buddha's dispensation. The passage says, the Buddha declared that he would not pass away until he had accomplished his mission of having disciples from each of the four assemblies—including bhikkhunis—who were competent, disciplined, self-confident and learned.

In certain Buddhist texts, it is said, the Buddha refused ordination to women. The Buddha's refusal needs to be considered in the light of an alternative suggestion by him, reported in several versions, that women can live a celibate spiritual life, shaving their head and donning robes, but that they should do so without wandering around on their own. It suggests that the Mahapajapati and her followers should live a renunciant life 'without wandering around'—to the households that are easily assailed and in the fields afflicted then by a disease. This may originally have illustrated the problems ordained women encountered in ancient Indian society if they were to wander around freely, since rape and similar abuse appear to have been far from uncommon at that time. 'If Sakyamuni Buddha were here in the world today, undoubtedly he would see to it that bhikkhuni communities establish themselves independently, as their own self-governing legal entities, with all of the rights and privileges completely equal to bhikkhu monastics (and individuals in the wider society), including the right to perform their own ordinations without any contingencies whatsoever imposed from without, by those who are not themselves ordained with bhikkhuni precepts.'[3]

The *Vimalakirti Sutta* teaches that maleness and femaleness, like other phenomenal distinctions, are essentially unreal. 'With this in mind, the Buddha said: In all things, there is neither male nor female.' The *Vimalakirti* is an essential text in several Mahayana schools, including Tibetan and Zen Buddhist.

It is the larger *Sukhavatvyuha Sutta*, also called the *Aparimitayur Sutta* (one of three sutras that provide the doctrinal basis of the Pure Land school) which contains a passage usually interpreted to mean that women must be reborn as men before they can enter Nirvana.

Institutionalised bias against Women

Some of the ways in which patriarchal views and actions manifest within Buddhism are the following: The misinterpretation which is taught by some influential temples, monks and scholars that *being born a woman is a result of previous bad karma* and is a misfortune because women will experience many difficulties in life. This includes also the teaching that the male body is sacred, higher and more important/superior than the female body. From this belief flows the theory that only male monks can teach and lead Buddhism.

Buddhist women, including nuns, have faced harsh discrimination by Buddhist institutions in Asia for centuries. There is gender inequality in most of the world's religions, of course, but is sexism intrinsic to Buddhism, or did Buddhist institutions absorb sexism from Asian cultures? Can Buddhism treat women as equals, and remain Buddhism?[4]

In many Buddhist countries, women are not allowed to take full ordination (as a female monk); the reason given by the Buddhist institution is that there is no lineage for female ordination in that country or in that school of Buddhism. Male monks and lay men are also served/sit first in temple ceremonies. The *Therigatha* tells us, the Buddha had said that allowing women into the Sangha would cause his teachings to survive only for 500 years instead of a 1,000. The other impossibilities are related to the inability of women to take up leadership roles in ancient Indian society. Women are seen as *not fit to occupy the heavenly rulership positions* as well as that of a wheel-turning king or a Buddha, a secular and spiritual leadership role on earth.

The impossibility of a female to be a *Pratyekabuddha* seems to imply that *women have lesser spiritual abilities.* To quote, the Buddha said to the woman: With a female body one cannot be a Buddha, a *Pratyekabuddha, Brahma, Sakra, Mara* or a wheel-turning king; these dignities are very lofty and cannot be attained with a female body. If it is your wish to attain these, you should relinquish your dirty embodiment and acquire a pure body.

According to this story, the woman placed her head at the Buddha's feet and asked, how to reconcile a past life of the Buddha as a female with the dictum that a woman cannot be considered a full-fledged *bodhisattva.* Even though this version also adheres to the doctrine of the superiority of a male body, it does so in a way that is considerably less offensive than its parallels. In other words, *by dint of their female nature women are polluted and sinful, for which they deserve to be punished.*

Jetsunma Tenzin Palmo argues that there appears to have been institutionalised bias against women from the beginning of Buddhism. The council of five hundred *arahants* (ordained disciples) that was held after the historical Buddha passed away did not document attendance by any woman. She thinks that the Buddha imparted teachings to women, but very few of these teachings were recorded due to the exclusion of women from the council. Centuries later, when the canon was committed to writing, men's privileged education enabled them to read and write. Therefore, they had the monopoly in choosing whose records to preserve for future generations. Consequently, the teachings and commentaries were recited and recorded from the male point of view.

The liability of a female birth is still emphasised in many parts of the Buddhist world where male dominance and gender hierarchy persist. This misogynistic attitude has been especially devastating for nuns, who face reduced economic support, inferior education, and, in some parts of the world, even the extinction of their ordination lineages because of long-established monastic rules that are excessive in the way they favour monks over nuns.

Rules for Bhikkhunis

The Buddha's rules for the monastic orders are recorded in a text called the *Vinaya*. The *Pali Vinaya* has about twice as many rules for bhikkhunis as for bhikkhus.

Wy Cheng, in her study of Buddhist nuns, writes 'socially, the idea of women's inferior karma might hinder nuns to compete in the same activities as monks. This problem seems to be more severe in Taiwan than in Sri Lanka'. In a passage in the commentary on the *Sutta-nipata*, the *Paramatthajotika*, a woman aspires to be reborn as a man and she notes how disgusting it is to be a woman—even the daughter of a wheel-turning monarch will be under the control of others. She, therefore, aspires to become a male. In this story, a bad deed results in becoming a woman, and a good deed enables becoming a man. A change from woman to man is always desirable while the reverse is always undesirable.

The *Vinaya-pitaka* section of the *Tripitaka* records that the rules for a bhikkhuni include subordination to monks; the most senior nuns are to be considered 'junior' to a monk of one day. Some scholars point to discrepancies between the Pali *Bhikkhuni Vinaya* and other versions of the texts and suggest the more odious rules were added after the Buddha's death. Wherever they came from, over the centuries the rules were used in many parts of Asia to discourage women from being ordained.

In a paper on 'Women and the Arahant Issue in Early Pali Literature', Ellison Banks Findly argues that women 'were not granted *arahant* status by virtue of the prevailing social standards'. According to her research, 'all the individuals to whom the term arahant is applied in the early Pali canon are men. There is not a single case of the term being applied definitively to a specific woman in the *Vinaya* (disciplinary texts) or the *Nikayas* (texts of the Buddha's sermons)'. This then leads her to the assumption that, even though the ability of women to reach the final goal is regularly affirmed, 'women renunciants are denied designation by the title because donors are less enthusiastic about giving to arahant petitioners who also happen to be women'.

The paucity of examples of the term *arahani* does not imply that the ability of women to reach full awakening was not recognised. Similarly, the use of the nominative bhikkhu does not reflect gender discrimination.

The Lineage Problem

In many parts of Asia women are not allowed to be fully ordained. The reason for this has to do with the lineage tradition. The historical Buddha stipulated that fully ordained bhikkhus must be present at the ordination of bhikkhus and *fully ordained bhikkhus and bhikkhunis be present at the ordination of bhikkhunis.* When carried out, this would create an unbroken lineage of ordinations going back to the Buddha.

There are thought to be four lineages of bhikkhu transmission that remain unbroken, and these lineages survive in Asia. But for bhikkhunis there is only one unbroken lineage, surviving in China and Taiwan. The lineage of Theravada bhikkhunis died in 456 CE, and Theravada Buddhism is the dominant form of Buddhism in South East Asia—in particular, in Burma, Laos, Cambodia, Thailand, and Sri Lanka. These are all countries with strong male monastic sanghas, but women may only be novices, and in Thailand, not even that. Often women who try to live as bhikkhunis are expected to cook and clean for the bhikkhus.

An estimated over 80,000 buddhist nuns live in South Asian countries. In all but Sri Lanka, the full ordination of women is forbidden at present. Theravada nuns are not even recognised as *sramaneria* (novice nuns) or considered to be members of the monastic community.

In Theravada countries, women and girls are often barred from entering sacred shrines and temples, and in some countries any monk who even supports the ordination of women is subject to severe punishment, which may include expulsion from his order.

SRI LANKA

When the orders of nuns died out in India and Sri Lanka centuries ago, conservatives used the rules that called for monks and nuns to be present at nuns' ordination to prevent the institution of new orders.

In Sri Lanka, with re-establishment of the Bhikkhuni Order, Buddhist nuns are seeking recognition and calling on the government to issue them with the 'Bikkhu identity cards' and register their monasteries.There are said to be around 2,000 Theranis in the Bhikkhuni Sasana in the country, while there are around 800 ordained Bhikkhunis in Sri Lanka. These Bikkhunis allege they are being treated unfairly and since their monasteries are not registered, they are deprived of government funding, which in turn deprives the young nuns of educational opportunities.

Although they want the same status as the monks in Sri Lanka and seek to be registered with the Bhudda Sasana Ministry, the chief prelates of Sri Lanka say, these nuns cannot be called Bikkhunis and cannot be ordained, and they are only 'Sil Mathas who have been ordained in the wrong manner'.The Maha Nayaka Theros (high-ranking monks) have voiced their disapproval saying, it is not possible to re-establish the Bhikkhuni Order according to the 'Dharmavinaya', the doctrine of the Buddha.

Records indicate that the Bhikkhuni Sangha that currently exists in Sri Lanka derives from a grand ordination held in 1996, where a ceremony was performed for bhikkhunis at Isipatanaramaya in Benares (Sarnath) in India. According to Buddhist monastic regulations, new bhikkhunis must be ordained by a quorum of both bhikkhus and bhikkhunis. In the absence of a living Theravada bhikkhuni lineage, South Korean and Taiwanese bhikkhunis, who follow Mahayana rather than Theravada Buddhism, made up the quorums that ordained the first Sri Lankan bhikkhunis (1996).

According to Anamaduwe Dhammadassa Thero, the Mahanayake Thero (the council of high monks) were not consulted prior to this ordination. Buddhist historical records indicate that even some of the Mahayana teachers do not accept a bhikkhuni tradition. 'If the ordainment of these nuns had been done in consultation with the Mahanayaka Theros of this country, and by bringing in representatives from a country that practices the Theravada doctrine with the mediation of the government as well, then we could have given consent. However, since it was done in an improper manner, we cannot accept them and disregard the traditional Theravada Buddhist traditions of this country.' Opponents of the bhikkhuni revival thus argue that all Sri Lankan nuns are really Mahayana nuns and should not receive formal recognition by the government or monastic authorities. However, in Sri Lanka, a section of the bhikkhu community openly cooperates in bhikkhuni ordinations. Without such cooperation, the revival of bhikkhuni ordination is not sustainable in the long run.

THAILAND

In Thailand and a few other Theravada (conservative) Buddhist countries, women are not allowed to sit beside and touch monks because they are told that they are temptations against the monks' enlightenment.

Women are also not allowed to enter certain sacred sites. Religious institutions opine, women who are abused by their husbands and partners 'are experiencing abuse as results of a previous life's karma'. The religious institutions cannot do anything about it and women must suffer and make more merit in this lifetime.

The fundamentalist view of male supremacy and heteronormativity also influence some Buddhist monks and nuns with regards to people who do not conform to gender and sexual norms. In Thailand, some monks and nuns teach that homosexuals and transgendered people are, like women, paying for their previous life karma because they indulged in inappropriate sexual behaviour. Buddha's original teachings do not see gender or sexual orientation as an issue.

In her study of the position of women in Thai Buddhism, Voramai Kabilsingh remarks, 'it is frequently said, for example, that women were born from their bad karma...many women are convinced that they carry a heavy load of negative karma due to the simple fact of their gender'. As a result of this, says Kabilsingh, 'Thai women seem to accept their suppression without complaint'.

Thai women do not share the cultural expectation or obligation to ordain; nor do they share the expedient institutional or cultural support to do so. Typically, when a man expresses the wish to ordain, he receives public support and encouragement; the same cannot be said for women.

The female renunciates are not designated with the comparable Pali female title of a bhikkhu, that is a bhikkhuni. They are called *mae chi*, this is Thai for 'mother ascetic'. Additionally, while monks receive a Pali *dhamma* name upon ordination, mae chis typically keep their lay names after ordination. The fact that mae chis are not technically part of the Sangha is visually reiterated by their appearance: mae chis don white robes rather than the traditional orange robes worn by bhikkhunis and bhikkhus of the Theravada tradition.

The invisibility of the mae chis in contemporary Thailand is noticeable. Their marginalised existence is due to the fact that many mae chis receive little, if any, familial, social or institutional support for pursuing the monastic path. Most single-sex mae chi nunneries belong to temples and thus fall under the jurisdiction of a bhikkhu sangha. Though mae chis are not technically part of the sangha, they are not wholly independent from it either.

At the institutional level, the ministries of the Thai government disagree over the status of mae chis. The Department of Religious Affairs classifies mae chis as lay women; thus, they do not receive government subsidised medical care or education (as do monks). Moreover, they are excluded from census data and absent from official records. Therefore, obtaining accurate statistical information regarding the mae chi population is problematic. One estimate says they range from 9,000 to more than 20,000 in number.

The Ministry of Communications also considers mae chis to be lay women; thus, mae chis do not reap the travel and transportation benefits allotted to bhikkhus and male novices. However, the Ministry of the Interior groups mae chis under the category of 'skilled ordinands', and thus they are prohibited from voting and political activity. The mae chi status is vague and contradictory, she is a Thai creation.

Prevailing stereotypes of mae chis include abandoned women, elderly women with no place else to go, or women who have failed at love. By and large, with the exception of some remarkable individuals, mae chis as a category 'are not particularly admired or respected'. Fundamentally, the mae chi institution is deemed 'a poor substitute' for the bhikkhuni idea.

In Thailand, feminism and demands for women's human rights are typically regarded as egotistical and aggressive, and are consequently viewed with suspicion and the bhikkhuni movement has been critiqued as a 'western feminist imposition'. Consequently, attempts made by Thai Buddhist women to change Buddhist practices surrounding gender are also seen as an attempt to 'westernise' the religion. According to the scholar Dhammananda, a leading proponent of the bhikkhuni movement in Thailand, mae chi organisations are 'politically motivated not spiritually motivated... The reason she wants to be a bhikkhuni...is for women's rights'. The motive of fighting for equality is deemed not only improper, but also antithetical to realising the spiritual fruits of the monastic life.

From a feminist perspective, mae chis do not emerge as progressive from a secular western feminist standpoint. In large part, this stance reflects adherence to Buddhist teachings and Thai cultural values, allegiance to the mae chi institution, an underlying contentment and satisfaction with mae chis' current role and status, and an implied skepticism that the bhikkhuni role is viable or necessarily carries more social or spiritual efficacy. For many Thai women, feminism emerges as intrinsically and extrinsically foreign and inappropriate for analysing the position and condition of Thai women.

The 12th Sakyadhita Conference in Bangkok, Thailand (June 2011) was held at Sathira Dhammasathan, a mae chi Buddhist community founded by Mae Chi Sansanee, and both mae chis and Thai bhikkhunis were in attendance. However, the mae chis' conservative views regarding gender identity and socio-religious roles in Thai Buddhism challenge the aims and achievements of the contemporary global bhikkhuni movement and basic underlying assumptions about global feminist vision and action.

As Bhikkhu Bodhi explains, when women have never had any role in the sangha for over 700 years that Thailand has been a nation, how is it possible for them to think otherwise. Thais have never known a bhikkhuni sangha. 'The main legal objection that conservative Vinaya legalists raise against a revival of bhikkhuni ordination is that it must be given by an existing bhikkhuni sangha, and to be a purely Theravada ordination, it must come from an existing Theravada bhikkhuni sangha', the scholar adds.

The unassuming monastery in Nakhon Pathom, an hour west of Bangkok, is the only temple in Thailand exclusively devoted to female monks. In 2003, its abbess, Dhammananda became the first Thai woman to ordain as a bhikkhuni in Theravada Buddhism—defying tradition by travelling to Sri Lanka for the ceremony. Her decision sent shockwaves through the deeply conservative Thai

Sangha Council, which explicitly banned the ordination of women in 1928. Technically Bhikkhuni activities are legal in Thailand and the Sangha cannot prevent women from becoming ordained in Sri Lanka and donning the robe. But activists say the government must do more to promote gender equality and the right to freedom of religion—as stipulated by the Thai constitution.

One of the key challenges is amending the 1962 Sangha Act, which excludes women from a number of special privileges afforded to male monks, such as healthcare coverage and public funding for temples. This can have a devastating financial impact on female monastics, forcing them to rely on alternative, sometimes unexpected, sources of funding.

TIBETAN BUDDHISM

Tibetan Buddhism also has an inequality problem, because the bhikkhuni lineages simply never made it to Tibet. No compelling evidence has been produced to indicate that Tibetan Buddhism has ever maintained a complete monastic community that included fully ordained women. But Tibetan women have lived as nuns with partial ordination for centuries.

The American Buddhist feminist scholar of religions, Rita Gross, asserts that male power in Tibetan Buddhism is maintained through the practice of discovering and installing successive reincarnations of the great lamas. No leaders in Tibetan Buddhism are more respected and honoured, or possess more power and influence, than these incarnations, particularly those who are heads of major lineages and prominent monasteries. It is generally taken for granted that each successive incarnation will be a *male* incarnation.

Although accomplished women practitioners existed throughout Tibetan Buddhist history, they did not enjoy the institutional support of their male colleagues. Inadequate androcentric record-keeping has deprived women practitioners from drawing inspiration from female role models and women were increasingly perceived as dangerous and threatening to the status of monks and to authority within the ecclesiastical hierarchy.

Over the past several decades, however, a number of women practitioners of Tibetan Buddhism, ordained as Mula novice nuns, have sought and obtained full-ordination following *Dharmaguptaka Vinaya* procedures preserved in Chinese Mahayana Buddhist societies. Demand for bhikkhuni ordination has led to the administration of several ordination ceremonies in various countries designed to accommodate the needs of international candidates, and to on-going questions among Tibetan Buddhists about whether it is possible and suitable for Tibetan Buddhist monastic groups following *Mula Vinaya* to directly offer full ordination to women.

In the Tibetan tradition, the full ordination of nuns has not been officially sanctioned because it is widely believed the nuns' lineage was never officially established in Tibet, and because, according to a rule in the *Mula-sarvastivadin Vinaya*, ten fully ordained nuns and ten fully ordained monks of an unbroken lineage of transmission must be present in order for a nun to be fully ordained.

The Dalai Lama has made numerous public statements advocating reform, including a message to the Fourth International Conference of Buddhist Women in 1995, which stressed that discrimination against women and other groups must be abandoned because it causes harm. He has also advocated that women be allowed to have full ordination, from the Chinese Mahayana lineages, but he lacks the authority to make a unilateral ruling on that and must persuade other high *lamas* to allow it.

The Dalai Lama suggests that Tibetan Buddhist Dharmaguptaka bhikkhunis conduct certain select functions in Tibetan society in the Tibetan language, following and conforming, as much as humanly possible, to the rest of Tibetan Buddhist society (Chodron). In that way, Dharmaguptaka bhikhuni nuns may be seen publicly to accommodate and uphold the moral perspectives conventional to the Tibetan Buddhist population. As the Dharmaguptaka formal social system condone gender discrimination and paternalism, the Dalai Lama says the nuns should temporarily, as formal ordination procedure requires, observe the patriarchal rules, and then resume self-sufficiency and independent self-governance for the majority of the time thereafter. He also wants this bhikkhuni sangha to become the true and perhaps only feasible refuge in the world for any and all Tibetan Buddhists with genuine universal ethics and a moral perspective seeking to practice a Buddhism that has extirpated itself from gender-based discrimination and domination (at least the majority of the time, full ordination procedures aside). Thus, the community must serve as an inspiration for those yet to entertain such principles, as being a suitable orientation for Vinaya practice. It is an osmosis method of Vinaya transmission.

In 2010, the 17th Gyalwang Karmapa, the spiritual leader of the Karma Kagyu lineage, announced that he is committed to improving women's rights and status, and to fully ordaining women as bhikkhunis in the Tibetan Buddhist tradition (*Damcho*). Other Tibetan leaders have also expressed a desire to improve women's status, but most appear to have more conservative agendas for achieving this. As these developments reveal, Tibetan Buddhism is moving incrementally towards greater gender equality. But at present, negative beliefs about women, and unequal rules and practices remain prevalent, and continue to be widely perpetuated.

The Tibetan Nuns Project

The Tibetan Nunnery Project works for women's empowerment and preservation of Tibetan culture. This can be a huge lesson to Indian Buddhist women and the priests its goals:

> Contribute to the preservation of Tibetan cultural and religious traditions.
>
> Improve the health and living conditions of Tibetan nuns in exile.
>
> Provide traditional as well as modern education for Tibetan women.

Provide highly educated female teachers to the Tibetan Buddhist community and the world at large.

Establish self-sufficient Buddhist nunneries.

Low assessments of women's worth have also been documented in Bhutan, Tibet, India, Sri Lanka, and Nepal. The Tibetan terms for woman, 'of lower birth' (*skye dman*) or 'black one' (*nag mo*), make explicit her lower or stained status. Tibetan refugees interviewed about the common myth have told scholars that it is believed women most resemble the ogress—impetuous, violent, witchlike—while men have inherited the cleverness of the monkey (a revered mythical figure in Tibetan-Chinese folk tradition). Women are said to be plagued by jealousy, greed, anger and desire, while men are more driven by ambition, logic and power. In the local vernacular, men have 'big hearts' (*snying chen mo*) while women have 'small hearts' (*snying chung*). Women are said to be fearful, bashful, and wicked, while men are brave, brash and good.

There is currently a movement in the Tibetan Buddhist tradition to establish full ordination for nuns. Michelle Hannah has criticised the non-Tibetan activists, western and Taiwanese, in this movement. She points out that non-Tibetan activists often lack the understanding about the local situation that ethnic Tibetan Buddhist women face and that ethnic Tibetan Buddhist women may even be barred from speaking for themselves in international platforms.

TAIWAN

The Taiwanese nuns whom Hannah criticises are likely to be feminists and academics and they are among the minority in Taiwan's female Buddhist clergy. One example of Taiwanese Buddhist nuns who actively engage in benefiting and empowering Buddhist women are from the Bhikkhuni Academy—the Bhikkhuni Sangha of Jiuhuashan Daxingshansi or the Daxingshan Nunnery.

Nuns of the Daxingshan Nunnery try to remain as inconspicuous as possible. Unlike many Buddhist establishments in Taiwan, Daxingshan has no website or publications to promote itself. Nevertheless, its fame has spread far and wide. Visitors to Daxingshan Nunnery are generally impressed by the modesty of the nuns; they are poorly dressed and avoid publicity. It also appears that they are aware of the international bhikkhuni movement even though they stay away from Buddhist feminist gatherings. A crucial question is whether the nuns of Daxingshan Nunnery are aware of the international Buddhist feminist movement that has been gaining pace since the late 1980s.

Even in Taiwan, a country where the nuns' status is highest and where nuns and laywomen far outnumber monks and laymen, only two leaders of orthodox Buddhist sects, Master Yin Shun and Master Xing Yun of Buddha's Light International have publicly rejected even part of the *Eight Garudhamma*s and other rules and teachings that imply that women are inferior to men and should be treated as such. Other notable Taiwanese Buddhists who have spoken out openly in favour of gender equality include Shih Chao-hwei, Shih Chuan-dao, Christie (Yu-ling) Chang and Yu-chen Li.

Taiwanese culture is changing quickly, however, and many, if not most, young people do not hold negative views of women. As women's empowerment in the country increases, it seems inevitable that the numbers of Buddhists who support gender equality will also rise.

IN THE WEST

In Buddhist orders in the west, sexism was once a considerable problem. But today approximately half of the teachers and leaders of western Buddhist groups are women and the vast majority of western Buddhists (including many Asians) view women and men equally and treat them as such. Zen monastic orders in the west often are co-ed, with men and women living as equals and calling themselves 'monastics' instead of monk or nun. Most see the unequal rules and negative teachings about women as unacceptable in a modern context, and either reject them as false Dharma or believe they arose due to the influence of androcentric/misogynist social forces in or after the Buddha's time—rather than due to the Buddha's own predilections.

A majority of the ordination lineages in Asia with which most western groups are affiliated, however, remain patriarchal and maintain fundamentalist interpretations of the unequal rules and negative teachings about women. In a number of Buddhist, former Buddhist, Muslim, and Hindu countries, low female status is also associated with unusually high male-to-female ratios at birth. An inequitable culture can also translate into inequitable personal laws. The whole discourse on ordination of women as priests and their subordinate status in the Buddhist religion could lead to the creation of personal laws which does not support the constitutional rights to equality for women in Buddhist and non-Buddhist countries.

Buddhist Culture and Women's Equality

There are several schools from whom the Indian Buddhists can learn how to protect culture as well as bring about gender equality. One of the gifts western bhikkhunis may give their Asian sisters some day is a big dose of feminism.

The Modern Bhikkuni

Today, the bhikkhuni tradition is thriving in parts of Asia. For example, one of the most prominent Buddhists in the world today is a Taiwanese bhikkuni, Dharma Master Cheng Yen, who founded an international relief organisation called the Tzu Chi Foundation. A nun in Nepal named Ani Choying Drolma has established a school and welfare foundation to support her dharma sisters.[7]

Yet, the reality that in many countries, patriarchal orientation reign supreme. At present, the vast majority of Buddhist orders throughout Asia teach that women are inferior to men and have more weaknesses and karmic obstructions. These organisations also discriminate against women in rituals and policies, and so, through their words and actions, teach their followers and cultures to do the same. This is true even in the most liberal Buddhist sects in Taiwan and Korea, where nuns generally enjoy higher standing and better opportunities than in other Asian countries.

A blogpost on Women's Status in Buddhism (ThinkWorth), enumerates discriminations and notes: They are also officially required to cede the positions they are allowed whenever a monk is present. Lay women and nuns are routinely made to eat after men have eaten (that is, to eat their leftovers); to speak after men have spoken; to sit, walk, and stand behind monks and laymen in ceremonies, rituals, classes, and retreats; and to chant, study, and teach sutras that contain disparaging messages about women.

In Dharma classes, and in books written by Buddhist leaders, it is taught that women have more negative qualities and heavier karmic burdens than men, and therefore they cannot become Buddhas. (However, it is usually taught that they can become arahants.) In some orders, the *Eight Garudhammas*—a set of rules in the *Tripiaka* that limit nuns' authority and status and place them under the control of the monks' order—are followed to the letter. Nuns are made to bow down to monks' feet, and even the most senior nuns are required to kowtow to monks who have just been initiated. Prevalent stereotypes, which strongly resemble statements attributed to Sakyamuni in the *Tripiaka* and other sutras, include the views that women are evil, weak, jealous, vain, ignorant, deceitful, short-tempered, sharp-tongued, given to complaining, more attached, less intelligent, less capable and have more karmic obstructions than men. Gender Equality is often dependent on interpretation of the Buddhist texts and doctrines.

IN INDIA

Need for Buddhist Personal Law

Following Independence, the Buddhists in India were clubbed together along with Jains and Sikhs to be governed by the set of four Hindu code bills: the Hindu Marriage Act of 1955 and the

Hindu Succession Act, the Hindu Minority and Guardianship Act and the Hindu Adoptions and Maintenance Act of 1956.

The draft Buddhist Marriage and Succession Act 2007, which deals with various aspects of marriage as per Buddhist traditions has provisions favouring women's causes. The Buddhist Personal Law Action Committee of India is working for the unification and education of the Buddhist community in India on a 'Buddhist Code of Conduct' and a 'Buddhist Personal Law'. It has submitted a memorandum to the President and Prime Minister of India on November 2013 for the 'Enactment' of a Buddhist Personal Law.[8] Once every few years, sections of Maharashtra's Neo-Buddhist community rise up to assert their religious identity by demanding their own personal law, separate from the Hindu Marriage Act that currently governs them.

The Indian Buddhist community has been persistent on this demand for more than fifty years. It is a growing community, with many Dalit Hindu groups voluntarily adopting Buddhism as their religions. Many individual intellectuals too prefer to adopt the Buddhist way of life rather than the Hindu way of life, they aver.

In Maharashtra, Buddhist scholar and a former State minister, Nitin Raut, has been campaigning tirelessly for a separate Buddhist Marriage and Succession Act. 'Lakhs of Buddhist women's legal rights are infringed and married women are helpless, exploited due to non-existence of the Buddhist Marriage Act', according to the 9th Maharashtra State Law Commission report. A Buddhist married woman is not a legal housewife but a 'keep' and her children are illegitimate.

It is a comment that finds an echo in the courts, where Buddhist men are more often than not granted divorce on the ground that marriages performed according to traditional Buddhist rituals are null and void. Raut says, there are about 75,000 such cases pending in the courts. Buddhist marriage are solemnised by a person eligible to solemnise a Buddhist marriage. They are called *bhante*, bhikkhu or a mendicant ie. a Buddhist monk authorised to solemnise marriage according to the Buddhist Marriage Ceremony. It can also be conducted by any Buddhist *upasaka.*

A separate personal law, according to those who support the demand, will ensure that Buddhist marriage rituals are always considered valid in a court of law. In Maharashtra, they claim, there have been several cases in which the High Court or various district courts have deemed Buddhist marriages illegal under the Hindu Marriage Act.

Technically, for a marriage to be registered under the Hindu Marriage Act, the wedding must include the ritual of *saptapadi*, or the seven steps around the holy fire. 'But this is a purely Vedic ritual applicable only to Hindus', say Buddhists. Raut believes that the provisions of customary laws within the Hindu Marriage Act have not been enough to safeguard the legal status of marriages that take place with Buddhist rituals. As examples of how things often go wrong, Raut and other activists frequently cite three landmark cases in the Bombay High Court where marriages of Buddhist couples were declared invalid.

In the Courts

The first court case is the Shakuntala-Nilkanth case of 1973, which involved a woman whose husband had abandoned her and remarried. Shakuntala's maintenance allowance plea was dismissed because the court held that her marriage was not valid. The couple had married through Buddhist rites even though they had not legally converted at the time of marriage and were still 'Hindu' on paper. The High Court ruled that, 'the fact that such marriages are taking place for the last 10 to 15 years is not enough to establish custom'. Judgment was from the Bombay High Court of Judicature at the Nagpur bench in *Smt Shakuntala vs Nilkanth & Others in Criminal Appeal No. 29 of 1970,* decided on 25-10-1972 byJustice Masodkar.

After two other similar cases of Baby-Jagtap in 1981 and Rekha-Ashok in 1985, says Raut, the High Court itself directed the

State government to consider making amendments to the Hindu Marriage Act. 'So far, nothing has been done', he points out.

The validity of marriage by converts to Buddhism in absence of *saptapadi* and *lajja homa mantra* is also a matter of great debate in India.

Hindu Marriage Act of 1955, Sec 7 & Penal Codes

Persons converted to Buddhism from scheduled castes (communities known as SCs/Dalits in India), entering into marriage ceremony comprising worship and garlanding of photographs of Lord Buddha and BR Ambedkar and thereafter reciting the marriage vows before those photographs should be considered valid, the HC said in the rulings in the *Babi w/o Jagtap vs Jayant Mahadeo Jagtap* (in 1981) and *Rekha vs Ashok and Others (in 1985).*

Garlanding each other and taking oath that as wife and husband they would henceforth conduct (accordingly) towards each other, the court said, would make the 'Marriage so performed is legal'. Husband after such marriage, marrying for the second time, commits offence under Sec. 494, it said.

In the Babi judgment in Para 13, the HC said, 'a copy of this Judgment is directed to the Government of Maharashtra Law and Judiciary Department for consideration. The Government of Maharashtra should persuade the Government of India to introduce necessary amendments to the Hindu Marriage Act 1955, as suggested by the Government of Maharashtra State Law Commission in its 9th report on some aspects of the Hindu Marriage Act since the issue effects millions of people and the matter of legitimacy of their children are involved'.

'The case cited was: Code of Criminal Procedure 1973 Section 125, wife's application for maintenance against alleged husband. Parties found as Mahar Hindu by caste. Marriage of Parties performed according to Buddha's rites. No proof of Conversion of Parties to Buddhism. Marriage not legal and applicant held as not entitled to maintenance under section 125

CrPC.' The High Court noted that by this ruling, women suffer if marriage is described as 'null and void' thus leading to rejection of provision of maintenance.

The High Court pointed out that such judgments 'created doubt in the minds of the people. Whether such marriages are valid or invalid? And created a confusion in the minds of the people whether the marriages which have been solemnised according to the Buddhist Ceremony are valid or otherwise'. Lakhs of Buddhist marriages have been held invalid in Maharashtra because of such court judgements.

A stage has been reached when codification at least of the law of Marriage and Succession have become virtually indispensable for fundamental changes, which have become inevitable to furnish fair and equitable solution to some of the most controversial questions in relation to the laws of marriage and succession of Buddhists in India.

A new Law for Property of a Female Buddhist

In India, the need for a new property and successions act is also felt, as the present Hindu Successions Act under which Buddhist fall is deemed to be inadequate.

> The Buddhist Personal Law Action Committee's draft proposal says: Any property possessed by a female Buddhist, whether acquired before or after the commencement of this Act, shall be held by her as full owner thereof and not as a limited owner.
>
> 'Property' includes both movable and immovable property acquired by a female Buddhist by inheritance or devise, or at a partition, or in lieu of maintenance or arrears of maintenance, or by gift from any person, whether a relative or not, before, at or after her marriage, or by her own skill or exertion, or by purchase or by prescription, or in any other manner whatsoever, and also any such property held by her as *stree dhana* immediately before the commencement of this Act.
>
> Nothing contained in subsection (1) of the Hindu Succession Act shall apply to any property acquired by way of gift or under

a will or any other instrument or under a decree or order of a civil court or under an award where the terms of the gift will or other instrument or the decree, order or award prescribe a restricted estate in such property.

In the case of *Baivijaya vs Thakuribai Chela bha in AIR 1979 SC 993,* the Supreme Court of India ruled that the recommended subsection (1) of Hindu Succession Act recognises equality of sexes and 'elevates the women from subservient position in the field of economy to a higher pedestal. Now the women can enjoy and have full powers as regards disposal of property held by them. They are to be taken as owners without putting any artificial limitations on their right of ownership'.

As of now the general rules of succession for female Buddhist are:

1. The Property of a female Buddhist dying intestate shall devolve according to the rules set out in section 14 of the Hndu Succession Act. a. Firstly, upon the sons and daughters (including the children of any predeceased son or daughter) and the husband. b. Secondly, upon the heirs of the husband. c. Thirdly, upon the mother and father. d. Fourthly, upon the heirs of the father and e. Lastly, upon the heirs of the mother.
2. Notwithstanding anything contained in sub-section (1):
   a. Any property inherited by a female Buddhist from her father or mother shall devolve, in the absence of any son or daughter of the deceased (including the children of any pre-deceased son or daughter) not upon the other heirs referred to in subsection (1) in the order specified therein, but upon the heirs of the father, and
   b. Any property inherited by a female Buddhist from her husband or from her father-in-law shall devolve, in the absence of any son or daughter of the deceased (including the children of any pre-deceased son or daughter) not upon the other heirs referred to in

sub-section (1) in the order specified therein, but upon the heirs of the husband.

The order of Succession among the heirs referred to in section 13 shall be, and the distribution of the intestate's property among those heirs shall take place, according to the following rules namely:

Rule 1. Among the heirs specified in subsection (1) of section 13 HAS. Those in one entry shall be preferred to those in any succeeding entry and those including in the same entry shall take simultaneously.

Rule 2. If any son or daughter of the intestate had pre-deceased the intestate leaving his or her own children alive at the time of the intestate's death, the children of such son or daughter shall take between them the share which such son or daughter would have taken if living at the intestate's death.

Rule 3. The devolution of the property of the intestate on the heirs referred to in clause (b) (d) & (e) of subsection in subsection (2) of section 13 of the Hindu Succession Act shall be in the same order and according to the same rules as would have applied if the property had been the father's or mother's or the husband's as the case may be, and such person has died intestate in respect thereof immediately after the intestate's death.

Need for Uniform Code vs Religious Laws

While Raut's demand for a separate Buddhist marriage law focuses heavily on these cases of 'wronged' couples, other community leaders see the issue as simply a matter of identity.

'Buddhism is entirely different from Hinduism. The point of converting with Babasaheb was to assert that we are not Hindus anymore', says Jogendra Kawade, president of the Peoples Republican Party and former MP from Nagpur. 'We don't walk around holy fires. Our marriage rituals need legal recognition of their own.'

For Prakash Ambedkar and his supporters, however, this idea of a separate law for Buddhists is against the spirit of Ambedkar's teachings. 'Babasaheb strongly believed that there should be a common personal code for people of all religions', says Ambedkar, referring to his grandfather's decision to resign from the Cabinet in 1951 when the government refused to pass his inclusive draft of the Hindu Code Bill. Muslims, Parsis and Jews already had their own personal laws, but with the Hindu bill, Ambedkar did not want codes that favoured any one kind of conservative Hinduism.

The current version of the Hindu Code Bills, amended over the years, is more inclusive than they originally were. 'Today the inheritance laws in the Hindu Succession Act, for instance, give women equal right to property and reflect the spirit of Buddhism that Babasaheb had envisioned', Sandeep Nandeshwar, a lawyer working at the Nagpur bench of the High Court points out. 'We don't really need a separate Buddhist law.'

Some community leaders believe that the government's committee to look into the issue of a separate personal law for Buddhists was appointed without widespread consultation with the community, and claim that the demand by Raut, Kawade and others is politically motivated. 'The feeling of community identity among Buddhists is a little weak in Maharashtra right now, so a small section of radical Buddhist leaders is demanding a separate law', says Maruti Kumbhar, Mumbai president of the Satyashodhak OBC Parishad, an organisation that is trying to convert Other Backward Castes to Buddhism.

According to Nandeshwar, there can simply be no legal debate about his view that Maharashtra must not have a separate law for Buddhists. 'There are many Buddhists outside the State and personal laws are clearly a national subject', he maintains. 'The State has no power to make laws for specific religions.'

Many features of Buddhism are more emancipatory than Hinduism for women and the need for separate Buddhist personal law can be thus justified. The debate, however, is still on whether a separate personal law is required for Buddhists or a Uniform Civil Code for the entire country, as Ambedkar would have liked it.

Conclusion

There is a deep contradiction between a hidden tradition of extremely accomplished female practitioners and the institutional preference for male practitioners. Nowhere is this better illustrated than in the *yogini-tantras* of Tantric Buddhism. Miranda Shaw notes that in Tantric Buddhism, the male principle is the consort to the female (199). Nevertheless, there is a great disparity between what ancient texts reveal and what some current Tibetan lamas articulate.

Tantras have a gynocentric world view which focuses on women as worthy of honour and respect. Those desiring to practice tantra must follow and accept this philosophy. Shaw concludes that people who pronounce upon the inferiority of women are generally monks who have built up a psychological resistance to women. Notwithstanding the favourable doctrinal attitude towards women, as illustrated by yogini-tantras and the profusion of female deities (for example, Tara, Vajrayogini and Kurukulla) in Tibetan Buddhist iconography, ambiguity still characterises the Tibetan Buddhist approach toward females, especially in connection with their monastic status.

According to the Dalai Lama, efforts need to be made to convene international conferences about this subject, but so far a clear conclusion has not been reached. The question of whether *gelong-ma*s (bhikkhunis or fully ordained nuns) can be ordained is something that must be determined by the sangha.

'However, regarding the opportunity for nuns to study—in India, nuns now have the opportunity to study the full curriculum leading to the *geshe-ma* degree. Some of the nuns in India have been studying for 17 or 18 years now and are making excellent progress. Jangchub Choeling is one of the best nunneries for getting a geshe-ma education', the Dalai Lama has said.

'I want you to consider yourselves as being totally equal to the men. In the *lamrim* (graduated stages of the path to awakening), one of the eight favourable qualities of an ideal human rebirth is being born male. But this is only in a physical sense, because men have stronger bodies than women. In terms of intellect, women and men are exactly the same. In fact, in terms of loving-kindness, women have a greater biological tendency to feel love and compassion. So, in this regard, you may be able to develop love and compassion more easily than men. In the world today, the quality of loving-kindness is rare, so it is especially important for women to contribute to the well-being of the world. It is not something that we Tibetans can resolve on our own. It needs to be resolved commonly by Buddhist countries in this world.'

According to the Dalai lama, discussion has been on for several years that Tibetan Buddhism should gradually allow the nuns to become geshe-ma (female *geshes*) 'after they have studied and passed the geshe examinations in whatever two or three fields (treatises) they have specialised in… if we can have *gelong-ma* (bhikkhuni), we can also have geshe-ma'. 'There are not only nunneries [among] us Tibetans, but several exist also [in other areas of Tibetan culture] from Ladakh in the west all the way to Mon [Arunachal Pradesh] in the east. In general, [the tradition of nuns is] not limited to Buddhist [culture] alone but can be found in several [other] countries'.

The world's tallest Buddhist leader, speaking at a conference on Women in Buddhism at the University of Hamburg in 2007, said:

> Warfare has traditionally been carried out primarily by men, since they seem better physically equipped for aggressive behaviour. Women, on the other hand, tend to be more caring and more sensitive to others' discomfort and pain. Although men and women have the same potentials for aggression and warm-heartedness, they differ in which of the two more easily manifests. Thus, if the majority of world leaders were women,

> perhaps there would be less danger of war and more cooperation on the basis of global concern – although, of course, some women can be difficult! I sympathise with feminists, but they must not merely shout. They must exert efforts to make positive contributions to society.

In 2009, at the National Civil Rights Museum in Memphis, Tennessee the DalaiLama said: I call myself a feminist. Isn't that what you call someone who fights for women's rights?

In 2007 he said that the next Dalai Lama could possibly be a woman, remarking, 'If a woman reveals herself as more useful, the lama could very well be reincarnated in this form'.

The Buddha did not place any premium on virginity. He admitted all classes, married, unmarried, widows and even prostitutes. Women from all walks of life, young and old, rich and poor, Brahmins and non-Brahmins were all admitted and had equal status in the Sangha. After conversion to Buddhism, the custom of *devadasi*s stopped completely in families converting to Buddhism, the spiritual leader pointed out.

Buddhist communities that preserve and condone archaic practices of domination and discrimination must ask themselves if they are thoroughly abandoning suffering and all of its causes, he has said. Buddhist ethics systems that fail to comprehend and accept contemporary socio-moral conventions upholding the dignity of all human beings equally will be of limited benefit to humanity, so long as they refuse to admit the beneficial moral imperatives of the societies they inhabit, he warns.

The Parsis in India

THERE ARE certain features that distinguish Parsis from other communities in India. The first Persians came to India from ancient Persia. The community that lives in India today trace back to references in the *Qissa-i Sanjan*. Followers of prophet Zoroaster, the Parsis migrated from Greater Iran to Gujarat, where they were given refuge between the 8th and 10th century CE, to avoid persecution by Muslim conquerors of Persia.

The Parsis are a very progressive community. Men and women are highly educated. For example, mean age of marriage is very high in contrast to other communities. People marrying outside the fold of the Parsi community are also very high. The percentage of never married men and women and childless women are high in the Parsi community. Estimated growth rate of Parsis in India since 1911 is also in the negative. Percentage of population below 14 is 10.4 in contrast to 35.3 all over India. Birth rate has been declining among Parsis.

Despite many progressive trend, women are far from equal in community and are discriminated in the personal laws. Some post-independence reforms were brought about, they were far from adequate.

Reforms in Parsi Personal Laws

During the eighties, while India was witnessing the emergence of a new women's movement, alongside there was the emergence of movements to bring about reform in various personal laws. The process for reform was initiated by the Board trustees of the Bombay Parsi Panchayat.[1] The BPP submitted the recommendations to the government. Most political decisions are taken by the Panchayat.[2]

While the amendment to the marriage laws was passed in 1988, the amendment to succession laws had to be shelved and was enacted in 1991, during the Congress rule. The provisions of marriage and divorce were modified along the lines of the Hindu Marriage Act. The grounds for divorce were further liberalised and divorce by mutual consent was introduced. The disparity between the rights of legitimate and illegitimate children was abolished. In 1991, by amending the succession laws, the discrimination between female and male descendants was abolished.

At each juncture, the process of reforms was initiated from within the Parsi community and a broad consensus was reached before the Bills were introduced. This was because Parsis are a small community which has no representation in Parliament, so first a consensus was needed within. Finally, when the Bills were presented to the legislature, they were passed unanimously without much debate. This is because on issues of equity Parsis in India have generally taken a sensible stand and thus there was not much confrontation within the community.[3] However, women from the community were conspicuously absent from the discourse.

Although the community is liberal and holds a progressive stand on women's issues, women's names do not figure in any phase of the reform.[4] This has been because till lately women have been conspicuously absent from Bombay Parsi Panchayat and other Parsi bodies. In fact, only in 2009 adult franchise was introduce in election of the BPP, which until then was composed of donors.

Although gender justice was the stated agenda, the motive of reform seems to be dual: (i) maintaining a separate community identity and once this is achieved (ii) ensuring that the laws do not lag far behind the dominant ideology—that is, the pre-independence period British statutes and Hindu Marriage Act of post-independence India.

Since the Hindu marriage Act grants the husband a right to maintenance, the same was also introduced in the Parsi laws.

Under the Special Marriage Act of 1954, husbands do not have a similar right. It is significant to note that the reform followed the provisions of the Hindu law rather than the Special Marriage Act, which is a secular legislation and more beneficial to women than the Hindu Marriage Act.

Moreover, even while modernising the statutes, the community has maintained its hold over matrimonial matters by retaining the jury system introduced in 1865. Constituting a special Parsi Matrimonial Court causes severe hardships and delays to the litigants. In the Bombay High Court, the Parsi Matrimonial Court is constituted twice a year and functions for about a week during each term.

The debate in Parliament when the Bills were enacted has been cursory. The members did not concern themselves with the implication of the Bills for Parsi women. The debate was essentially confined to two spheres: (i) now that the Parsis have willingly modified their laws, it is time to enact a Uniform Civil Code (ii) praises for the Parsi community that they are an enlightened and progressive community and thereby insinuating that other communities (more specifically the Muslims) are backward and reactionary. The fact that the Parsi community has also opposed the imposition of a UCC and the Adoption Bill, that they retain the jury system in matrimonial adjudication and that relief of divorce by consent was introduced as late as in 1988, did not even figure in the debates.

Discrimination in Parsi Personal Law

Though Parsi community is referred to by many as 'post-feminist', several areas are still discriminatory within the Parsi personal law.

Inter-Faith Marriages

Among the Parsi community, no issue is more controversial than the exclusion of offsprings of a 'mixed marriage', that is where one parent is a Parsi and the other is not, from all rights. Within a wider scope, the issue extends to questions of gender equality (whether males and females are to be treated differently), exclusion of women (and men if the gender equality question is taken into account) that marry out of the community.

Whether Zoroastrians who are not Parsis have a right to use the Parsi-Zoroastrian facilities such as the Fire Temples and Towers of Silence is also a matter of debate. The Parsi marriage and divorce acts are discriminatory against women.[5]

Inte-caste marriages among the miniscule community of Parsis, specially highly educated and economically independent Parsi women, are increasing day by day. A large number of Parsi boys going to foreign countries for higher studies do not return to India but settle down in those countries to improve their prospects in life. Thereby the community in India loses the educated youth. This causes a dearth of suitable spouses for educated Parsi women, ultimately leading them to engage in inter-faith marriages.

However, the orthodox sections within the community have been denying rights to people who marry out of the community's fold. This discrimination is faced more by women than men who inter-marry. The children of the men married to a non-Parsi Zoroastrian do not seem to face any discrimination or rejection by the priests and the community. Women often face discrimination in ceremonies and have been denied rights on marrying outside the community.Navjote ceremony is denied to children of Parsi women married to a non-Parsi. An example is the use of the *baughs* and *agiaries*, which are not available to inter-married ladies for Navjote ceremonies or wedding dinners.

There was an incidence in 1990, when a young Parsi Zoroastrian woman died tragically in a car accident, leaving behind a non-Parsi husband and two children. The natural instinct of her parents was to consign her body to the Tower of Silence and perform her last rites as she was a practicing Zoroastrian and had married under the Special Marriage Act of 1952. The Parsi Panchayat trustees refused to accept the body of Roxan Darshan Shah at the *Dokhma* despite being assured by her parents that she was a practicing Zoroastrian and had married under the SMA. The trustees presumed that she had converted to Hinduism subsequent to her marriage under the Special Marriage Act. The Parsi Panchayat was caught in the crossfire between the community's orthodox and liberal factions. High priests, eminent lawyers and certain section of the community opposed the move by the parents.

The high priest said that all inter-faith married women were engaged in 'adultery' and their children were subsequently 'illegitimate bastards'. 'Hysterical rhetoric was heard at hurriedly called meetings to ban the inter-married ladies' access to all fire-temples.' When it was brought to the notice of the orthodox that Parsi men married to non-Parsis should also be included in the ban, they half-heartedly agreed to include them in the denouncement. This is because Parsis are largely a patriarchal society. The orthodox high priests held that according to the holy dictates, texts, customs and traditions of the religion, a women married to a non-Parsi Zoroastrian under civil law cannot be considered a Parsi Zoroastrian after such marriage, and hence she cannot take advantage of or make use of any religious institutions like the Fire-temple or Tower of Silence. Eventually, this highly respected high priest was dismissed from his post. This particular incident is, however, not representative of all the priests.

Several liberals within the community feel that it is high time that this obnoxious and individual custom which now prevails, and which is invalid and unconstitutional and against the basic human rights of the Parsi mother and the spirit of the Zoroastrian religion, is now put to an end by the panchayat board trustees.

The community had sought the opinion of the then Chief Justice of India, YV Chandrachud, whom the panchayat had consulted on the legal niceties arising from the situation. In his first draft, Chandrachud is said to have opined that the trustee's presumption of Roxan's conversion to Hinduism was unjustified and that her marriage under the SMA entitled her to claim her rights to the use of community properties, in this case the dokhma.

In the meanwhile, 32 Parsi womens married to non-Zoroastrians wrote to the Panchayat requesting an assurance that, as they have married under the SMA and have continued to profess the Zoroastrian faith, on death they will be interred at the *Doongerwadi* without undue stress to their families. Claiming equal rights with men who are married to non-Parsis, the women also demanded that their children be permitted to witness the obsequies.

Homi Taleyarkhan, member of the Government of India's Minorities Commission, wrote in the *Bombay Samachar* that, '...we have got through laws in Parliament for the removal of discrimination between the sexes by having several laws affecting the Parsi community amended. On the other hand, by denying a Parsi woman, the wife of a non-Parsi, her right to the Tower of Silence on her death, we are perpetuating such discrimination'. Another scholar in the same paper opined that, 'undoubtedly, where the civil laws are not clear, it is permissible to resort to religious prescription to resolve a doubt—as was done in the case of *Sir Dinshaw M Petit vs Jamsetji Jejeebhoy* (known as the Parsi Punchayat case). But where civil law is clear, religious prescriptions are immaterial. Thus, for example, Hindu law as revealed in the Shastras advocates sati, prohibits a Hindu widow's remarriage and excludes females from inheritance to a man's estate. Civil law has now changed this. Can a Hindu contend that that the Shastras continue to prevail? Child marriage was practiced in all communities including Parsis. But no one can say it is still legal. Parsis were also a polygamous community earlier, but no one can contend so now. A priest is entitled to express his views and act by beliefs, but he has no right to foist them on others in defiance of civil law. A trustee cannot act contrary to civil law'.

At its core, the conflict is a manifestation of centuries-old anxieties and fears of assimilation and the loss of identity. Those in favour for restriction of the term 'Parsi' or even 'Zoroastrian' to only those whose parents are both Parsis/Zoroastrians are most numerous among those that come from deeply conservative backgrounds, in particular (but not always) among the priesthood and the priestly class (the *Athornan*). These conservative Parsis are largely settled in Mumbai and Gujarat. Consequently, the exclusionist stance is frequently equated with fundamentalism and its by-products of social and religious intolerance. Inversely, the inclusionist stance, ie. that Zoroastrianism is a world-religion not limited by boundaries of gender, race or national origin, is denigrated as 'heterodox', and its defenders are accused of being 'anti-traditional' and 'neo-liberal'.

The official position of the community is often one of exclusion. This is, however, not necessarily a stance that has been democratically determined since the panchayat or *anjumans* (the local trusts that manage and maintain community property—primarily the Towers of Silence—and administrate policy as to their use) are predominantly conservative, usually having five priests on a nine-member board.

In accordance with Indian statutes, the anjumans have the domestic authority over trust properties and have the right to grant, prohibit or restrict entry and use. Thus, they can (and do) legally prohibit their use by anyone they might consider unentitled, or—in the case of properties administered by less exclusionist trustees—the priests employed at that facility make their opinion known by other means, for instance, by refusing to recite the names of half-Parsis or non-Parsi spouses during the *tan-darosti*.

In cities with larger Parsi communities, there is almost certainly at least one fire temple run by priests that are not exclusionist. In any event, the Zoroastrian faith does not prescribe worship in a fire temple, so—in principle—a Zoroastrian who has been banned from entry to a particular temple could worship from his/her own home. Self-help groups such as the Association of Inter-Married

Zoroastrians for 'those who still believe that equality is a basic tenet of Zoroastrianism' attempt to ensure that the 'rights of intermarried Parsis are not compromised' by organising the initiation rites (Navjote) for children of mixed parentage or by maintaining a list of fire temples where Parsi spouses of mixed marriages are not ostracised. Nonetheless, with respect to last rites and use of the Towers of Silence, the anjumans continue to be selective about who may be interred according to Zoroastrian tradition.

Recent years have also seen an increasing unwillingness in the communities to accept a priests' exclusionary stance. Where a priest's opinion had previously been accepted as canon, this is gradually changing with respect to who may and who may not be considered a Parsi.

The priests in Calcutta, for instance, have for decades been pragmatic when it came to implementing the exclusionary stance of their superiors in Navsari—they 'import' priests from Jamshedpur when ceremonies need to be performed for individuals that would otherwise not be considered eligible.

Conversion

Conversion is not acceptable to orthodox sections within the Parsi community. According to them, Parsi personal law does not accept conversion. A large number of orthodox Indian Parsis have said a resounding 'no' to taking 'outsiders' into their fold, arguing that conversion goes against the tenets of the religion.[6] And they are a strong voice, since over 69,000 of the estimated 1.25 lakh-strong community lives in India.

According to orthodox Zoroastrian scholar Khojste Mistree, conversion is not advocated in Zoroastrianism. So, those advocating the move 'are not adding to numbers within the Parsi community as conversions go against the tenets of our religion'. Mistree had opposed the proposal to form a world body that will have both Zoroastrians and 'converts' and encourages conversion. A controversy was sparked about Indian Parsis joining the new world body. Mistree argues that to begin with, the term 'fire-temple' is a misnomer for what can, at best, only be a prayer hall. He explains that an *agiari* can only be consecrated by the highest echelons of the clergy, after three weeks of rituals. According to Mistree, a group of renegade priests officiating in a cult movement certainly don't qualify.[7]

The proposed world body includes the Association of North American Zoroastrians, Zoroastrians' Federation of Europe, some groups based in Australia, Singapore and China and some Parsi anjumans from India.The issue of forming this organisation was raised at a meeting of the Federation of Parsi Zoroastrians' Anjumans of India (FPZAI) in 2004. It resulted in a split in the federation. In a letter to all anjumans, the Ahmedabad Parsi Panchayat president and FPZAI vice-president, Areez Khambatta said, 41 out of 69 member-anjumans of the federation are 'against joining such a world body'. High priests of the Parsi community too came out against the decision. Seven high priests in India wrote to the FPZAI that the proposed body that encouraged conversions, did not have their sanction. They opined that the move was unacceptable to them as the body would have 'self proclaimed converts' who could not be accepted into the fold.

However, there have been attempts within the community by liberals to include the non-Parsis within their fold. Individuals like Ali Jaffree in North America have been converting people to Zoroastrianism.[8] On *Khordad Sal*, Prophet Zarathustra's birthday, a group of Parsis quietly inaugurated a new 'universal agiari' or Fire Temple in a Colaba apartment. It was for the first time in the community's history that a temple was thrown open to non-Parsis. Almost a hundred people, both Parsis and non-Parsis, turned up for the agiari's *jashan* and the *humbandagi*—traditional prayers recited strictly for and by Parsis. The prophet encouraged conversion, but Parsi women who marry outside the fold are still pariahs, debarred from fire temples, from converting their families.[9]

Dwindling numbers—the census recorded 69,601 at last count—have prompted progressive Parsis to adopt a more practical approach, says Kerssie Wadia, a trustee of the radical Association for Revival of Zoroastrianism (ARZ), which spearheaded the universal agiari.[10] Parsi women who are stopped from attending ceremonies in agiaries and fire temple can appeal to the courts and the courts, on the principle of equity, will not accept orthodox line followed by some Parsis. In a case when the Parsi Panchayat tried to stop some women from entering Dokhma, the courts upheld women's rights and allowed them to attend the *Dokhmenishini* ceremony. The court said, '...while the Parsi race could die out in a few decades, we cannot allow our great religion to do the same'.

ARZ was formed to fight discrimination against women. In its first three years ARZ performed 200 Navjotes. Vispy Wadia says, the ARZ is very similar to the Hindu Arya Samaj, which is also reformist in nature.

The solution is to admit non-Parsi spouses and children of community members into the clan. Already, Parsi priests have started offering ritual services at Navjots, marriages and funerals for a sizeable number of ostracized clients. Wadia points out that orthodox priests initiated a French woman Suzanne into the Parsi religion in 1905, but they disallowed conversion. According to ARZ trustees, it is for more of social rather than religious cause that the orthodox sections have been opposing conversion. These sections want to avoid division in charity, trust and housing facilities. They insist their movement has no personal agenda: All six trustees of the ARZ are married to true-blue Parsis. Crishna, a founder member of the Association of Intermarried Zoroastrians (AIMZ), has pointed out that Zarathustra wanted his devotees to spread his gospel to the four corners of the Earth. Parsi religion can be followed as the Prophet preached it.

By claiming that conversion is prohibited in their scriptures, the Parsi clergy have also prevented any debate on the important issue of the community's diminishing population as it is linked to the issue of conversion. The question of conversion tends to divide the community to such an extent that even genuinely good Parsis, who are otherwise kind and loving, are prepared to disown their sons or daughters if they get married outside the community, and are not prepared to do the Navjot of their grand children, as they consider it as a conversion.

Orthodox Parsis argue that Parsis have preserved separate racial identity over the centuries and have distinguished themselves. They should not allow Parsi identity to be diluted or submerged in the vast country that is India by allowing open conversion.

A organisation calling itself the World Alliance of Parsi-Irani Zarthoshtis (WAPIZ) has been formed to prevent any persons who are not pure Parsi Zorastrians entry from the back door and because the World Zoarastrian Organisation does not restrict its membership to only Parsi-Irani Zorastrians.

If one were to look at work of scholars and learned high priests and examine the old records to see what the most eminent scholars of the 19th and 20th century have said and done, we find that scholars such as Shenshai high priest Dasturji Jamaspi Minochurji Jamas Asa, Shenshai high priest Dastur Peshotan Sanjana, KR Cama and several others favoured mixed marriages, conversion and the Navjote ceremony. These are a few of the examples where the most eminent scholars and dasturs have openly admitted that conversion is permitted and actully performed it, not selectively for rich persons only but even for the dock worker of Mazgaon. Later, those who had the courage to openly state and practice conversion like Dasturj Bode were ridiculed and ostracised. Since the average Parsi could not read the original scriptures, they accepted what the high priests and pseudo scholars told them.

Once it is clear that Parsi religion does not prohibit conversion, then the debate becomes one of the desirability for conversion from the social standpoint. Even if it is permitted, should they encourage it?

This issue needs to be examined from a purely social aspect, viz the issue of the survival of the community as its numbers are diminishing rapidly and what measures, including selective conversion, should be considered to preserve the community. The debate should be among sociologists and demographers and medical experts and not amongst priests and religious scholars, as it has been so far. Liberal Parsis feel that it is very necessary for the educated Parsis, who realise how the community is declining in numbers, to start to consider how they can go beyond the traditional remedies to slow down the decline in the Parsi population. It is not in Parsi interest to allow the community to get wiped out. They need out of box thinking for survival.

Discriminatory Adoption Laws

Parsis have no general law of adoption in India. Adoption was made illegal way back in 1908 in the *Dinshaw Petit (Sir) vs Jamsetji Jeejeebhoy (Sir)1909, ILR 33 Bom 509* case. In order to prevent the Parsi trust property and fire temples from going away from the Parsi fold, in the *Saklat vs Bella 1925 ILR 53* case, the court held that in a marriage between a Parsi woman and a non-Parsi man, there is a presumption that the wife will have to accept the religious faith of her husband. So, it would follow that the children will be brought up according to the religion of the father.

Adoption is violently opposed by the orthodox Parsi body.[11] Government can only pass a law when some kind of consensus emerges among Parsis. Parsi couples anxious to adopt a Parsi child find it extremely difficult to find one (specially a male child). This has left them with no alternative but to adopt a non-Parsi child. But the non-Parsi child is not entitled to the benefits of a Parsi. A non-Parsi child adopted by a Parsi will not automatically become a Parsi. Consequently such a child is not entitled to enjoy rights and privileges available to a natural born child and other members of the Parsi community.[12] The non-Parsi child cannot be taken into Zoroastrian faith by performing his Navjote ceremony, since that wiil amount to conversion of a non-Parsi child into the Zoroastrian faith, which is not permissible under the long-standing custom against conversion.

As per the Parsi customary practice, the adopted non-Parsi child is not entitled to rights which are otherwise available to a Parsi child. This child cannot on attaining majority get married, ried to a Parsi undergoing the *ashirvad* ceremony under the Parsi Marriage and Divorce Act, 1936, which applies only when both the spouses are Parsis. Persons belonging to different religions, castes or communities have their marriages solemnised under the Special Marriage Act, 1954 without renouncing their religion. Inter-caste marriages (known as civil marriages) almost invariably take place under this Act. The child cannot claim any right or benefit under the trusts or schemes related to *atash beram*, agiaries, *dar-e-meher*, baug, dakhmas, *aramgahs*, cemeteries etc meant for Parsi Zoroastrians only, eg. for jashan, *afringan*, *geh saran* and *uthamna* ceremonies.

Inheritance

The right of adopted non-Parsi child to inheritance is not recognised by community customs. Similarly a *behedin* (Parsi) child adopted by an *athorman* (priestly class) will not on adoption automatically become an athorman. The non-parsi child cannot claim inheritance rights. Such a child can make such a claim if a bequest is made to him under the will of the deceased parent.[13]

All these disabilities create an embarrassing situation for an adopted child being a non-Parsi vis-à-vis the adopted child being a Parsi under the Parsi law applicable to Parsis.The courts too, in some of the cases, have held that adoption is not allowed within the Parsi culture.

The Bombay High Court in 1929 held that although in the Baroda State a custom prevailed among the Parsis of taking a *palak* (adopt) son, such custom could not be recognised in respect of succession to immovable property in British India. In 1998, the

Bombay High Court held that the Parsi community does not have any right to adopt children. It is thus authoritatively laid down by the High Court that *the custom of adoption does not prevail among the Parsis residing in India.*[14]

The premise that gender equity was not the primary object is substantiated by the retention of certain outdated discriminatory notions inherited from the British statutes in 1865. The law provides for settling the property of an adulterous woman in favour of the children (Sec 50). The statute also treats women as legal minors and provides for a trust to be set up in respect of the maintenance allowance with the power to restrain women's access to maintenance.

In the Bombay High Court, the Parsi Matrimonial Court with a jury system is constituted twice a year and functions about a week during each term.

Parsi Women as Priests

Noshir Dadrawala, one of the trustees of the Bombay Parsi Panchayat, points out, 'Nowhere is it mentioned that women cannot become priests, but it is also true that traditionally there were no women priest amongst the Parsis. It is like any other religion where certain rituals like touching of the holy books is not allowed during the monthly cycle of women'.

The prominent researcher and university professor, Katyoon Mazdapoor notes the significant role of women in Zoroastrian society and says, 'although throughout history there is no mention of female Mobeds, but women always had an important role in the safe-keeping and guarding of the religion'.

In February 2011, in the Tehran Mobeds Anjuman, (Anjoman-e-Mobedan) for the first time in history of the Zoroastrian communities worldwide, eight women have joined the group of *mobeds* (priests) in Iran as *mobedyars* (lady priests).These mobedyars are well educated and have passed all the religious tests set by the Mobeds Anjuman on religious matters.Esfandiayr Ekhtiyary, representative of the Zoroastrians in Iran's Parliament, said on the occasion: Today is an auspicious day because we learn what it means in reality when Zoroaster said that females and males have equal status... we have many educated females and they are qualified to be Mobedyar.

Mobed Ardeshir Khoshridan comments, 'after Sweden, it is the Parsis and the Zoroastrian societies that have the lowest illiteracy rate and this achievement is due to women's efforts. They now hold a certificate and apart from the lower-rung religious functions, they can even initiate people into the religion'.

But in India, women priests are absent as it is not accepted by the patriarchal system here. Vipsy Wadia argues, *if Iran, despite being an Islamic republic, can have Zoroastrians being this liberal, why not in democratic India?* It is the so-called orthodox who are of the view that only males can become priests.

State and the Parsi Community

In 2009, a Public Interest Litigation, perhaps the first of its kind, was admitted in the Gujarat High Court where a Parsi woman married to a non-Parsi sought the court's intervention to avail the fundamental right to worship and to access the religious places of Parsis she was denied by her community after her marriage.

The petition was filed by Goolrokh Adi Contractor, now Goolrokh Mahipal Gupta, who married a non-Parsi in 1991. Following her marriage, she was denied entry to the Parsi religious temple, agiari, as well stopped from participation in Parsi rituals. She approached the court seeking directions to the authorities of the Fire Temple in Mota Pariwad in Valsad and to other members of community to allow her in the agiari.

Goolrokh feared that the trustees of the agiari, which belongs to the Valsad Parsi Anjuman Trust, would deny her entry even when her elderly parents die and would restrain her from performing their last rites.

According to the petition, Goolrokh continuously practiced Zoroastrian religion both before and after her marriage and has not changed her religion to Hindu. She contended that being an Indian citizen, barring her from following her religion and to stop her from enjoying privileges of the religion were violations of the rights given by the Constitution of India. She added that there was no scripture or text book denying Parsi women their rights to worship and practice the religion after marriage to a non-Parsi.

Goolrokh had, therefore, asked the High Court for directions to the Respondents to allow her to enter and worship in the Fire Temple and to participate in the funeral ceremonies at the Tower of Silence for her old parents. The respondents claimed that as per Parsi tradition, Parsi women married to non-Parsis are barred from entering religious places such as agiari and the Tower of Silence and performing rites and rituals.

The High Court ruled that the petitioner ceased to be a Parsi Zoroastrian on account of her marriage to a non-Parsi (even though she married under the SMA) and, consequently, her prayers on the basis of her status as a Parsi Zoroastrian did not require consideration.

This verdict was challenged in the apex court on the ground that, 'The Special Marriage Act, 1954 was enacted as a special legislation to provide for a special form of marriage by registration which does not require either party to the marriage to renounce his/her religion'.

The petitioner contended that the decision of the Gujarat High Court is in violation of the fundamental rights guaranteed under Articles 14, 15, 21 and 25 of the Indian Constitution and Sec 4 of the SMA. Goolrokh challenged the proposition of the Gujarat High Court that the wife would automatically acquire the religion of her husband on marriage, alleging that it amounted to the denial of the fundamental right of the woman to freely profess and practice her religion as guaranteed under Article 25 of the Constitution.

Alleging that the interpretation of the High Court tantamount to relegating 'women to the class of cattle' she also contended that the 'feudal concept that a woman loses her legal identity on marriage, and it merges with the identity of her husband, is no longer acceptable today'. In December 2017, the Supreme Court in a major ruling said, 'a Parsi woman, who marries outside her community must be allowed to enter fire temples and participate in other religious rituals'.

Divisions within Community

The Parsi community in India is a clearly divided community on the issue of conversion, status of intermarried spouse, adoption etc. Two major issues of contention evidently are: intermarriage and the method of disposal of the dead among the Parsi community.

There is a concentration of orthodox sections in areas of Mumbai and Gujarat while Delhi has a more liberal and reformist environment. The Mumbai and Gujarat Parsis have been orthodox in their response to outside community marriage. However, in Delhi from the 1970s, a need has been felt by the Delhi Parsi Anjuman to accommodate these Parsis and their families as members.[15] The Parsi spouses and their children, after their Navjote was performed could avail of the facilities of the Dar-Meher and aramgah, while their non-Zoroastrian spouses were welcome to all social gatherings and activities, the Delhi Anjuman says. Delhi's response to the changing times has been in line with the more progressive Zoroastrian communities in North America and other western countries.

While the orthodox section everywhere have opposed mixed marriages, scholars find this acceptable and much needed to secure the future of the small community. Some of them feel that the community cannot afford to lose even a single member. To them, a good percentage of Parsis married outside the community are more conscious of their roots and see their earlier lifestyle and value system which they had otherwise taken for granted, with greater appreciation. In other words, they tend to become more concerned and better Parsi Zoroastrians.

Difference within the FPZAI

The Federation of Parsi Zoroastrian Anjumans of India (FPZAI) is the governing body of the Parsi Panchayats across the country. However, there are differences amongst different panchayats. Some like the Bombay Parsi Panchayat and its allied panchayats from Delhi, Madras, Hyderabad, Secunderabad and Jamshedpur are seen as reformist in nature, while those from Gujrat, Ahmedabad, and some fifty panchayats across India are seen as traditionalist in nature.

The clash between the 'reformist' Bombay Parsi Panchayat and its allies and the 'traditionalist' panchayats goes back to a December 2004 meeting of the panchayats at Thane. At the meeting, the 'reformist' panchayats initiated a change in the century-old Parsi Constitution by bringing in a new voting pattern in the Federation. This, the Ahmedabad Parsi Panchayat, believes leave Gujarati and other 'traditional' Parsis in the minority.[16] The president of the Ahmedabad Parsi Panchayat, Areez Khambatta, who is also the vice-president of the Federation declared at the meet that they would not allow the Gujrati representation to become less. According to Khambatta, the current voting pattern at the federation is one vote per panchayat. While the number of panchayats in Gujarat is large, the number of Parsis is relatively fewer. The new voting pattern will reduce Gujarat Parsis into a minority group.[17]

The major reformist agenda includes legalising adoption and accepting children of Parsi girls who are married to non-Parisis, a move many say can increase the Parsi population in India. The debate within the community is also over opting for or against Dokhmenishini and funerary rites performed at the Doongerwadi.

Dokhmenishini is the ancient practice amongst the Parsis of disposing of the dead. The bodies are kept in a well for vultures to feed in a tradition dating back to the 16th century. Doongenwadi is the area where the funeral rite for the deceased are performed. The Parsi community is now divided over how to dispose of their dead. Many Parsis are now opting for an alternate and more dignified system of disposal of the dead. From time to time, residents of nearby buildings have complained of a nauseating stench emanating from the direction of the dakhmas. Reformist Parsis are now alleging that the Towers are becoming unhygenic and succumbing to decay. The vultures, who are supposed to eat the bodies, are in fact disappearing and as a result, dead bodies are rotting for years.

The second issue is about the use of Doongerwadi bunglis (bunglows) by Parsis who choose to opt out of the Dakhmenashini system.[18]

In an attempt to seek clarity over the use of the Doongerwadi bunglis, eminent Parsi senior counsel in the country sought civil action, an Originating Summons, to be filed in Bombay High Court. The summons ask the court to interpret the 122-year trust deed, which enjoined to permit the use of Doongerwadi facilities and trust land use for the performance of religious rites and ceremonies to the members of the Parsi community professing the Zoroastrian religion who in the present situation opt for an alternate mode of disposal of body. The petitioners were eminent members of the community, including a former municipal commissioner while the defendants were the trustees of the Bombay Parsi Panchayat.

Framroze Mirza and Khushroo Madon were banned in June 2009 from praying or performing religious ceremonies in Towers of Silence at Malabar Hill, Godavara Agiari at the Fort and SF Jokhi Agiari at Godrej Baug, Napean Sea Road because they had been conducting Navjotes for children from mixed marriages and offering after-death prayers for those who had opted for non-traditional funerals. Following the ban, former municipal commissioner Jamshed Kanga and former Tata Chemicals MD Homi Khusrokhan filed originating summons seeking the HC's assistance in interpreting legal documents (in this case, the BPP's Deed of Trust made in 1884) to find out whether the document gave trustees the authority to decide on a religious matter.

The originating summons provides the court with a detailed history and background of the traditional Parsi method of disposal of the dead and the reason why the Doongerwadi lands at Malabar Hill were acquired for the purpose. The first *dakma* was built there in 1669 when the area was a jungle and there was no dearth of scavenging birds. In fact, tigers freely roamed around Bombay and a tiger was last spotted in Malabar hill in 1822. In today's urbanised Bombay, the pressure of unbridled population has resulted in a dearth of scavenging birds. There are no vultures left at the Doongerwadi, leading to a failiure of the traditional method of disposal of the body.

In 2011, The High Court said, 'Trustees of the Bombay Parsi Punchayet cannot arrogate powers to themselves in a mistaken belief that they are custodians of religion' and it lifted the ban on the two Zoroastrian priests from praying at the BPP's facilities. The judges added, 'The court has carefully gone through the Deed of Trust and we do not find any provision that empowers the trustees to prevent a duly ordained Zoroastrian priest from performing religious rites and ceremonies as far as it is for Parsi members'.

In order to solve the problems the Doongerwadis now face, the petitioners conceived the idea of installing solar concentrators over the dakhmas in 2001. These solar concentrators concentrate the rays of sun on to the corpses in order to dehydrate and decompose the corpses faster.

The petitioners submitted that the General Trust Deed provides that the Doongerwadi lands are to be used for every member of the Parsi community professing the Zoroastrian religion, as a place for exposure of the dead and for performance of religious rites and ceremonies.

Conclusion

From within the community there have been suggestions to reconciling the issue of preservation of the Parsi culture with gender equality. Several groups and individuals have made efforts to preserve Parsi heritage and culture on one hand, and on the other hand there has been a movement to bring about equality for women within the community.

As far as cultural preservation is concerned, for example there is a foundation in Delhi, by the name of PARZOR, which has been engaged in Parsi cultural preservation. From its inception the most pressing need of the Parzor Project was to immediately start recording the intangible aspects of Parsi Zoroastrian heritage, as the most valuable resource people, both priests and laity, are of advanced age. The scope is wide, and it is often a race against time. The Project attempts to record intangible heritage before knowledgeable people are lost—priests, musicians, artists and traditional medical practitioners.

Community leaders like Adi Sethna and Shernaz Cama have been engaged in getting intermixed couples to get their rights. Organisation like ARZ and AIMZ have been engaged with the same purpose. The Delhi Parsis have been active in performing Navjote ceremony for inter-faith couples. There are priests who are specially willing and happy to perform Navjotes of children of intermarried ladies. Navjotes can be performed at any age. In Mumbai, the main objective of an organisation by the name of Association of Inter-Married Zoroastrians is to assert, establish, agitate for, protect and safeguard the rights, privileges, benefits of and available to Parsi Zoroastrians married to any person who is not a Parsi. The Association's main concern is to ensure the rights of the children.

The amendment to the marriage laws was passed in 1988, the amendment to succession law was enacted in 1991. The provisions of marriage and divorce were modified along the lines of the Hindu Marriage Act. Grounds of divorce were further liberalised and divorce by mutual consent was introduced. The disparity between the rights of legitimate and illegitimate children was abolished. In 1991, by amending the succession laws, the discrimination between female and male descendents was abolished. However, the debate within the Parsi community between the reformists and conservatives still continue in India, especially for children, community inheritors.

Jews: Anti-choice Community and Women

THE JEWS of India are now less than 5000 in number. They first arrived in India's west coast about 2,500 years ago, as traders, later as persecuted communities seeking shelter. They came in search of a peaceful land to live out their lives and worship their god. The Indian subcontinent offered them this. The Jews never tried to convert the native population to the Judaic faith. Inevitably, while they assimilated many native practices into their culture, they guarded their own religious and cultural practices zealously in essentialy what the early settlers considered a 'refuge' and a 'foreign' land. In their mind's eye, Israel was their home. They remained quietly in the west coast, always as a minority community. About seventy years ago, when Israel was created many of the Jews went back to the new state of Israel.

They are, however, not granted a minority status in India.Thus, they are deprived of the privileges which come with recognition of a community as a minority. They are deprived of cultural, educational and linguistic rights granted to minorities by the Indian Constitution. While many of the Indian Jews are affected by the theory of political Zionism, the fact is that Jews here have had a lot of intermingling with the Hindu culture.[1]

Just as they have had to struggled to keep their Jewish culture alive in India, they are now struggling to keep their Indian culture alive in Israel. Unlike most European immigrants to Israel, Indian Jews were never persecuted in India. Hence their memories of India are not sour, and they don't want to break ties with India completely.

No Personal Law for Jews

In India, Jews are governed by the Special Marriage Act. They do not have their own personal laws. Interestingly, during Indira Gandhi's government when there was a debate in Parliament on the need for a Uniform Civil Code, the Indian Jews emphasised on the need for a Uniform Code, unlike India's Muslims.[2]

Women in Jewish Culture

Jews are largely a matrilineal culture. Women, when married to a non-Jew, can retain all the rights of the Jewish community. For the Jews, bloodline is passed to daughters if no male heirs were born. Matrilineal descent still is the rule within Orthodox Judaism. Orthodox Judaism holds that anyone with a Jewish mother also has irrevocable Jewish status. In other words, even if someone with a Jewish mother converts to another religion, that person still is considered Jewish.

However, the Indian Jews are also Indians. They are influenced by India's caste and class culture. So the Jews of Cochin are concerned not just about the woman's 'substance' but also about the purity of a father's substance. This reflects the south Indian identification of substance with semen rather than blood.

In India, a Jew woman and a non-Jew man cannot get married in a synagogue. In a synagogue, women and men are not allowed to sit together. Jewish women pray thrice in their houses. They know the law of *Niddah* (period of separation during and after women's menses). They are strict about the days of menstruation and will not enter the kitchen during the period of separation. This prescription exceeds *halakhic* standards (Jewish religious laws), which at maximum prohibit handing of food by a woman to her husband directly or pouring wine for him within his sight but in no way limits a woman's access to the kitchen. This Niddah reflects Hindu menstrual taboos which bar women from the kitchen.

Inequitable Divorce

The *ketubah*, the Jewish marriage contract, is one of the oldest continuously used documents within Judaism. Over the course of the past thirty years or so, many ketubahs have undergone a makeover so that rather than simply act as a business document that lists the items in the bride's trousseau and the amount of *zuzim* (silver pieces) that the groom has to set aside for her well-being, many contemporary ketubahs reflect the equal partnership that the marrying couple are entering into.

One addition that many liberal Jews have made to their ketubahs is the Lieberman Clause—a section of the ketubah that states that both partners can initiate a divorce. This seems logical and obvious, but under traditional law, only men have the power to give a *get*, the Jewish divorce. As a result, there have been too many cases to count of *agunot*, women who because their husbands refuse to give a get, end up chained in dead (and sometimes abusive) marriages, without the ability to remarry within Jewish law. The Lieberman Clause has been one response to this problem, as has the Jewish Orthodox Feminist Alliance's (JOFA) Advocacy for Agunot programme.

Jew Marriage and Divorce

The law of marriage and divorce are not codified in India. In India, Jews can obtain dissolution of marriage in the civil court.

The couple, both, the man and the woman, cannot, however, legally get married after divorce unless they get divorced according to jewish religious law. They cannot also remarry. It is the *biet-din* (the rabbis' court) that grants religious divorce. Jews have no codified divorce laws. They are fully codified by customary laws. If the Jew spouse opts to register the marriage under the Special Marrige Act, their divorce shall be settled under this Act.The SMA is a secular option for all religious communities.[3]

Judaism does not accept that marriage is a permanent sacrament. Tradition has always recognised that not all marriages work and has sought uncomplicated ways to dissolve failed marriages. Divorce is mentioned as early as in the *Torah*. Because the Torah reflects the culture of its time, the laws of marriage and divorce were based upon the then-prevailing notion that women were property. Women were rarely allowed to have control of their own destinies. Thus, according to *Torah law*, only the husband can grant a divorce, and the woman has no say in the process. Under *rabbinic law* the woman can initiate divorce proceedings in some situations and obtain help from the beit din (rabbinic court) in doing so. But in the end, the husband must still give her the get (bill of divorce) for the divorce to be valid. This practice continues to this day.

At present, the Orthodox and Conservative movements follow halakhic (Jewish legal) norms and will only process a religious divorce (get) if the husband initiates the procedure. Rabbis from these movements are not allowed to perform second marriages where there is no get. The Reform and Reconstructionist movements do not require a get, and will process a get initiated by the wife, but these alternative *gittin* (plural of get) are not accepted by the Orthodox or Conservative movements.[4]

A woman can petition the beit din to coerce the husband to participate in the divorce process in limited circumstances:

1. Where the husband has a physical condition or occupation that the rabbis deem to make him repulsive to his wife. In mishnaic times, these included a disease or trade that caused the man to have a terrible smell or a skin disease. A woman was entitled to petition for a divorce in these circumstances

even if she married the man knowing of these conditions, unless she had explicitly stated before getting married that she was willing to marry him despite the condition.

2. Where the husband will not provide the wife her marital rights. The ketubah (marriage contract) requires the husband to maintain and support his wife. If he fails to do so, he has violated his contract and the wife can petition for divorce. Similarly, the husband is obligated to provide the wife a certain number of opportunities for sexual activity a month. If he refuses to have sexual intercourse for more than a limited period, the husband has violated his obligations, and his wife can petition for divorce.

3. The wife claims that her husband is sexually repulsive to her (ma'isalai). The law in this area is very difficult. The original mishnah (oral tradition) that introduces this concept contrasts two types of women who refuse to have sex with their husbands: those who merely want to torment their husbands and those who say my husband 'is repulsive to me'. The mishnah concludes that the wife should not be forced to respond to the husband's needs. Rashi (Shlomo Yitzchaki 1040-1105, today generally known by the acronym Rashi, was a medieval French rabbi and author of a comprehensive commentary on the *Talmud* and the *Tanakh*) says, 'she is not compelled [to stay married], but he gives her a get'. Later authorities, including the Shulhan Arukh (Code of Jewish Law), interpret Rashi as saying the man should give the get, but we cannot force him to do so.

4. Wife beating. There are widely differing opinions as to whether physical abuse of the wife is grounds for a beit din to compel a divorce. Some rabbis hold that it clearly is sufficient grounds, others that it is not. An intermediate view, is best expressed by Ramo (the Polish Rabbi Moshe Isserles 1530-1572), the premier Ashkenazic (Judaic) authority.

> Ramo holds that certain types of beatings are considered acceptable, for example: if she curses him, or denigrates his father and mother, and he warns her beforehand. However, if he beats her for no ascertainable reason, then she can petition the beit din for a divorce. Interestingly, Ramo says if it is not clear who is the cause of the altercation between the spouses, the wife's testimony over the husband (Even Haezer 154:15) holds.

However, it should be stressed that if the coercion used by the beit din, or the secular courts at the behest of the beit din, is not effective to force the husband to participate in the get process, the beit din itself can do nothing. Only the man can do the act (give) required for a valid Jewish divorce; the Jewish court has no more power to declare a man divorced against his will than it does to declare a man married against his will.

It is important to note that a civil divorce is not sufficient to dissolve a Jewish marriage. As far as Jewish law is concerned, a couple remains married until the woman receives the get. This has been a significant problem: many liberal Jews have a religiously valid marriage, yet do not obtain a religiously valid divorce. If the woman remarries after such a procedure, her second marriage is considered an adulterous one and her children are considered *mamzerim* (bastards, illegitimate).[5]

Inequality of the Sexes

The position of husband and wife with regard to divorce is not an equal one. According to the Talmud, only the husband can initiate a divorce and the wife cannot prevent him from divorcing her. Later rabbinical authorities took steps to ease the harshness of these rules by prohibiting a man from divorcing a woman without her consent.

In addition, a rabbinical court can compel a husband to divorce his wife under certain circumstances: when he is physically repulsive because of some medical condition or other characteristic, when he violates or neglects his marital obligations (food, clothing and sexual intercourse), or, when there is sexual incompatibility. The biblical text *Old Testament* that is the basis for the laws of Jewish divorce provides that a marriage is dissolved where the husband 'writes a bill of divorcement, hands it to [the wife], and sends her away from his house' (*Deuteronomy 24:1*).[6]

- It is clear from this passage that a divorce is accomplished through specific acts of the husband.
- Neither wife nor beit din (Jewish court) is mentioned as a possible initiator of the divorce process. The rabbis in the Talmud also mandated that the husband's act must be done 'with his full consent'.
- The Mishnah (the early rabbinic legal code) does provide, however, that a wife is permitted, under certain circumstances, to request that a Jewish court compel the husband to perform the acts required for a divorce. These circumstances include: where the husband has physical defects that are deemed unendurable; where the husband fails to perform his marital duties; and, according to some, where the wife says, 'he is repulsive to me', or where the husband beats his wife.

The Special Marriage Act and Abandonment

As far as divorce under the SMA is concerned, if the Jewish couple register the marriage for civil purposes under SMA, then divorce shall also be under Special Marriage Act.

A peculiar problem arises, however, if a man disappears or deserts his wife or is presumed dead but there is insufficient proof of death. Under Jewish law, divorce can only be initiated by the man. If the husband cannot be found, he cannot be compelled to divorce the wife and she cannot marry another man. A woman in this situation is referred to as *agunah* (literally, anchored). The rabbis have agonised over this problem, balancing the need to allow the woman to remarry with the risk of an adulterous marriage (a grave transgression that would affect the status of offspring of the marriage), if the husband reappears. No definitive solution to this problem exists yet.[7]

To prevent this problem to some extent, it is customary in many places for a man to give his wife a conditional get whenever he goes off to war, so that if he never comes home and his body is not found, his wife does not become agunah.

Conclusion

- Jewish law permits divorce.
- Civil divorce does not dissolve a Jewish marriage.
- A man can divorce a woman for any reason or no reason, but rabbinical law requires the woman's consent.
- In traditional Jewish law, a woman cannot initiate a divorce.

These rules apply to a normal situation. However, there are some specific circumstances where a divorce can be enforced by a Rabbinical court whether or not the husband agrees. This can be done in the case of spousal abuse or some other specific circumstances. So, there are a few limited times when a woman can initiate and force the divorce, but they are few and very specific.

The problem of agunot has a long and painful history in Judaism and it remains even more problematic today, especially outside of Israel, since the Jewish establishment has relatively little power in terms of domestic law.

In Israel, however, steps have been taken to ensure that the problem of agunot is mitigated. In 2012, the Israeli parliament, the Knesset, ruled that a husband has 45 days maximum to provide his wife with a get, once a rabbinical court has ruled that one is needed. If the husband refuses to do so within that time frame, the court must hold a hearing to arbitrate whether to impose punitive sanctions, which can include preventing the husband from traveling abroad, confiscating his driver's license, and even incarceration.

7

A couple who has had a legally Jewish divorce are forbidden from remarrying each other. Both men and women are permitted to remarry after a divorce; however, a Kohen, a descendant of the holy priests, cannot marry a divorcee.

Such a mechanism may also provide a solution to one of the most tragic and vexing problems of modern Orthodox family life, the plight of those thousands of women whose husbands refuse them a religious divorce though they themselves have remarried after receiving a civil decree. In India, provision of the Special Marriages Act can be more equitable than traditional marriage and divorce principles of Jewish law.

Conclusion

Hope of Reconciliation

> We have no words to speak about our oppression, our distress, our bitterness, and our revolt against the exhaustion, the stupidity, the monotony, the lack of meaning of our work and our life, against the contempt in which our work is held; against the despotic hierarchy of the factory; against a society in which we remain the underdogs and in which goods and enjoyments that are considered normal by other classes are denied to us and are parceled out to us only reluctantly, as though we are asking for a privilege. We have no words to say what it is and how it feels to be workers, to be held in suspicion, to be ordered around by people who have more and who pretend to know more and who compel us to work according to rules they set and for purposes that are theirs, not ours. And we have no words to say all this because the ruling class has monopolised not only the powers of decision-making and of material wealth; they have also monopolised culture and language.
>
> —Andre Gorz

The book began with the question whether cultural diversity can accommodate gender equality and if multiculturalism can coexist with women's equality.

As India, among the world nations, is considered the most diverse in terms of religions practiced, continuing cultural traditions and legal dos and don'ts, I have looked at personal laws in India as this issue has been raised on and off since the Constituent Assembly Debates, 1946-49.This study has taken into account most of the minority communities in India—that is Christians, Parsis and Muslims, Jains, Buddhists and Jews because the state has already brought about changes in the majority community, that is the laws for the Hindus.

The key concern of this book has been to see whether personal laws violate women's rights and whether multicultural issues go against feminist concerns for equal treatment. Are the fragile gains of feminism eroded by heightened multicultural sensitivities?

This is of great importance because in India, religious minorities have been granted the right to keep their own personal laws. These laws have, however, been very discriminatory against their own women—for example, for the Muslim women. Some communities like the Buddhists and Sikhs—who have not been granted their personal laws by the Indian Constitution—feel that if *their* women were granted rights under *their* personal laws (and not Hindu laws as of now), it would have been more egalitarian for women. Nanak's teachings were extremely egalitarian. Similarly, Buddhist laws could have been more equitable under the Buddha's *Dhamma*. The Dalai Lama has even said that a woman can be the next Dalai Lama.

In this book I have discussed minority communities which have personal laws granted under the Indian Constitution and some who have been equated with Hindus. The debate over Sikh, Jain and Buddhist personal laws after Jains have been granted minority status has be reignited in the new century. However, proponents of separate personal laws feel, and rightly so, that the application of Hindu laws to them gives an impression that their religions are not independent and are merely off-shoots of Hinduism. They take it as an attempt to denigrate and subordinate their respective religions.

What can be the solution then?

Three minority communities in India show different way-out models being applied.

In a democracy, the need is to draw the boundaries for permissible diversity. To highlight this, I have tried to point out how property and inheritance rights are discriminatory in most personal laws. If one is to look at the Hindu Succession Act, it does not challenge the Mitakara coparcenary (joint inheritance), or the exemption for women to equal inheritance in agricultural land. This law is based on north Indian Brahmanical patriarchy and marginalises the rights of matrilineal communities for the question of *Hindu succession*.

Even within north Indian communities, it erodes the property rights of widows who had customarily been entitled to marital property despite remarriage, by making remarriage an event wherein all Hindu widows are forced to forgo property. According to Srimati Basu, 'The Hindu Succession Act (1956) stands as a prime signifier for the contemporary position of Indian women with respect to personal law.... It includes some change that gives Hindu women greater access, while veiling the significant patriarchal and patrilineal scripts on which personal law is grounded'. Numerous studies also show that the inheritance provision for daughters are rarely availed of, that women generally turn down shares of natal inheritance.

As far as Muslim laws are concerned, the Sharia grants the right to inherit property as embodied in the Muslim Personal Law. However, this is not actually implemented. Studies by Srimati Basu, Zoya Hasan and Ritu Menon have similar findings as far as property rights are concerned. Women trade away the right of inheritance for what they perceive as more long-term gains, in the way of maintaining good relations with brothers, these researchers say.

Among Parsis, in 1991, by amending the succession laws, the discrimination between female and male descendants was abolished. However, up to 1991, Sec 51(1) of the Indian Succession

Act, 1925 dealing with the death of a male intestate, divided the share between the daughter and the son/widow in the ratio of 2:1. The amending act of 1991, premised on the recommendations of the 110th Law Commission Report, brought about complete equality by removing ISA Sec 52 and substituting the old ISA Sec 51 to deal with the division of property of men and women (amongst widows and widowers) which would divide equally between the sons and the daughter.

Sec 51(2) of the ISA recognises the rights of the parents in the share of their children's property, they get half the share of their grandchildren. Therefore, although the share of the children might be reduced as compared to the Hindu law, for Indians, it is more uniformly divided, providing support for parents in their old age.Christians do not have their own succession act and follow the Indian Succession Act 1925, which is more equitable than other religion-based succession acts. Though it is a law made during British time, with amendments, it now grants equal rights to daughter and son.

Marriage and Divorce acts have been made relatively more equitable in most religions.

Parsis and Christians have followed the Hindu Marriage and Divorce Act. The Hindu Act introduced the husband's rights to maintenance. The Parsis follow the Hindu Act rather than the more progressive Special Marriage Act which does not have the right of husbands to maintenance. The Christian law does not have the right of husbands to maintenance.

For Muslims, Triple Talaq and maintenance of wife and children are problematic areas. Muslim laws as operative in India and clerics do not consider it inappropriate that a man's responsibility for his wife should end after the three-month iddat period. The Muslim Women Act 1986 made divorced Muslim women ineligible to file suit for maintenance against their former husbands under section 125 of the CrPC. As per this Act, if a Muslim woman has no other means of subsistence, she may instead appeal under the Muslim

Women Act to obtain financial support from parents, siblings, other natal relatives, adult children, grand children or if they are lacking or without sufficient means, from the the Waqf boards of the States in which they reside.

As far as other minority communities are concerned, it is a cause of great heartburn for Buddhists, Jains and Sikhs that Explanation II of Article 25 (freedom of conscience and free profession, practice and propagation of religion) of the Indian Constitution classifies them as 'Hindus', subject to Hindu personal laws. The explanation has been challenged legally many times, but still has not been altered. It reads as follows:

> ...The reference Hindus shall be construed as including a reference to persons professing Sikh, Jaina or Buddhist religion and the reference to Hindu religious institutions shall be construed accordingly.

Therefore, the reconciliation between personal laws and women's rights or multiculturalism and feminism is a difficult thing to attain.

Certain communities in India without personal laws are more inequitable for women as they are equated with the Hindus, whose personal laws are extremely inequitable for women. Theorists like Susan Moller Okin say, when the state cannot intervene because of personal laws of communities, or due to culture rights of communities, then women are on the receiving end of multiculturalism. Says Moller Okin, *group rights are detrimental to women's rights.* Bonnie Honig points out that after struggling for long to increase gender equality in hiring, wages and promotions, and to decrease violence against women, concessions to differences may negate all achievements in this area.

Women in several cultures have been denied the right to become priests for example, the Parsis, Jews, Sikhs and Buddhist. We see that due to group rights given to these communities, the state cannot intervene in India. Even the courts at times rule against

Constitutional guarantees on freedom to practice religion, marriage, divorce and inheritance. Communities accorded cultural freedoms tend to suppress women and, therefore, granting of group rights only mean sanctioning women's oppression.

I have looked at three models that theorists feel can continue to protect cultural diversity and gender equality. Exit option theorists like Chandran Kukathas emphasise that the individual's right to exit is the most fundamental right which individuals need. Critics have pointed out that the exit option is no real choice for women and other sections within minorities as it increases their vulnerability. Legally, it expects the individual to choose between community or state. This penalises the vulnerable sections who have to opt out of their cultures to be governed by secular laws of the state.

Liberal multiculturalists like Will Kymlicka, Bhikhu Parekh and Joseph Carens espouse that 'granted rights' does not mean cultural groups can commit atrocities against vulnerable group members. Their contention is, all cultural practices cannot be accepted within liberal democracies as they tend to harm minority groups. Thus, the requirement of internal liberalism rules out the justification for group rights of fundamentalists of all political and religious stripes.

Joseph Carens says, there are certain principles of human moral equality which no cultural community seeking cultural rights can give up. Any practice (such as genital mutilation of young girls) which goes against the equal moral worth of persons cannot be supported.

Laws of marriage, divorce, inheritance and adoption, which are discriminatory against women are tougher problems which have not been addressed by these theorists. Parekh is of the opinion, the operative public values as enshrined in the Constitution should provide the basis for what is acceptable in society. However, operative values do not provide safeguard against discriminatory practices. This is because Parekh and many others miss out the point that constitutions reflect the consensus in society when they were initially formed.

There are theorists who believe that deliberative democracy offers for women and disadvantaged sections a robust, egalitarian model of power sharing in public deliberation and decision-making.

It also provides a political framework for democratic and respectful resolution of both inter-and intra-cultural conflicts in socially plural, liberal democratic states. In contrast to other models of democracy, the deliberative democracy model emphasises on the 'need for inclusive decision making' which can contribute towards 'more just and political judgements'.

The deliberative model advocates that conflicts are best addressed and provisionally resolved by actual deliberation. The give and take of arguments is respectful of reasonable differences. It advocates the need for openness of politics to all reasonable people and perspectives, providing especially to marginalised groups like women and minorities access to deliberate on forums.

It admits all reasonable arguments to the national political agenda for decision-making purposes. However, deliberation seems to work for softer issues but as far as the so-called irreconcilable issues are concerned, deliberation has yielded lesser results.

Ayelet Shachar points out the paradox of multicultural vulnerability—namely the unintended consequence of well-meaning state policies that aim at cultural accommodation but result in the women and children of such groups bearing a disproportionate burden. In her work, *Multicultural Jurisdictions*, Shachar specifically addresses the issue of conflict between community groups and women's rights in a multicultural polity.

In a country like India, Shachar suggests that religious groups must be convinced to voluntarily surrender their power over family laws or other issues, as 'communities' in India mean religious groupings.

The deeper the cleavages run between the communities comprising a body politic, the more difficult it becomes to alter the current balance of power between state and the groups. In Shachar's argument, there is a certain privileging of the legal at the expense of the political and cultural. Minority practices which do not violate public values can be permitted within liberal democracy, she believes.

India is a rather a complex multicultural polity. Deliberative democracy has been a popular option in the Indian context because it does not involve external pressure from the state. Both, Christians and Parsis have relied heavily on dialogue and deliberation within their communities. Within the Muslim community, deliberation has taken the form of internal reform. Since most nikahnamas prepared by local *qazi*s or elders gave women a raw deal in cases where the marriage was called off, reformists and women's groups put pressure on the All India Muslim Personal Law Board to design a uniform code for marriages in the community and, more important, abolish the practise of triple talaq. Significantly, the AIMPLB model nikahnama did not not take on the contentious issue of triple talaq and it completely ignored areas such as marriage of minors and polygamy. Although the model nikahnama does put together some guidelines, its greatest fault is that it makes none of these mandatory.

In a recent example of state intervening, in December 2017, finally a draft Muslim Woman Protection of Rights on Marriage Bill has been okayed by the Indian Pariament.It says, any form of triple talaq, oral, electronic or written is a cognisable offence where the husband can be imprisoned for three years.

Yet, one has to admit, all communities in India, whether, Christians, Parsis or Muslims have seen the successful usage of deliberation dialogue. Deliberation has shown way in a deeply diverse country like India. The informal exit option has also been used extensively in India. The Working Group on Women's Rights and several women activists in India have suggested that all citizens should be guranted the common secular gender-just law but can choose to opt for their personal laws. However, this is not possible because it means bringing about change in the Constitution itself.

Multicultural jusrisdiction also can be seen as a model, as applied in the Indian context. Community leaders, priest and women activists have for long suggested that some uniform laws could be with the state while separate laws could be with the community. For example, laws like adoption rights and property laws could be with the state, while marriage and divorce laws could be with the community. It is thought that though reconciliation between cultural diversity and gender equality is difficult, yet it is possible to be achieved.

Kymlicka points out that the interesting debate, as far as multiculturalism and feminism is concerned, is not whether to adopt multiculturalism or not, but rather *what kind of multiculturalism* to adopt. Reconciliation would require, as Anne Phillips says, not just equitable treatment of minority and majority cultures but alongside, other considerations of equity—that is between men and women in every small and big community in a truly multicultural society. India may take several decades to get to such an ideal political position.

References

Introduction

1. Gurpreet Mahajan, *The Multicultural Path*, Sage, New Delhi, 2002.
2. T Saujanya: Understanding Dalit Feminism, https://www.academia.edu/10225419/Understanding_Dalit_Feminism.
3. Bonnie Honig, My Culture Made Me Do It, in *Is Multiculturalism Bad For Women*, ed Joshua Cohen, Mathew Howard and Martha Nussbaum, Princeton University Press.1999. p39.
4. Tamanna Khosla, Is Democracy Bad For Women, *Mainstream*, March 2013.
5. Tamanna Khosla, Feminist responses to multiculturalism: An Examination, Unpublished. Dissertation, 2001. JNU.
6. Homi Bhabha, Liberalism's Sacred Cow, in *Is Multiculturalism Bad For Women*, op cit, p79-84, p80.
7. ibid.
8. Uma Narayan, *Dislocating Cultures: Identities, Traditions and Third World Countries*, New York, Routledge,1997, p54.
9. Homi Bhabha, op cit, p81.
10. Kumkum Sangari, Which Diversity, *Seminar* 484, December 1999, p24-30, p26.
11. Homi Bhabha, op cit, p 82.
12. ibid. p82.
13. ibid.

Common Call for Diversity & Gender Justice

1. Rita Felski, *The Doxa of Difference*, Signs, Vol.1.No.232
2. Chandran Kukathas, 'Liberalism and Multiculturalism', *Political Theory*,Vol.26(1), No.5, Oct
3. Unlike Iris Young who uses the term 'oppression' to describe the status of minority groups, I would prefer using a stronger phrase, 'ideological genocide'. Ideological genocide works in the present system and follows a certain pattern. Certain groups get marked and their ideologies or identities are seen as threats and are systematically annihilated.
4. Distributive injustice include issues which are concerned with allocation of resource, income and wealth.
5. This to Young would include understanding the reasons for present oppression which can be resolved through a politics of difference.
6. Iris Young, *Justice and Politics of Difference*, Princeton University Press, p15.6./20 ibid.
7. ibid
8. ibid.
9. ibid.
10. ibid p16.
11. ibid.
12. Many writers have cogently argued that this Marxist concept of exploitation is too narrow to encompass all forms of domination and oppression. In order to understand exploitation in contemporary world, we need to take a holistic picture. While workers exploitation has been the prominent agenda of the left movement, a somewhat similar yet different problem has gone unnoticed. This is the problem of the real producers or as Ayn Rand would term them as 'primary producers'. It is important to understand in countries like India where there is scant Intellectual Property Rights Safeguards. So the thinkers' work point out how such a system creates a reverse discrimination for these primary workers in favour of the second-handers

and mediocres. So while the left movement stands for workers' rights, similar is not happening for the real producers such as scientists, thinker, architects, engineers etc or the primary producers. Ayn Rand in her work *Fountainhead* showed how second-handers and mediocres gained from the work of primary movers. In the present world, with increase in cyber crime there is need to protect the intellectual property of the real producers, especially in countries like India, where there is no system in place to ensure this.

13. Iris Marion Young, *Justice and politics of Diff*erence, Princeton University Press, New Jersey, 1990, p50.
14. *Marxist feminism* is a sub-type of feminist theory which focuses on the dismantling of capitalism as a way to liberate women. Marxist feminism states that capitalism, which gives rise to economic inequality, dependence, political confusion and ultimately unhealthy social relations between men and women, is the root of women's oppression in the current social context. While at this point I would like to employ Young's Marxist feminist critique of patriarchy, I am fully aware that Marxist Feminism provides only an incomplete interpretation of women's oppression as it limits itself to working within the Marxist framework. An adequate critique is provided by radical and socialist feminists. *Radical feminist:* Patriarchy on the other hand is more complicated and needs a more nuanced understanding. Radical feminism, which emerged in the 1970s, also took issue with Marxist feminism. Radical feminist theorists have stated that modern society and its constructs (law, religion, politics *etc*) are the product of men and therefore have a patriarchal character. According to those who subscribe to this view, the best solution for women's oppression would be to treat patriarchy not as a subset of capitalism but as a problem in its own right. Thus, eliminating women's oppression means eliminating male domination in all its forms. Like most feminists, however, radical feminists believe in replacing such domination with a culture and policy of equality.
15. *Socialist Feminists:* Some contributors to this perspective have critiqued traditional Marxism for failing to find an inherent

connection between patriarchy and classism. Marx and Engels were largely silent on gender oppression except to subsume it underneath broader class oppression. Marx felt that when class oppression was overcome, gender oppression would vanish as well. According to socialist feminists, this view of gender oppression as a sub-class of class oppression is naive and much of the work of socialist feminists has gone towards separating gender phenomena from class phenomena.

16. Young, *Justice*, 51.
17. Thus, oppression in the present world system is much more complicated than just a pure attribution to class and several other factors a play a dominant role in it.
18. Young, *Justice*, 51.
19. https://en.wikipedia.org/wiki/Polyandry_in_India. In Contrast Political thinker Kancha Illiah argues for the need of dalitisation of India, where cultural symbols which are more egalitarian in nature come to fore in contrast to Sanskritization and Brahmanization.
20. Charles Taylor, 'Politics of recognition' in *Multiculturalism: A critical reader,* ed David Goldberg, UK, Blackwell,1994, p.81.
21. See Axel Honneth, 'Integrity and Disrespect-Principles of a Concpt of Morality Based on Theory', *Political Theory*, 20;1992.
22. Taylor, 'Politics of Recognition' ,75.
23. ibid.
24. Nancy Fraser, 'Rethinking Recognition', *New Left Review*, May-June 2000, p-107-120.
25. Taylor, 'Politics of Recognition', p 81.
26. ibid.
27. Young, 'Justice and Politics of Difference',p.164.
28. See Glenn Jordan and Chris Weedon, *Cultural Politics-Class , Gender, Race and Postmodern World*; UK, BlackWell,1995.
29. Mary Wollstonecraft similarly sought to show that reason has no sex, knowledge has no sex and mind itself is sexless. Therefore stress on right to vote, equal opportunity, equal pay etc.

30. This was exemplified in works of feminist theorists like Carol Gilligan and Nancy Chodorow.

31. This is represented in works of theorists like Iris Young, Bonie Honig, Gayatri Spivak, Chandra Talapade Mohanty etc.

32. By unified category they are trying to say is that all women suffer same kind of oppression. However third world women are more oppressed than the White women.

33. Glenn Jordan and Chris Weedon, 'Cultural Politics', p 290-298.

34. Native American and Stereotype reality, nwindian.evergreen.edu/curriculum/Stereotypes.pdf, retrieved on 14july 2008.

35. ibid.

36. ibid.

37. ibid.

38. ibid.

39. ibid.

40. Caste Based Exploitation Still Rampant in India, Special Correspondent, *The Hindu*, April 6, 2014.

41. ibid, p 58.

42. ibid, 52.

43. ibid.

44. ibid.

45. ibid.

46. ibid.

47. Polyandry in Ancient India by Sarva Daman Singh.

48. Yogendra. Singh, *Modernization of Indian Tradition* (A Systematic Study of Social Change), Jaipur, Rawat Publications, 1994. p11.

49. Taylor, op.cit. p 81.

50. Axel Honneth, Integrity and disrespect-principles of a concept of morality based on theory, political theory, 20:1992.

51. ibid.

52. taylor, p 75.

53. ibid.

54. Nancy Fraser, Rethinking Recognition, New Left Review, May-June 2000, p 107-120.
55. Nancy Fraser, p 120.
56. ibid. p 107.
57. Young, p 164.
58. ibid.
59. ibid.
60. ibid.
61. Vinay Lal, "Anti-Christian Violence in India". Manas: India and Its Neighbors. UCLA College of Letters and Science.
62. Annop Singh, 'French Sikh Schoolboys Lose Turban Case in French Court', *The Panthic Weekly*, 24 April 2005.
63. Bhikhu Parikh,'Equality', p 230.
64. ibid.
65. ibid.
66. Bhikhu Parekh, 'What is Multiculturalism', *Seminar,* 484, December 1999, p 14.
67. Charles Taylor, 'Politics of Recognition' In *Multiculturalism: A Critical Reader*(ed) David T Goldberg Cambridge Mass, Blackwell, 1994.
68. Bhikhu Parekh, 'What is Multiculturalism', p 15
69. See Ann Brooks , *Post Feminism:Feminism, Cultural Theory and Cultural Forms*, London, Routledge, 1997.
70. Chandra Talapade Mohanty, 'Under Western Eyes: Feminist Scholarship and Colonial Discourse', *Boundary*, 213 (1), 1984, pp333-357.
71. See Sylvia Walby, Theorizing Patriarchy, Oxford, UK, Cambridge, MA, USA ,Basil Blackwell, 1990.
72. See John Rawls, *Theory of Justice*, Cambridge, MA, Harvard University Press, 1971.The liberal view has in recent time been most eloquently represented in works of John Rawls who in *Theory of Justice* points out that civil and political rights and primary social goods such as education and employment should

not be distributed on the basis of ascriptive identities that are arbitary from the moral point of view. Rights and benefits, privileges and power, should be distributed in a manner that is blind to social differences. At minimum, justice requires a regime of fair equality of opportunity, ungirded by a system of equal rights and liberty for all citizens. Rawls' theory of 'Justice as fairness' defined from within an original position, models an ideal of impartiality which is meant to be purely procedural in nature.The veil of ignorance (which is thick and not thin) represents the commitment to treat individuals as equals without regard to morally arbitary characteristics, such as race, class, religion and so on. To Rawls, under the veil of ignorance, since the difference among parties are unknown to them and everyone is equally rational and similarly situated, therefore we can view the choice in the original position from the standard point of the worst-off person. Thus, difference is automatically eliminated at the very outset from his thought. However, in Rawls later work, *Political liberalism*, the political seems at last to come to the fore because problem of diversity appears to be directly confronted. He poses the question, how over time a stable and just society of free and equal citizen profoundly divided by, reasonable though incompatable religious, philosophical and moral diversity can exist? To him answer is provided by the idea of an overlapping consensus that embraces all reasonable doctrine and is embodied in an ideal of political justice.

73. See Gurpreet Mahajan. *The Multicultural Path*, Sage,2005.p 32.
74. Young, 'Justice and Politics'p.168.
75. ibid, p.171.
76. ibid, p171.
77. ibid.
78. ibid.
79. ibid, See p 188.
80. ibid p 185. According to her special rights are needs and emerge not from a need to compensate for an inferiority as some would interpret it, but from a positive assertion of specificity in different

forms of life. Thus equal treatment is unjust because it denies these cultural differences or makes them a liability. She takes up the example of special rights in workplace-pregnancy and birthing, physical disability and being old, which challenge according to her the normal healthy worker and typical work situation.

81. ibid,184.
82. Kymlicka, *Liberalism, Community and Culture*, Oxford, Clarendon Press,1989, p-182-205., Also See, *Multicultural Citizenship, A Liberal Theory of Minority Rights,* Oxford, Claredon Press,1995.
83. ibid,191.
84. ibid.p 218.
85. ibid.
86. See Bhikhu Parekh,*Rethinking Multiculturalism: Cultural Diversity and Political Theory*, Cambridge, MA, Harvard University Press, 2000,pp 217-218.
87. ibid, p 218.
88. Feminist critics of a universalistic citizenship stress on-
    a) Not only the need to overcome liberal suppression of women's gendered subjectivity in public realm which would require access being made easier for women to enter the public/political realm, example through affirmative action.
    b) However, alongside they need a range of activities in private realm as forms of citizenship which are relevant to different women's lives. So that the spirit of liberal laws of justice should be applied whole heartedly to issues of so called private domain-Pornography, violence against women, rape, marital rape, co-parenting etc. Therefore need would be for a notion of differentiated citizenship which is at once political and intimate. Thus both public and private realms are crucially interconnected by the fully human selves that characterize both spheres, which however take cognizance of lived experiences of different women.
89. Kathleen Jones, Citizenship in a women-friendly Polity, *Signs*,1990, Vol. 15, No. 4, p781-812.

90. Multiculturalists too advocate in order to facilitate emergence of a multiculturally constituted common culture, both private and public realms need to encourage intercultural interaction. a) So far as the private realm is concerned, the development of a multiculturally constituted common culture requires a flourishing civil society providing ample opportunity for different cultural community to treat and pursue common cultural, economic and other interests on a regular and relaxed basis. Museums and art galleries which define and celebrate the national heritage should include and suitably integrate minority contributions which are also an integral part of a multicultural arts, exhibitions, literary, musical and other events and film festivals, build up a shared source of pleasure and foster multicultural ethics in society at large. As far as public realm is concerned, the development of multicultural-constituted common culture requires a different pattern of intercultural interaction. Since public realm sets the tone of rest of society and wields considerable power and prestige, it should ensure adequate representation to cultural community. Because of prejudice of wider society there is a strong case for affirmative action programme for excluded communities,for example-as in case of India untouchables have been to a considerable degree brought into the mainstream. When both public and private create such conditions-for equal intercultural interactions with such judicious government, a multicultural constituted culture is possible. See Bhikhu Parikh,*Rethinking Multiculturalism*, Hound Mills, Macmillan Press,1999,p222-223.

91. Since every definition of national identity is necessarily selective, both multiculturalist and feminist point that is stresses one of these stands and visions and delegitimises or marginalizes others. The history of a community too is necessarily complex and can be read in several different ways and a definition of national identity runs the risk of oversimplifying it and glorifying the role of some groups and denigrating that of others. A definition of national identity can also become a vehicle of silencing dissident voices and moulding the entire society in a particular image with all its authoritarian and repressive implication.

92. Young, ibid.
93. In Contrast Political thinker Kancha Illiah argues for the need of dalitisation of India, where cultural symbols which are more egalitarian in nature come to fore in contrast to Sanskritization and Brahmanization.
94. Young, 151.
95. ibid.
96. Iris Marion Young, *Justice and Politics of Difference*, p 121.
97. From TH Marshall to Jawaharlal Nehru: Citizenship as Vision and Strategy Jivanta Schoettlifile:///C:/Users/YOGA/Downloads/9783642345678-c1.pdf.
98. ibid.
99. Mushrirul Hasan, *Nationalism and Communal Politics in India*, 1916-1928, Manohar, New Delhi, 1979.
100. Young, 184.
101. ibid.
102. ibid.
103. Parekh, Multicultural citizenship, p 340.
104. ibid.
105. ibid.
106. Amy Gutmann, The challenge of multiculturalism in political ethics, philosophy and public affair 22:3(summer 1993)171-204.p 199.
107. ibid, 203.
108. Parekh, Multicultural citizenship, p 340.
109. Young,191.
110. ibid.

Conflicting Practices of Diversity & Feminism

1. Will Kymlicka, 'Liberal Complicancies', in *Is Multiculturalism bad For Women?*, Susan Moller Okin ed.by Joshua Cohen, Matthew Howard and Martha C Nussbaum, New Jersey, Princeton,Princeton University Press. 1999.p 34.

2. Brian Barry, 'The Muddle of Multiculturalism', *New Left Review*,(March-April),pp-49-77.
3. Susan Moller Okin, 'Multiculturalism and Feminism: No Simple Questions and No Simple Answers' ,in ed *Minorities within Minorities Equality, Rights and Diversity,* Avigail Eisenberg and Jeff Spinner-Halev(ed) Cambridge, Cambridge University Press, 2005.
4. Susan Moller Okin , in *Is Multiculturalism Bad for Women,* ed by Joshua Cohen, M Howard and M Nussabaum, Princton: Princeton Universit Press,1999, p10.
5. Katha Pollitt, ' Whose Culture?', in *Is Multiculturalism bad for Women* , p.27.
6. ibid.
7. ibid.
8. Bonnie Honig, 'My Culture Made Me Do It', in *Is Multiculturalism Bad For Women',* p.35-36.
9. ibid.
10. Bonnie Honig, 'My Culture Made Me Do It',p.35-36.
11. Susan Moller Okin, '*Is Multiculturalism Bad For Women',* p12.
12. ibid.
13. Gurpreet Mahajan, 'Rethinking Multiculturalism', *Seminar* 484, p 60.
14. See Bhikhu Parekh, 'A Varied Moral World,' In *Is Multiculturalism bad for Women*,p 71. However multiculturalist and several feminists have a different view on the issue of circumcision. According to Parekh circumcision on children is unacceptable because it causes irreparable harm to helpless victims.
15. In some communities, however it is freely undergone by adult, sane and educated women after birth of their last child as a way of regulating their sexuality or reminding themselves that they are from now onwards primarily mothers rather than wives, or as a religious sacrifice of what they greatly value for the sake of their children and family or as a symbolic break with one phase of life.

16. What Culture Got To Do With It? Excising The harmful tradition of Female Circumcision', *Harvard law Review*, July 1993, Vol 106;No.3: 1944-1961 at 1959.
17. Browyn Winter, 'Women, The Law and Cultural Relativism in France, The case of Excision', *Signs*, Summer,1994 Vol 19, No.4: PP 939-974 at 939.
18. ibid.
19. Veena Meetoo and Heidi Safia Mirza , 'There is Nothing Honourable about Honour Killings-Gender Violence and Limits of Multiculturalism', *Women Studies International Forum*Volume 30,Issue 3, May-June 2007,p 187-200.
20. ibid.
21. ibid.
22. Susan Okin, ' *Is Multiculturalism bad for Women*', p15.
23. ibid.
24. ibid.
25. According to Parekh, Polygamy is unacceptable if limited to men, and what if women were also given the right to marry multiple partners? It then does not offend against principle of equality of sexes. Indeed it does not seem to violate any of central liberal values for it is based on uncoersed choice by adults, respects individual differences of temperament and emotional needs, encourages experiment in living, relates to the realm of privacy with which the liberal state is expected to interfere and so on. See Bhikhu Parekh,op.cit.p.71. Bonnie Hónig in her article points out that the institution of monogamy, presented as unambiguously preferable to polygamy, from a feminist perspective famously violates women from each other and privatizes them.In contrast institution of polygamy puts women in situation of solidarity. The struggle of monogamous wives against their husband's power are small, individual rebellion, usually unsupported these days by any network. See Bonnie Honig, My Culture made Me Do.
26. Alida Brill, 'Womb vs Women, Politics of Accusation and Protection,' *Dissent*, Summer,1991,p395-399 at 395.
27. Bonnie Honig, 'My culture made me do it'p, 35.

28. Okin, p. 17.
29. Iris Young , 'Stuctural Injustice and the Politics of Difference', In *Multiculturalism and Political Theory* (ed) Anthony Simon Laden and David Owen, Cambridge, Cambridge University Press, p 86.
30. ibid.
31. Seyla Benhabib, *The Claims of Culture: Equality and Diversity in the Global Era,* Princeton: Princeton University press,2002.
32. Okin.
33. ibid.
34. See Martha Nussbaum, *Women and Human Development, The Capabilities Approach,* Kali for Women, New Dehi,UK 2000. In western philosophy,thinkers like Bertrand Russell attacked religion explicitly. Kant viewed religion within the limits of reason alone. JS Mill too advocated liberalism as a comprehensive doctrine of life rather than as simply the basis of the core political principles. Others are hostile to religion as such but simply insist that it fall in line with a rational secular understanding of value. Joseph Raz and Suan Okin would seem to be in this group.
35. Also see Jacques Derrida, 'Taking a Stand For Algeria' in *Acts of Religion* ed by Jacques Derrida with an Introduction by Gil Anidjar,New York, Routledge, p 306.Jacques Derrida in his work writes,'Our idea of democracy implies a separation between the state and religious powers, that is, a radical religious neutrality.
36. ibid. Faultless tolerance which would not only set the sense of belonging to religions, cults , and thus also cultures and languages away from reach of any terror-whether stemming from the state or not-also protects the practices of faith and, in this instance, the freedom of discussion and interpretation within each religion.
37. ibid.
38. See Yael Tamir, 'Siding With The Underdogs,' in *Is Multiculturalism Bad For Women?*
39. Gurpreet Mahajan,'Rethinking Multiculturalism,' *Seminar,484,* December, p.61.

40. Valntine Moghadam, 'Islamic Feminism and Its Discontents: Toward a Resolution of the Debate'. *Signs*: *Journal of Women in Culture and Society*, 27 (4), 1141-1165.at 1159.
41. Haideh Moghissi, *Feminism and Islamic Fundamentalism: the Limits of Postmodern Analysis,* London, Zed Books,1999, p 146.
42. Egyptian feminist openly wrote against the practice of female circumcision. Finally Egypt has banned the practice of circumcision.
43. See: Hameed Shahidian, 'The Iranian Left and 'The Woman Question in the Revolution of 1978-79.' *International Journal of Middle East Studies*, vol. 26: 223-247, 1994.Also see Hameed Shahidian, 'Feminism in Iran: In Search of What?', *Zanan*, no. 40: 32-38, 1998.
44. See Nadje Al Ali, *Secularism, Gender and the State in The Middle East The Egyptian Women's Movement,* UK, Cambridge University Press, 2000.pp154-155.
45. ibid; In Egypt this also holds true for the debate around the Nationality or Citizenship Law, which is likewise considered to be discriminatory and therefore widely rejected in its current form. The law does not grant this right to children of Egyptian women married to foreigners while Egyptian men are granted this right. This is seen as the ultimate example of the confining of women to second class citizenship and like the personal status law, many activists argue, the nationality law is unconstitutional and in conflict with Convention on the elimination of all forms of discrimination against women (CEDAW).
46. Martha Nussbaum, 'A Plea For Difficulty', in *Is Multiculturalism bad for Women;*105.
47. ibid.
48. Susan Heschel, *On Being a Jewish Feminist,*2nd edition, New York, Schocken Books,1995,p xii.
49. For more on these debates in recent works see, Kecia Ali, 'Progressive Muslims and Islamic Jurisprudence: The Necessity of Critical Engagement With Marriage and Divorce Law', in *Progressive Muslims on Justice, Gender and Pluralism* ed.

Omid Safi, Oxford, One World Publications, 2003; Aziza Al-Hibri, 'Islam, Law and Custom : Redefining Muslim Women's Rights', *American University Journal of International Law and Policy*,12,1997,p 1-44; Ziba Mir-Hosseini,*Islam and Gender: The Religious Debate in Contemporary Iran*, Princeton, Princeton University Press, 1999.

50. Irshad Manji, *The Trouble With Islam Today:A Muslim's Call for Reform in her Faith*, New York, St. Martin Press.
51. ibid.
52. See http: //www.irshadmanji.com/ Project-Ijtihad, retrieved on 10 january 2009 According to Manji is a charitable initiative to promote the spirit of Ijtihad, Islam's own tradition of critical thinking, debate and dissent. We support a positive vision of Islam that embraces diversity of choices, expression and spirituality. To achieve this, Project Ijtihad will help build the world's most inclusive network of reform-minded Muslims and non-Muslim allies. Reform-minded Muslims already exist in spades. Our goal is to bring them out of the shadows.
53. ibid. Islam gives them the permission to be thoughtful and faithful at the same time. Because they're not alone, they can have such faith without fear.Progressive non-Muslims are crucial partners in our mission. When non-Muslims work with reform-minded Muslims, they're sending notice that moderates and fundamentalists are no longer the only voices that count in Islam. When non-Muslims recognize reform-minded Muslims, they're spurring a healthy competition of ideas and interpretations. Above all, they're affirming that reform-minded Muslims are as authentic as the mainstream, and quite possibly more constructive.
54. Noel 'O Sullivan, 'Difference and Concept of Political in contemporary Political Philosophy', *Political Studies*, Vol. XLV, 1997; 739-754 at 739.

Diversity & Feminism: Theories of Reconciliation

1. See Chandran Kukathas *The Liberal Archipelago: A Theory of Diversity and Freedom* ,Oxford, Oxford University Press, 2003.

2. Oonagh Reitman, 'On Exit', In *Minorities Within Minorities: Equality, Rights and Diversity* Ed. By Avigail Eisenberg and Jeff Spinner Halev. Cambridge University Press, Cambridge.2005. p 189.
3. See Ayelet Shachar, *Multicultural jurisdiction, Cultural Difference and Women's Rights*, UK,Cambridge University Press, 2001.
4. Gurpreet Mahajan, 'Can intra group equality Coexist with Cultural Divesity?' *Re-examining multicultural Frameworks of Accomodation,in Minorities within Minorities, Equality, Rights and Diversity*, (ed) A Eisenberg and Jeff Spinner Halev, Cambridge University Press, 2005 ,p 102.
5. ibid.
6. ibid.
7. Ayelet Shachar ' Multicultural Jurisdiction,'.p 41.
8. ibid.
9. See Will Kymlicka, 'Multicultural Citizenship'. Oxford, Clarendon Press, 1995.
10. Kymclika, op.cit. p 15.
11. ibid.
12. Susan Moller Okin 'Is Multiculturalism Bad For Women?' p 21.
13. Gurpreet Mahajan, *The Multicultural Path*, New Delhi, Sage, 2002, p 175.
14. ibid.
15. Joseph Carens, *Culture, Community and Citizenship: A Contextual Exploration of Justice as Evenhandedness,* Oxford, Oxford University Press, 2000, p 107-139.
16. Gurpreet Mahajan, 'The Multicultural Path', p 192.
17. Bhikhu Parekh, 'Fairness and the Limits of Diversity', *Innovation*, Vol.7, no.3.1994.pp 298-308.
18. Gurpreet Mahajan,, 'The Multicultural Path', ,p185-186.
19. ibid, p 186.
20. ibid.
21. ibid.

22. Gurpreet Mahajan , 'The Multicultural Path', p 98.

23. Several works have been done on deliberative democracy in the present context.See Iris Marion Young, *Inclusion and Democracy*, Oxford University Press, 2001; Joshua Cohen in 'Deliberation and legitimacy' in Alan Hamlin and Philip Pettit(ed)*The good polity*(London, Blackwell,1989) , Cass Sunstein, *The partial constitution* (Cambridge, Harvard University Press,1993. Jane Mansbridge , ' A Deliberative Theory of Interest Representation' in Mark P Patracca(ed).The Politics of Interest:I nterest Groups Transformed,(Boulder, 1992) Jurgen Habermas, *Between facts and norms* Cambridge, MIT Press,1996. Seyla Benhabib, *The Claims of Culture* ,Princeton University Press,2002; Amy Gutmann and Dennis Thompson, *Democracy and Disagreement*, Harvard University Press ,1996; Robert Goodin, Reflective Democracy,(2003)

    In the Indian context ,see Gurpreet Mahajan, 'Can intra group equality co-exist with cultural diversity? Re-examining Multicultural framework of Accomodation' ,in *Minorities within Minorities Equality ,Rights and Diversity* ,2005.

24. MoniqueDeveaux, 'A Deliberative Approach to Conflicts of Culture 'In *Re-examining multicultural Frameworks of Accomodation ,in Minorities within Minorities, Equality, Rights and Diversity*, (ed) A. Eisenberg and Jeff Spinner Halev, Cambridge university press, 2005 ,p 102.

25. Iris Young, *Inclusion and Democracy* Oxford, Oxford University Press, 2001p 31.

26. Amy Gutmann, 'The Challenge of Multiculturalism in Ethics', *Philosophy and Public Affairs*, Vol 22-23, Summer 1993.

27. Robert E Goodin, 'Democratic Deliberation Within' , *Philosophy and Public Affairs*, Vol.1.29, No.1,2000.

28. Young, 'Inclusion and Democracy',p 31.

29. ibid.

30. ibid.

31. ibid.

32. ibid.

33. ibid.
34. See Monique Deaveux,, 'A Deliberative Approach',.p.103.
35. See Ayelet Shachat, 'Multicultural Jurisdiction',p 203.
36. ibid, p 204.
37. ibid, p 424
38. The other three models discussed by Shachar based on multiple jurisdiction are:
    a) Temporal Accommodation-Jurisdiction according to this model may be split between state and the nomoi group e.g.- while marriage ceremony could be by state divorce permitted only by any state authority.
    b) Consensual accomodation-This model more suitable to deal with cases of marital oppression.The parties in this retain the option of resorting to either secular or religious authority inorder to get divorce and separation.Once civil divorce has been filed by one party, the other party must comply by removing all religious barriers to remarriage.
    c) Contingent accommodation-Here the state yields jurisdictional autonomy to groups in certain well defined legal arenas ,but only so long as their exercise of this autonomy meets certain minimal state defined standards .If a group fails to meet these minimal standards, the state may intervene in the groups affairs and override its jurisdiction by applying states residual powers.
39. ibid,119.
40. ibid,p120-123.
41. ibid,p123-126.
42. Shachar, *Multicultural Jurisdiction* 147-148.

Personal Laws in India: Laws for Hindus

1. See Ayelet Shachar *Multicultural Jurisdiction Cultural Differences and Women's Right, Cambridge* University Press,UK, 2001.
2. ibid, p.81.
3. ibid.

4. Five members were Mohd Ismail Sahib, Nazirrudin Ahmed, Mehboob Ali Baig Sahib Bahadur, B Pocker Sahib Bahadur, Hussain Imam.
5. CAD, VII,p 545.
6. ibid.
7. *Constituent Assembly Debates* VII , p 550.
8. B Shiva Rao, *The Framing of India's Constitution*, IIPA, New Delhi, 1967, p 122.
9. ibid, p 547, Take for instance Turkey and Egypt.
10. ibid, p 548.
11. ibid, p 549-550.
12. Granville Austin, *Religion, Personal Law, and Identity in India In Religion and Personal law in Secular India A Call to Judgement,* ed by Gerald James Larson, Delhi:Social Science Press, Social Science Press,Delhi, 2001. p 16.
13. Also See, Reba Som, Jawaharlal Nehru and the Hindu Code: A Victory of Symbol over Substance? *Modern Asian Studies,* 28:1,1994:165-94.
14. ibid, p 18.
15. ibid.
16. Thus while thinkers like Herder criticized the enlightenment homogenizing project, enlightenment was followd by pluralism, which then together worked in west.Both worked together, the enlightenment project and pluralism project.
17. See Giovanna Borradori, *Philosophy in the Time of Terror Dialogues With Jurgen Habermas and Jacques Derrida,*Chicago, The University of Chicago Press, 2003.
18. see ibid.
19. ibid.
20. ibid.
21. Ratna Kapur and Benda Crossman, *Subversive Sites: Feminist Engagements with Law in India,* New Delhi, Sage Publications, 1996.

22. For a discussion on Feminist critique of Multiculturalism See, Tamanna Khosla, *Feminist Responses to Multiculturalism: an Examination,* MPhil Dissertation (Unpublished),CPS, JNU,2001, p 121-165.
23. Also see, Rajeswari Sunder Rajan, *The Scandal of the State: Women, Law and Citizenship in Postcolonial India*, Durham, NC, Duke University Press, 2003.
24. Nivedita Menon, (2000), 'State, Community and the Debate on the Uniform Civil Code in India', in Mahmood Mamdani (ed.). *Beyond Rights Talk and Culture Talk*, New York,, St Martin's Press.
25. Flavia Agnes , p 98.
26. ibid.
27. ibid.
28. ibid.p99.
29. ibid.
30. ibid p 100.
31. ibid.
32. ibid.
33. ibid.
34. ibid.
35. ibid.
36. ibid p 101.
37. ibid.
38. ibid.
39. ibid.
40. Chandran Kukathas, 'Are their any Cultural Rights?' *Political Theory*, 20, 1992,pp 105-139.
41. Amrita Chacchi, 'Civil Codes and Personal Laws: Reversing the Option Working Group on Women's Rights', p20-24., *Women Against Fundamentalism ,http://waf.gn.apc.org/.*
42. For the Liberal approach and need for internal reforms within communities seeWill Kymlicka, *Liberalism, Community and Culture*, OUP, 1989.UK.

43. Partha Chatterjee, 'Secularism and Tolerance', *Economic and Political Weekly*, 9 June, 1994,11.

44. Rajeev Bhargava, 'Should we abandon the minority-majority framework' In Gurpreet Mahajan and D.L Sheth (ed) *Minority identities and nation state,* OUP, 1998.p191; Also see Partha Chatterjee, ' Secularism and Tolerance', *EPW,* 9 July, pp 1768-79.

45. ibid p.193.

46. Imtiaz Ahmed,1994, 'Personal Laws:Promoting laws from within', *EPW*: pp 2851-52.

47. Nivedita Menon, 'Women and Citizenship' In Partha Chatterjee (ed) *Wages of Freedom*. New Delhi.New Delhi.Oxford University Press,p 256-261.

Laws for the Indian Muslim Community

1. By anyway and anyhow, I mean, in a discriminatory manner.

2. Asghar Ali Engineer, 'The Need for Codification and Reform in Muslim Personal Law in India', Dossier 22, *WLUML*, January2000.

3. ibid.

4. See for reforms in other Muslim countries, Nandini Chavan and Qutub Jehan Kidwai, *Personal law Reforms and Gender Empowenment A Debate on Uniform Civil Code*, Hope India, Gurgaon, 2006.pp-224-244.

5. This is only one of the factors to bring about change. Changes have come about by changes in AIMPLB, changes in Muslim countries legal system etc.

6. Ashghar Ali Engineer, 'The Need for Codification and Reform in Muslim Personal Law in India', Dossier 22, *WLUML*, January2000.

7. Ashghar Ali Engineer' 'Indian Muslims and Muslim Personal Law Board', *Secular Perspective,* Feburary 16-28 2005.Also See, Syed Shahabuddin, 'The Turmoil in the Muslim Mind', *Onlooker,* 16-31 March, 1986.

8. ibid.
9. ibid.
10. ibid.
11. ibid.
12. Tahir Mahmood, 'Progressive Codification of Muslim Personal Law' in Tahir Mahmood(ed) *Islamic Law in Modern India,* ILI, New Delhi, p. 88-89.
13. ibid, p.89-90.
14. Kashi Prasad Saksena, 'Need for a Code of Muslim Law', in Tahir Mahmood(ed) *Islamic Law in Modern India,* ILI, New Delhi, p.137.
15. ibid, p 138.
16. Seema Mustafa, 'A Farce of a Nikahnama', Sabrang Alternative News Network, *www.sabrang.com*, May 21,2005.
17. Also see Ashghar Ali Engineer, *The Shah Bano Controversy*, Hyderabad: Orient Longman,1987.
18. Sona Khan , 'Veil of Ignorance: Muslim Women Talaq Trap', *www.express India.com*, August 24, 2004.
19. ibid.
20. ibid.
21. Southern states in India such as TN, AP and Karnataka deleted the phrase 'save questions relating to agricultural land' in 1949. Kerela followed similar model in 1963. In other states like Maharashtra, Gujarat and Bengal there was no strong presumption in favour of custom even before the 1937 act. Here even without the Sharia Act , the Sharia could be presumed to cover agricultural land.
22. Also See, Bina Aggarwal, 'Gender, Resistance and Land: Interlinked Struggles over Resources and Meanings in South Asia' , *Journal of Peasant Studies*, Volume 22, Issue 1 October 1994 , pages 81 – 125.
23. ibid.
24. ibid.

25. For example right to culture in fundamental rights discriminates against women of all communities.

26. ibid.

27. Here it needs to be pointed out that this form of divorce which gives absolute and unilateral power of divorce is upheld only by the Hanafi school. The other three schools—Maliki, Shafai and Hambali – do not approve of it.

28. https://www.aljazeera.com/news/2017/12/house-passes-bill-criminalise-triple-talaq-171228113118141.html.

29. There is considerable debate on what can be considered justice in this situation. Justice itself is interpreted variously by conservative/ orthodox interpretations and liberal and now feminist debates.

30. Syeda Saiyidain Hameed, 'Now We Shall Speak', *The Times of India*, 20 June, 2001.While Muslims were found to be least polygamous of other religions and caste groups. However the fact remains that among Muslims it is legally permitted and some Muslims do take advantage of it by taking more than one wife. Here legality and not the incidence of its occurrence is the main problem. See Asghar Ali Engineer, *The Rights of Women in Islam*. New Delhi Press inc, India.2004.p. 185.

31. ibid. It is precisely in this backdrop that feminists in these counries are working because it is hardly a fair system even in this form. So it is a curb not removal of unfairness.

32. Firoze Bakht Ahmed, 'Muslim women In India-Prisoners without Parole', *Women Living Under Muslim Law*,27 May 2005.

33. Ashghar Ali Engineer, 'Uniform Civil Code or Legal Pluralism', *Institute of Islamic Studies and Centre for Study of Social System*, August 1-15 2003.

34. http://womenpla.net/supreme-court-judgment-bans-polygamy-in-india-completely.

35. Vasundhara Dhagamwar, *'Towards the UCC'*,Indian Law Institute, New Delhi, 1989, p.11.

36. Daniel Latiffi, 'Adoption and Muslim Law', 16 J.I.L.I., 120-122(1971) as quoted in Tariq Modood, *Muslim Personal Law in India*,p.112.

37. T Mahmood, ' A Secular Law of Adoption,'*Hindustan Times*, New Delhi, 13, August 1972.
38. Tariq Mahmood, Muslim Personal Law in India, p.114.
39. According to Qutub Kidwai (in an interview on 23 June 2007) of CSSS adoption is not such a burning issue within the Muslim community. Other issues such as maintenance, triple talaq and polygamy have required more attention from the womens movement. However according to Hasina Khan of Awaaz-e-Niswaan, all issues require equal attention and therefore the need for secular gender just laws is essential.
40. https://www.indiatoday.in/india/story/supreme-court-gives-adoption-rights-to-muslims-181849-2014-02-20.
41. ibid.
42. ibid.
43. ibid.
44. Here I would like to point out that in an telephonic interview, Jyotsana Chatterjee of JWP pointed out to me that while the Christians have been open to the idea of a all India adoption bill, Muslim community have been wary of it. According to her Muslim community people have been unable to gather courage to speak against the religious leaders.
45. This was pointed out to me by Ms. Hashmi in a telephonic interview on the 8 June 2007.
46. ibid. Also see Wit petition filed by Shabnam Hashmi APPENDIX.IV.
47. This was pointed out by Kamal Farooqui, Member AIMPLB and Chairman ,Delhi Minority Commission in an interview on 23rd May 2010.
48. Ashghar Ali Engineer, 'Women's rights and Islam,' *PUCL Bulleitin*, January 2007.
49. Ashghar Ali Engineer, 'The concept of Ijtihad in Islam', Progressive Dawoodi Bohras, *www.daewoodi-bohras.com.*
50. ibid.

51. However Kamal Farooqui in an interview pointed out that Ulema,andMaulavis are also from rich backgrounds. Thus it is mixed bag.

52. See F Ahmed, 'Fatwa needed to make Talaq revocable', *The Pioneer* , 17 May 1994; Ashghar Ali Engineer, 'Personal Law and Gender Justice', *The Times of India,* 10 June 1995. Syed Shahbudin, 'A Mountain is Being Made out of a Mole Hill,' *The Hindustan Times,* 28 May 1995.

53. Tahir Mahmood, 'Muslim Personal Law :Clearing the Cobwebs', *Hindu,*p.14, July 30, 2006.

54. Tahir Mahmood , 'Why Fear Marriage Registeration', *Milli Gazzette,*1-15 May 2005.

55. ibid.

56. ibid.

57. Nandini Chavan and Qutub Jehan Kidwai, *Personal Law Reforms and Gender Empowerment,* Hope India Publication, Gurgaon, 2006, p.256

58. Ibid, p 259.

59. Interview with Kamal Farooqui, Chairman , Delhi Minority Commission on 23 rd May 2010.

60. Flavia Agnes, 'Law and Gender Inequality',p 131.

61. Yoginder Sikand, ' Interview: Flavia Agnes on Personal Law, UCC and Muslim Personal Law Board', *www.insaf.net,* Feburary 25, 2005.

62. Ibid.Also see Tanu Thomas K, 'Diverse Justice', *Times of India,* 29 August 2003. Flavia Agnes she is opposed the demand for a uniform civil code as she feels that in the highly vitiated political climate that exists today, the demand will be used to whip up an anti-minority hysteria. A uniform code is not a magic wand that will ameliorate the sufferings of women in general and Muslim women in particular. working more concretely on the question of safeguarding women's rights within diverse laws. Need would be to working more concretely on the question of safeguarding women's rights within diverse laws.

63. Anupama Katakam, 'Reluctant Reform,' *Frontline,* Volume 22, Issue 11, June03, 2005,Retreived on 27th May 2007.
64. ibid.
65. ibid.
66. ibid

    The AIMPLB is a body of 400 members representing almost every sect of Islam in India. It was essentially created to protect Sharia laws in the country, it has become an influential body with the power to lay down rules for the community.
67. ibid.
68. Kamal Farooquiin an interview on 27th May 2010, pointed out that in a democracy like India it is up to people to decide how many additional clauses they want to add to a nikahnama.
69. ibid.
70. ibid.
71. Tarannum Manjul , 'Four Law Boards : Will Muslim Women Find A 'Masiha'?', South Asian Women's Forum,09 Sep2005.
72. ibid.
73. ibid.
74. Venkitesh Ramakrishnan,, 'Shia Personal Law Board seeks Political Representation', *The Hindu,* Sunday, January , 2005. The new Board consists of 69 members. Maulana Ghulam Hussain Raza Agha of Hyderabad was elected as the general secretary. The projected strength of the SMPLB is 200, same as the All-India Muslim Personal Law Board.
75. Massod Hasan, 'Women Personal Law Board', *Milli Gazette online,*16-28 Feburary 2005.
76. S Anand, 'Getting Ready For World's First Women's-Only Mosque', *Counter Currents.Org* , 2 September,2004.
77. ibid.
78. Papri Sri Raman, 'Muslim Woman Builds her own Mosque At Risk to Her Life,' *New American Media,* October 23, 2006.

79. Soutik Biswas, 'Storm over Indian Women's Mosque', *BBC News*, Tuesday, 27 January, 2004.

80. The idea of a women's jamaat and mosque faced resistance even from progressive Muslim groups like the Tamil Nadu Muslim Munnetra Kazhagam (TMMK). According to them, a women's mosque is unacceptable and also women cannot be represented in jamaats.

81. SAnand, 'Getting Ready For World's First Women's-Only Mosque', *Counter Currents.Org* , 2 September,2004.

82. Pointed out in a telephonic interview by Shia scholar Kalbe Sidiqui, on 17 May 2010.

83. Hasina Khan of Awaaz-e-Niswaan,Mumbai based Muslim womens organisation pointed out this to me during a telephonic interview on 13 June 2007.

84. Hasina Khan of Awwaz e Niswaan,during a telephonic interview,said we should not wait for the community to get ready and should initiate changes irrespective of communities readiness for change. Also irrespective of communal environment reforms should be brought about. Also changes have to come about irrespective of government in power. The idea being that reform should be a continuous process. According to her the view that one needs to wait for the right time to come is a fundamentalist view.

85. Pointed out by Hasina Khan. On 13th June 2007.

86. Amrita Chacchi, 'Civil Codes and Personal Laws: Reversing the Option Working Group on Women's Rghts', *Women Against Fundamentalism*,Journal no.8 1996. p20-2.

87. Several Scholars such as Zoya Hasan, Tanika Sarkar, Farida Khan, Kum Kum Sangari, Urvashi Butalia, Uma Chakravarti , Nivedita Menon, Ritu Menon have supported this model. See ,Amrita Chachhi, Civil codes and Personal laws.

88. Also See, Amrita Chachhi, 'Civil codes and Personal laws'p 21.

89. ibid.

90. Interview of Hasina Khan , Awaaz e Niswaan on 13th June 2007.

91. Interview with Javed Anand of Muslim for Secular Democracy in a telephonic interview taken by me on 18th June 2007.

92. Javed Anand , telephonic interview, 18 June 2007.

93. On being asked about four new board formation, Anand replied the more they splinter, much better it would be for Muslim community. I also conclude that in turn it would add to democratization process within the Muslim community.

94. Tariq Modood,(ed*) Islamic law in Modern India,*New Delhi, 1972.p.1.

95. Tariq Modood, 'Progressive Codification of Muslim Personal Law', in Tariq Modood (ed) *Islamic law in Modern India,*New Delhi, 1972.p.96.

96. M.C. Chagla , 'Plea for a Uniform Civil Code', *Weekly Round Table*, 25 March, 1968. p.7.

97. Hamid Dalwai, Vide, letter in the Hindustan Times, New Delhi, 1 November,1970.

98. Pointed out by Javed Anand during a telephonic interview.

99. Vrinda Narain , *Gender and Community Women's Rights in India*, University of Toronto Press, Toronto, 2001,p 24.

100. Narendra Subramaniam, 'Legal Pluralism, Legal Change and Gender Inequality : Changes in Muslim Family LawinIndia',2004profspolisci.mcgill.ca/subramanian/papers/legalpluralismandlegalchangechangesinmuslimlawinindia.pdf.p.7, Accessed on 26 June 2007.

101. ibid, 109.

102. However it is not Black and White situation. Orthodox doesn't mean that they cant be modern in other aspects. Could be against several issues but favour several others. They can for example be against internal reform but favour a more liberal nikahnama.Also See, Thomas Metcalf, *Ideologies of the Raj*, New York, Cambridge University Press, Gail Minault (ed), *The Extended Family*, Delhi, Chanakya Publications, 1981.

103. While the largely uncodified nature of India's Muslim laws left considerable room for judicial interpretation, the common law

tradition of respect for precedent governed adjudication in the formal courts much more through much of the twentieth century than the more flexible techniques of adjudication used for long in Islamic legal history (such as eclectic reasoning (taqlid) and interpretation (ijtihad).

104. Aziz v. Ashghari, AIR, 1960, Allahbad.684.
105. This however did not trigger a flood of divorce litigation from Muslim women.
106. In fact their have been two other legislations which tried to restrict and check the right of the Muslim male in India to practice polygamy. Though the Dissolution of Muslim Marriage Act, 1939 has not expressly provided to abolish the practice of polygamy, yet it has very effectively sought to control it under section 2 clause(f) , which states ' if has more wives than one, does not treat her equitably in accordance with injunctions of Quran. Another modern legislation , Special Marriage Act, 1954 has directly abolished the practice of polygamy, and contains under section 4 (a)'" neither party has spouse living. At present, very frequently the young Muslim women prefer to marry under the said Act so they may not be shared in the matrimonial home by another woman.
107. Shahnaz Sheikh v. Abdul Rab Kavish, Petition No. 13451 of 1980.
108. Khan Noor Ephroz, *Women and Law, Muslim Personal Perspective*, Rawat Publications, Jaipur and New Delhi, 2003 , p128.
109. Marieme Helie Lucas, 'Strategies of women and women's movements in the Muslim world vis a vis fundamentalisms:From entryism to internationalism', WLUML,Global Solidarity Dialogue.
110. A Yusuf Rowther v. Sowramma, AIR, 1971 Ker. 261.
111. Marrium v. Shamsi Alam, AIR 1979 ALL.257.
112. Ziauddin Ahmad v. Anwar Begum, AIR1978, Guhwati, 145.
113. Ahmedabad Women's Action Group (AWAG) case and others v. Union of India, (1997) 3 SCC 573.
114. Shamim Ara v. State of UP and another, (2002) 7 SCC 518.

115. See, Zeenat Fatema Rashid v Mohd. Iqbal (ii (1993) DMC 49); Saleem Basha v Mumtaz begum (1998 Cri. Lj 4782); Zelukha Begum v Abdul Rehman (ii(2000) DMC 99), Sheik Alimuddin v (I (1998) DMC 233).

116. See Narendra Subramaniam, Legal pluralism, Legal Change and Legal Inequality, Changes in Muslim Family Law in India, 2004. The Daniel latifi judgement did not evoke a conservative backlash like that during Shah Bano because of changed political context since 1985, the greater strength of Hindu nationalism,increased violence against Muslims and the Hindu nationalist BJP leading the alliance in power also deterred conservative Muslim leaders who gave greater priority by 2001 to protecting Muslims from further violence and preventing the construction of Ram Temple at the former site of Babri Masjid in Ayodhya.

117. TK Rajalakshmi, 'Restraint on Talaq', *Frontline*,Vol, 19, Issue 15, July 20-August 2 2002.

118. ibid.

119. ibid.

120. ibid.

121. Flavia Agnes., 'Law and Gender Inequality',p 186.

122. ibid.

123. Ali v Sufaira (1988 (2) KLT 94) , Also see Aliyar v Pathi (1988(2) KLT172), Nizar v Hyru nneessa (I(2000) DMC 229).

124. PK Saru v P.A Halim , Also see Karim Abdul Shaikh v Shehnaz Karim Sheikh (2000 Cri.L J 3560)

125. Syed Fazel Pookoya Thangal V union of India(II (1993) DMC 285);Tamil Nadu Wakf Board v Syed F Nachi (1996 Cri. LJ 3488).

Church Laws in Modern India

1. Interview with Jyotsana Chatterjee on 22nd January 2007.
2. Flavia Agnes, *Law and Gender Inequalty*, New Delhi, Oxford University Press,1999,p 45.

3. Pointed out by Jyotsana Chatterjee , Director, Joint Women's Programme in an interview on 22nd January,2007.
4. ibid.
5. ibid.
6. ibid.
7. Flavia Agnes, 145.
8. ibid, 141.
9. Law Commission Report, *Ninetieth Report on the Grounds of Divorce amongst Christians in India ,Section 10 Indian Divorce Act ,1869*, Government of India , Ministry of Law, p9 Section 10, IDA , 1869-*When husband may petition for dissolution*-Any husband may present a petition to the district Court or to the High Court , praying that his marriage may be dissolved on the ground that his wife has, since the solemnization thereof, been guilty of adultery.

   When wife may petition for dissolution-Any wife may present a petition to the District Court or to the High Court, praying that her marriage may be dissolved on the ground that, since the solemnization thereof, her husband has exchanged his profession of Christianity for the profession of some other religion, and gone through a form of marriage with another woman;

   Or has been guilty of incestuous adultery,

   Or of bigamy with adultery,

   Or of marriage with another woman with adultery,

   Or of rape, sodomy or bestiality,

   Or of adultery coupled with such cruelty as without adultery would have entitled her to a divorce *a mensa et toro,*

   Or of adultery coupled with desertion, without reasonable excuse for two years or upwards (LC 90th).
10. 'Indian Church Women get Divorce Rights', *Christian Monitor*, September 12, 2001.
11. Jean D' Cunha, 'The Antiquated Christian Law', *Paper presented in National Workshop on Gender Just Laws* Bombay 30-31 May-1-2 June 1996 ; Human Rights Law Network : Source CWDS.

12. Ninetieth Report Law Commission of India, *The Grounds of Divorce amongst Christians in India: Section 10 Indian Divorce Act, 1869.* Law Commission of India, Government of India,1983., p-2-3.
13. Anna Chandy: *A Community in Peril; Christian Womens Struggle for Equal Inheritance Rights in Kerela*; ISI ; New Delhi; 1995. p 39.
14. Flavia Agnes ,p 149 ; See Sebastian Champappily , 'Christian Law of Succession and Mary Roy Case',1994,4 SCC (Jour) 9.
15. Flavia Agnes,p 149; See Anna Chandy, *A Community in Peril*; See, Amali Philips, 'Stridaharam: Rethinking Dowry, Inheritance,and Womens Resistance amongst Syrian Christians of Kerela', *Anthropologica* 45(2003) , p 245-263. See Sindhu Thulaseedharan, Report on *"Christian women and Property Rights in Kerela, Gender Equality in Practice"*,Thiruvanthapuram, p.1-120,13 January,2004.
16. 'Anna Chandy', p.35, Also See Amali Philips,' Stridaharam'
17. Anna Chandy, p 36.
18. See Sindhu Thulaseedharan, 'Report on *Christian women and Property Rights in Kerela, Gender Equality in Practice*'.
19. Interview with Jyotsana Chatterjee, 18 January 2008. Also pointed by Babu Joseph, Spokesperson CBCI, on 27 June 2009.
20. Babu Joseph; *The Indian Express* August 2005, Pointed by Babu Joseph on 27 July 2007.
21. Interview of Jyotsana Chatterjee and Anjana Messey, Advocate , NCCI on December 9 2009.
22. ibid.
23. ibid.
24. ibid.
25. Vasudha Dhagamvar *IndianExpress*, Aug 19,2005.
26. Interview of Jyotsana Chatterjee on 22nd January 2007.
27. ibid.
28. Flavia Agnes, The Supreme Court, the Media and The UCC Debate in India, *Qualander*, December 1994.

29. Preman vs. Union of India reported in 1998(2) KLT 1004.
30. Vallomattam v Union of India, 2003 Indian Law SC 53.
31. Vallomaotam v Union of India,2003(P11- 12).
32. Also See Agnes, 'SC, Media and UCC',1994.
33. Sanu George, 'People in Kerela Welcome UCC'; *Indo- Asian News Service*, July 23,2004.
34. Pointed out by sister Julie George, lawyer, Stree Vani.
35. *Gender Policy of Catholic Church of India*, CBCI Commission for Women Catholic Bishops' Conference of India, 2010.
36. *Letter to Women by John Paul II, 29th June, 1995).*
37. Interview with professor Christopher Raj, a priest and professor in JNU on 5th June 2014.
38. Fifteenth Report, *Law relating to Marriage and Divorce in India*, Law Commission of India, Government of India,1960.
39. Twenty Second Report, *Christian Marriage and Matrimonial Causes Bill, 1961*, Law Commission of India, Government of India, December 1961.
40. Ninetieth Report Law Commission of India, *The Grounds of Divorce amongst Christians in India: Section 10 Indian Divorce Act, 1869.* Law Commission of India, Government of India,1983.
41. One Hundred and Sixty Fourth Report; The Indian Divorce Act (IV of 1869) Law Commission of India, Government of India,1983.
42. Swapna Ghosh v Sadananda Ghosh AIR,1989. Cal.1.
43. Youth Welfare Federation v. Union of India, 1996,Andhra Pradesh. 1138.
44. N Sarada Mani vs G Alexander,AIR,1998, 161-162.
45. Ammini EJ vs Union of India and ORS, 1995, DMC, 252(FB).
46. Pragati Varghese vs Cyril George Varghese and ORS,1998, DMC, 375 (FB).
47. Mary Sonia Zachariah vs Union of India and ORS, 1990(1) KLT 130.

48. Interview with Jyotsana Chatterjee, 10th December 2009.
49. Pointed out by Mary Scaria, Advocate, CBCI on 8th August 2009.
50. ibid.
51. ibid
52. Interview with Jyotsana Chatterjee on 10th December 2009.
53. ibid.
54. ibid.
55. ibid.
56. ibid.
57. ibid.
58. Mary Scaria. Interview on 8th August 2009.
59. Rita Monterio, Paper presented in National workshop on Gender Just Laws, Bombay, 30-31. May- 1-2 June, *Human Rights law Network*, Source CWDS.
60. interview with Jyotsana Chatterjee,10th December 2009.
61. interview with Mary Scaria.on 23rd January 2009.
62. ibid.
63. Rita Monterio, *Paper presented in National Workshop on Gender Just Laws* Bombay 30-31 May-1-2 June 1996 ; Human Rights Law Network : Source CWDS.
64. ibid.
65. ibid.
66. ibid.
67. ibid.
68. ibid.
69. Interview by Jyotsana Chatterjee on 22nd January 2009.
70. ibid.
71. Flavia Agnes, 'Law and Gender Inequality',pp151-152.
72. ibid.
73. ibid.
74. ibid.

75. Interview with Jyotsana Chatterjee on 14th March 2008.

76. ibid.

77. ibid.

78. ibid.

79. ibid.

80. Interview with Anjana Messey. 23rd December 2009. See Appendix I.

81. Indian Feminist Theology and women's concerns reviews, resources and remembrences,vol 21,2013.

82. Jyotsana Chatterjeeinterview on 17th January 2007.

83. Gurpreet Mahajan, 'Can Intra-group Equality Co- Exist With Cultural Diversity? Re-Examining Multicultural Frameworks of Accomodation, in Minorities Within Minorities, Equality, Rights and Diversity' ed, by Avigail Eisenberg and Jeff Spinner-Halev, p 108.

84. ibid.

85. Pointed out by Jyotsana Chatterjee on 17th January 2007.

86. ibid.

Sikhs: Women and Cultural Diversity

1. http://www.mrsikhnet.com/2006/11/27/women-in-sikhism-gender-inequality.

2. Baldev Singh, Relocating gender in Sikh History, A Critical Analysis. It is amply clear that Gurus' mothers, wives, sisters and daughters were active participants in the Sikh movement. For example, Guru Hargobind and Guru Gobind Singh were very young when they assumed Guruship after the execution of their respective fathers by the Muslim rulers and Guru Har Krishan was a mere child of five when he took over as Guru after the death of his father. What was the major influence on these Gurus at that very critical period in Sikh history when the Sikh movement was under attack not only from the Muslim rulers, but more so from other dangerous foes, the schismatic groups and the defenders of the caste ideology? The answer, of course,

is the influence of their mothers: Mata Ganga, Mata Gujri and Mata Krishan Kaur, respectively. Further, it was Mata Sundri (Jito)—wife of Guru Gobind Singh—who guided the Sikh community through a very difficult period of external repression and internal divisions after her husband's death—about forty years (1708-1747 C.E.), longer than any of the nine Gurus subsequent to Guru Nanak.Guru Amar Das' daughter, Bibi Bhani, according to Sikh tradition, was the one who selected her groom herself, Guru Ram Das.

3. Many feminists would consider this to be derogatory. Iris Marion Young in justice and politics of difference speaks about the derogatory work given to women.
4. SR Tater, SK Jha, Women and Sikhism (Women and religion-6), Regal Publicaton, New Delhi, 2011.
5. ibid p 125.
6. Nikki Guninder Kaur, the introduction of the system of separate personal laws struck at the roots of Enlightenment principles (which has been the aim of both liberal and socialist societies). By this arrangement, India temporarily made space for cultural diversity, but sacrificed values of a scientific society based on enlightenment.

   aur Singh, 'A feminist interpretation of Sikh Scripture', *The Oxford handbook of Sikh studies*, in ed Pashaura Singh, Louis E Fenech, OUP, 2014.
7. Karamjit K. Malhotra. Issues of Gender among the Sikhs: Eighteenth-Century Literaturehttp://www.global.ucsb.edu/punjab/journal/v20_1_2/4-Karamjit%20Malhotra%2020.pdf.
8. Banerjee, Anil Chandra (1983), *The Sikh Gurus and the Sikh Religion*. Delhi: Munshiram Manoharlal Publishers Pvt. Ltd.
9. McLeod, W H (1997), Sikhism. London: Penguin.
10. R Tater, SK jha, op.cit. p 164.
11. Ibid.
12. ibid.

The Case of the Jain Community

1. Among Svetambara sects, there tends to be more female mendicants than male. Traditional sources name several distinguished women who play important roles in the tales of the Jinas, while goddesses are significant cultural and religious figures. In addition, the soa sati – 16 virtuous women – are female role models whose stories highlight desirable religious qualities.
2. Nalini Balbir Sharma, Arvind (1994). *Religion and Women.* SunyPress, p. 121.
3. ibid.
4. VA Sanghave, *Facets of Jainology*, Popular Prakashn, Mumbai, 2001. p 20.
5. Upinder_Singh,_*A History of Ancient and Early Medieval India: From the Stone Age to the 12th Century*, Pearson Education India, 2008.
6. ibid.
7. ibid.
8. ibid. Also see Anne Vallely, *Guardians of Transcendent,* University of Toronto Press, Canada, 2002.
9. VA Sanghave, op.cit.p 12.
10. Padmanabbh S Jaini, Gender and Salavation, Munshiram Manoharal Publishers, 1991.

Do we need Buddhist Personal Laws?

1 Richard F Gombrich, *What the Buddha Thought,* London, Equinox, 2009.
2. I B Horner, (trans.). *The Book of the Discipline* (Vinaya Piaka). 6 vols. Oxford, The Pali Text Society, 1938-66.
3. Doniger, Wendy, *Splitting the Difference: Gender and Myth in Ancient Greece and India*, New Delhi: Oxford University Press, 2000 (first published 1999).
4. ibid.

5. Hannah, Michelle, 'Transmigratory Buddhists and travelling feminism: globalisation and cross-cultural difference', *The Australian Journal of Anthropology* ,(2010), 332-349.
6. Scherer, Burkhard. 'Gender Transformed and Meta-Gendered Enlightenment: Reading Buddhist Narratives as Paradigms of Inclusiveness', *Revista de Estudos da Religião, 3 (2006), 65–76.*
7. ibid.
8. ibid, Conditions For A Buddhist Marriage:

   https://scroll.in/article/759598/do-maharashtras-neo-buddhists-really-want-and-need-a-separate-marriage-law.

The Parsis in India

1. BPP is the nodal decision-making body of Parsis in Mumbai. Reform was based on the recommendation of the 110th Report of the Law Commission of India.
2. Interview with Rusi Gai, Former Secretary to Ministry of Law and Justice, on 7th June 2009.
3. Flavia Agnes.
4. Interview with Shernaz Cama on 14th June 2008.
5. Interview with Naursheed Dadarwala, Member BPP on 10th June 2009.
6. TR Andhyarujina was a former Solicitor-General of India and senior advocate the Supreme Court. Interview on 5th June 2009.
7. Amarendra Jha, 'Conversion by Diaspora split Parsis' *Times of India,* http.timesofindia.indiatimes.com, 24 Feburary, 2005.
8. Interview with Meher Amersey, President, Association of Inter-Married Zoroastrians. Interview on 10th June 2009.
9. Farah Baria, 'On Prophet's birthday, new fire temple shakes 500 years of exclusivity', August 26, 2007, *Mumbai News Line,* cities. expressindia.com.
10. Interview with Vipsy Wadia, Trustee of ARZ. on 10th June2009.
11. The court explained that while Zorastrianism is a religion, Parsis are a race and there cannot be conversion to a race. Just like a person cannot convert and become an Englishman or a

Frenchman, in a similar manner no one can convert and become a Parsi, the court explained.

12. Rustom S Gae, 'Adoption not an Option', *Parsiana*, March 2004 p. 92.
13. ibid; In 1999, the Bombay High Court gave an important judgement regarding adoption by Christians. The Court held that in the absence of any general law regarding adoption, persons who have taken a child in guardianship under the GAWA,1890 will have the right to move the court to adopt that child. It further held that the legal consequence of an order for adoption passed by the court will be that the personal law of the adoptive parents will apply to the adopted child whose rights to inheritance will be the same as of the natural born child. However, the same cannot be applied in case of Parsis as a non-Parsi child does not become a Parsi and therefore cannot claim the estate of the deceased parent on intestacy (dying without leaving any will).
14. Armin Wandrewala, 'An avoidable divide', *Parsiana,* January ,2002, p 40.
15. Ava Khullar, 'The Open-Minded Anjuman', *Parsiana*, August 2002. p.136. Khullar, a trustee of Delhi Parsi Anjuman felt that her marriage outside the community did not lead to any tension or break with the Parsis of Delhi. But it would have been very different if she and her family were settled in some other State. Also pointed out by Rusi Gai on 5th June 2009.
16. Kumar Anand, 'Split in the Parsi Parivar', Farvahr. Org, June 5 2006.
17. See for the criticism of the Thane meeting of FPZAI, Areez Khambatta,'A one man army throws a spanner at the work of FPZAI,' *The Parsi Voice*, March 2006, Vol II.7.
18. Sherene Vakil, 'The Rites Issue', *Parsiana,* January 7, 2007 p.23.

Jews: Anti-choice Communities and Women

1. Like every immigrant community, Indian Jews faced troubles being accepted in Israeli society, especially because their traditions were quite different from those of other Jews and

incorporated various Hindu practices. In the 1950s, when the Indian Jews began to migrate, they were among the darkest of all the new immigrants and experienced racism. Shalva Weil, senior researcher on Indian Jews, Hebrew University, Jerusalem, says, 'In India, they never had to fight for their basic rights but in Israel they did, and this was something new for them'.

2. Interview with Rabbi Malekar on 5 September 2014.

   In Delhi under Rabbi Malekar many of the interfaith marriages take place where women and men sit together.
3. Shiv Sahai Singh, *Unification of Divorce Laws under Divorce Laws in India,* New Delhi, Deep and Deep publication, 1993.
4. http://www.myjewishlearning.com/life/Life_Events/Divorce/Contemporary_Issues/Agunot/Annulment.shtml?p=2.
5. Viva Hammer, Can A Woman Initiate Jewish Divorce Proceedings?"http://mobile.myjewishlearning.com/life/Life_Events/Divorce/History/Women_Initiating_Divorce.shtml.
6. http://www.jewfaq.org/divorce.htm.
7. Interview with Ralphy Jhirad on 10.8.14.
8. http://www.jewfaq.org/divorce.html.